THE
RHODESIAN WAR
A MILITARY HISTORY

THE
RHODESIAN WAR

A MILITARY HISTORY

PAUL L MOORCRAFT AND
PETER MCLAUGHLIN

Pen & Sword
MILITARY

First published in South Africa in 1982 by
Sygma Books (Pty) Ltd and Collins Vaal (Pty) Ltd

Published in this format in 2008 by
Pen & Sword Military
An imprint of
Pen & Sword Books Ltd
47 Church Street
Barnsley
South Yorkshire
S70 2AS

ISBN 978 1 84415 694 8

A CIP catalogue record for this book is
available from the British Library

Printed and bound in England
By CPI UK

Pen & Sword Books Ltd incorporates the Imprints of Pen & Sword Aviation,
Pen & Sword Maritime, Pen & Sword Military, Wharncliffe Local history, Pen
& Sword Select, Pen & Sword Military Classics and Leo Cooper.

For a complete list of Pen & Sword titles please contact
PEN & SWORD BOOKS LIMITED
47 Church Street, Barnsley, South Yorkshire, S70 2AS, England
E-mail: enquiries@pen-and-sword.co.uk
Website: www.pen-and-sword.co.uk

CONTENTS

List of Maps and Illustrations

List of Photographs

About the Authors

Professor Paul Moorcraft lived in Rhodesia and Zimbabwe from 1976-81. He covered the war, *inter alia*, for *Time* magazine, and also taught politics and history at the University of Rhodesia/Zimbabwe. His doctorate was on the intelligence and military failures of the Rhodesian government. He also served in the A Reserve of the BSAP/ZRP for 18 months, after December 1979. In addition, he worked extensively as a journalist covering the conflicts throughout southern Africa from 1981-88. Later, he was the editor of a range of UK security and foreign policy magazines, including *Defence Review* and *Defence International*. He worked for most of the Western TV networks as a freelance producer/war correspondent, as well as lecturing full-time at ten major universities in journalism, politics and international relations. He was a Distinguished Radford Visiting Professor in Journalism at Baylor University, Texas. He has worked in 30 war zones in Africa, the Middle East, Asia and the Balkans, often with irregular forces, most recently in Afghanistan, Iraq, Palestine/Israel, Darfur and Nepal.

Paul Moorcraft is a former senior instructor at the Royal Military Academy, Sandhurst, and the UK Joint Services Command and Staff College. He also worked in Corporate Communications in the Ministry of Defence in Whitehall. In 2003 he was recalled temporarily to government service in Whitehall and Iraq.

He is the author of a wide range of books on military history, politics and crime, as well as being an award-winning novelist. Paul Moorcraft is a regular broadcaster and contributor to UK and US newspapers (with frequent columns in the *Washington Times, Business Day* [Johannesburg], the *Guardian*, etc.), as well as a pundit on BBC TV and radio, Sky, Al-Jazeera, CBC, etc. His most recent co-authored book is *Axis of Evil: The War on Terror* (2005); the updated US edition is *The New Wars of the West* (2006). His co-authored study on combat journalism, with Professor Phil Taylor, *Shooting the Messenger: The Political Impact of War Reporting*, was published in 2008.

Professor Moorcraft is currently the director of the Centre for Foreign Policy Analysis, London, as well as being a Visiting Professor at Cardiff University's School of Journalism, Media and Cultural Studies.

Dr Peter McLaughlin was born in Northern Ireland and lived in Southern Rhodesia, Rhodesia and Zimbabwe from 1956 to 1983. He is a history graduate of the University of Rhodesia. His doctorate was a study of the role of British Imperial defence policy in shaping the Rhodesian armed forces from the 1890s to the 1950s. During the Rhodesian war, he served in operational areas as a field reservist in the British South Africa Police. Peter McLaughlin taught modern political and economic history at the University of Rhodesia/Zimbabwe from 1977 to 1983. He set up the War Studies course at the university and was awarded an Association of Commonwealth Universities Post-doctoral Fellowship to the London School of Economics to study the British munitions industry in the First World War. He left the world of research and lecturing to carve out a successful career as a headmaster at major independent schools in England. From 1999 to 2005 he was Principal of The British International School in Cairo and kept the school functioning smoothly throughout the Islamist terrorist campaigns in Egypt, as well as during the turmoil in the Middle East of 9/11, the Afghanistan invasion and the Iraq crisis.

Other related books by Paul Moorcraft

A Short Thousand Years: The End of Rhodesia's Rebellion (1979)

Contact 2: The Struggle for Peace (1981)

Africa's Superpower (1981)

Stander: bank robber (with Mike Cohen) (1984)

African Nemesis: War and Revolution in Southern Africa, 1945-2010 (1990)

What the hell am I doing here? Travels with an occasional war correspondent (1995)

Guns and Poses: Travels with an occasional war correspondent (2001)

Axis of Evil: The War on Terror (with Gwyn Winfield and John Chisholm) (2005)

The New Wars of the West (with Gwyn Winfield and John Chisholm) (2006)

Shooting the Messenger: The Political Impact of War Reporting (with Phil Taylor) (2008)

Peter McLaughlin

Ragtime Soldiers: The Rhodesian experience in The Great War (1981)

The Occupation of Mashonaland (1982)

Preface to the
Pen and Sword 2008 edition

This new version of the classic account of the Rhodesian war has been produced 25 years after it was originally published. It was the first comprehensive military history of the war, presenting a balanced account of the struggle from both sides. The main thrust of the book was concerned with the dramatic final years of the war. No punches were pulled and the book caused controversy, not least in South Africa, where the logic of the book pointed clearly to Nelson Mandela's victory.

It was widely praised by military experts worldwide and became a standard text for the study of counter-insurgency, including its application to the current 'war on terror'. Such has been the demand for the book that it has been updated and revised to produce a fresh version of this 'military classic'.

It was originally written immediately after the end of the war when nearly all the official sources were still secret. As very little open material was available in 1981, our book was based primarily upon direct experience of the conflict, and detailed interviews, perforce nearly always anonymous. Hence we had to dispense with references. The bibliography at the end of this book is purely to support further reading, and does not necessarily tally with our interpretation of events. A few of the intelligence details – for example, concerning Rhodesian raids into neighbouring states – were challenged by subsequent histories and memoirs, but the structure, and stature, of the book remained undiminished, according to military experts. Sandhurst historian John Pimlott, for example, included the book alongside Guevara, T E Lawrence, Mao, Debray and Marighela in his brief list of recommended texts on insurgency.

The text uses the place-names current during the war; many have changed since 1981. Also some terms, especially in quotations – although today considered politically incorrect or downright racist – have remained to maintain historical accuracy and consistency. We have made a number of minor revisions, particularly on matters relating to intelligence, though some of the later books of Rhodesiana, often from disgruntled exiles, must be treated with caution. Nevertheless, after nearly three decades, and in the light of the near-total destruction of the state by Robert Mugabe, many will look back and reflect that the Rhodesian rebellion, although doomed, was perhaps not so damned.

Professor Paul L Moorcraft
Dr Peter McLaughlin
July 2007.

Preface to the 1982 edition of the book, originally entitled *Chimurenga*

Many books have been written on the politics of the UDI years, but this is the first military history. We recognise that it is a pathfinder exercise. The heavy guns will undoubtedly follow in the form of memoirs and official histories. The Joint High Command of Zimbabwe has already probed this issue. It was suggested that ZIPRA, ZANLA and the security forces organize their own histories of the conflict. The three accounts would be locked away for five years. Then they would be synthesized into the official history. We suspect, however, that this grand design will not materialize. Already many records have been destroyed or lost and others spirited away to vaults in South Africa or Britain. And former combatants seem to be suffering from selective amnesia. We hope future historians will appreciate how difficult it was to write in the immediate aftermath of this often secret, undeclared war. *Chimurenga* is a contribution to the general study of the conflict. We believe it represents also a portent of the greater conflagration which is looming in southern Africa.

Besides the general problem of piecing together a history from scattered information and trying to separate fact from fiction, there were other practical difficulties. Material on the Rhodesian forces and their operations is more abundant. Although few great war photographs emerged from the conflict, the Rhodesians took more, and better, photographs than did the guerrillas. The Zimbabweans took few photographs and those that survive are often of poor quality. This accounts for the imbalance in pictorial content.

In a fairly short general history of the 15-year conflict it is difficult to convey the atmosphere of the war. There were no major battles; it was a conflict of short, sharp contacts and fleeting encounters. We have included the 'boxes' describing specific incidents and the Green Leader transcript to try to give the reader some idea of what the war was like from the soldier's point of view.

....Our thanks go to all those informants who asked to remain anonymous, but without whom we would not be confident that this is an accurate account...

Paul L Moorcraft and Peter McLaughlin
Salisbury, Zimbabwe
July 1981.

PROLOGUE

'Making war on rebellion,' wrote T E Lawrence, 'is slow and messy – like eating soup with a knife.' Crushing Rhodesia's revolt took 14 years at a cost of more than 30,000 lives. The tiny white minority defied the world, its enemies and friends, and, in the end, its inevitable fate: black rule. Rhodesia's first concern, according to Prime Minister Ian Smith's followers, was to prevent the spread of godless communism. But the war led to the triumph of a self-professed communist, Robert Mugabe. The most right-wing British prime minister in modern history, Margaret Thatcher, had inadvertently created the conditions for the first democratic electoral victory of a Marxist leader in Africa. Instead of preserving white privilege, the conflict hastened the destruction of many elements of European dominance. Comfort was replaced by the sheer struggle for survival.

The greatest paradox involved South Africa. Rhodesia broke away from Britain to avoid black rule and then, with the onset of the guerrilla war, became completely dependent upon an apartheid regime which subsequently became even more determined than London to establish a black premier in Salisbury, soon to be renamed Harare. Above all, Pretoria dreaded the possibility of a victorious Marxist army marching through the streets of Salisbury and Bulawayo, a precedent which it feared could be replicated in the Transvaal. For the major international issues raised by Rhodesia's revolt – the pace of Soviet advance in Africa, the role of the UN, and the future of race relations worldwide – threatened to explode with magnified intensity elsewhere.

Rhodesia's diplomatic history is a long melodrama punctuated by angry encounters on train and ship, foolish estimates and silly superlatives. It has been retold many times by those who have sought to comprehend Rhodesia's courageously futile defiance. But what does a military analysis, at tactical, operational and strategic levels, reveal?

In the first decade of the twenty-first century it is hard to recreate in memory and imagination the context in which the Rhodesian war was fought and lost: the crushing of the Prague Spring by Soviet tanks; America's withdrawal from Indochina and the subsequent fall of Saigon, Laos and Cambodia; Israeli reverses in the initial stages of the Yom Kippur War and the oil embargo on the West; the collapse of Portugal's 500-year-old overseas empire; the Soviet invasion of Afghanistan to prop up the Afghan Marxist regime. At the time, Western governments steadfastly refused to see the war as anything more than the struggle of unattractive and unintelligent white supremacists to defend the indefensible. Then, the tide of history was flowing in favour of the guerrilla brandishing his Soviet- or Chinese-supplied AK-47 in a gesture of defiance against US capitalist imperialism and its running dogs. Now that the tide of history has turned in favour of the global consumer brandishing his iPod and there is creeping 'Che-ification' of Osama bin Laden and his al-Qaeda franchisees, the time may have come for a revisionist perspective on the historical meaning of the struggle.

The fall of the white Rhodesian republic added powerfully to the mystique of the guerrilla in the developing world. Vietnam had laid the groundwork for the thrall in which guerrilla warfare holds Western minds. The conflicts in southern Africa appeared to demonstrate further the invincibility of the nationalist or communist guerrilla. First Portugal's colonial armies, their will and morale sapped by more than a decade of insurgency, gave up the struggle against insurgents in Mozambique, Angola, and Guinea-Bissau. But this could be explained away, like the American defeat in Vietnam, in terms of metropolitan conscripts refusing to fight any longer in dirty little wars in remote corners of the globe.

Rhodesia was often seen as a different case. The Zimbabwean nationalists called the whites 'settlers', but the 'European' population thought of themselves as Rhodesians, a nation in themselves, or a white African tribe at least. South Africans watched Rhodesia carefully. Afrikaner racism extended to the Portuguese, who were seen as idle, incompetent and poorly disciplined. In Rhodesia, however, white Anglo-Saxons were up against the wall. Would a committed white Rhodesian population allow itself to be defeated by black guerrillas?

Rhodesia did fall to the guerrillas, Zimbabwe emerged, and the world drew its own conclusions. White rule in Africa was certainly doomed. Rhodesia had been the final test to prove the hypothesis. The tide of black majority rule was irresistible. Africa could only be free when the whole continent was purged of white supremacy. The long continental struggle ended in 1994 when Nelson Mandela became president of South Africa.

In surveying the history of the war in Rhodesia, one question is predominant: can Western soldiers win guerrilla wars in the developing world? The British experience in Malaya is often held up by counter-insurgency experts as a model campaign. In long-term perspective, however, it may have been a freak in time and place, and the price of 'success' was a further British retreat from shrinking Empire anyway. Northern Ireland was perhaps a better measure of British endeavour in guerrilla warfare in 'foreign' lands. That war ended, after three decades, though it still constituted modern Europe's longest conflict.

The American debacle in Vietnam showed how wide the cultural gap between soldiers of the so-called first and third worlds could be. The rival armies fought completely different wars – the Viet Cong and the North Vietnamese army happened to fight the right one in Asia. At the beginning of the twenty-first century, American and British armies were again facing the same dilemma in the quagmires of the occupation of Iraq and Afghanistan. History, as ever, was repeating itself as farce. Britain had fought and essentially lost three wars in Afghanistan, and had also occupied Iraq twice before – now it was trying simultaneously to do both again, albeit in alliance with the world's only superpower.

In Rhodesia the technological gap between the Rhodesian soldier and the

Zimbabwean guerrilla was not as great as that between a US Marine and a Viet Cong cadre. But could soldiers infused with a sense of racial superiority, who rode to battle in helicopters or fought from mine-proofed vehicles, supported by jet fighter aircraft, hope to defeat guerrillas who slogged everywhere on foot, who could live on a ball of cold maize porridge and tepid water, and who were, except for their ubiquitous AK-47s, often indistinguishable from the rest of the impoverished peasant population? The insurgents believed they could not hope to win a head-on clash of arms and so adopted the weapon of the weak – guerrilla warfare.

THE MAJOR TRIBAL GROUPINGS IN RHODESIA WITH APPROXIMATE PERCENTAGE OF AFRICAN POPULATION (1970s)

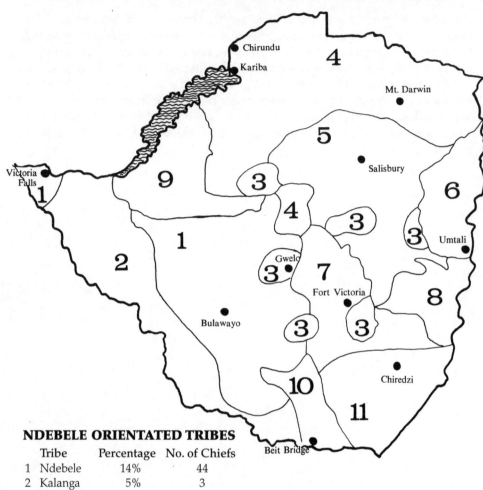

NDEBELE ORIENTATED TRIBES

	Tribe	Percentage	No. of Chiefs
1	Ndebele	14%	44
2	Kalanga	5%	3

SHONA ORIENTATED TRIBES

	Tribe	Percentage	No. of Chiefs
3	Rozwi	9%	20
4	Korekore	12%	20
5	Zezuru	18%	22
6	Manyika	13%	9
7	Karanga	22%	35
8	Ndau	3%	11

OTHERS

	Tribe	Percentage	No. of Chiefs
9	Tonga	2%	27
10	Venda	1%	6
11	Shangaan	1%	5

NOTE

1. The three above divisions are based on historical fact. They do not necessarily mean that a modern African from the KALANGA group, for example, automatically considers himself to be NDEBELE orientated in matters of politics, sport or any other aspect of organized life.

2. Some of the above groups have further sub-groups. The NDEBELE, for example, have 12 such sub-groups, the ZEZURU have 8, and the KARANGA have 15.

3. The SHONA language group have approximately 65 sub-groups.

Chapter One

THE ROOTS OF CONFLICT
1890-1965

White Rhodesia was the deliberate creation of a man pursuing a complex dream of wealth and power, of a river of British red flowing from Cape Point to the Nile delta, drawn by the magic attraction of gold. Cecil Rhodes's invasion of the lands north of the Limpopo, which legend depicted as the location of King Solomon's mines and of gold deposits which dwarfed those of the Rand, was the gamble of a megalomaniac with the wealth to indulge his fantasies. Rhodes secured by deceit a mining concession from Lobengula, the Ndebele king who claimed dominion over most of the territory between the Limpopo and the Zambezi rivers. He used it as a legal basis to secure a Royal Charter from the British Crown, which empowered him to establish a settler state in Mashonaland ruled by Rhodes's British South Africa Company.

In 1890 several hundred men of the British South Africa Company's Pioneer Corps and Police, the kernel of the self-contained frontier society, defied Lobengula's threats to unleash the tens of thousands of warriors in his regiments. He had belatedly realized his folly and forbidden the settlers' entry. But, outsmarted by Rhodes's multinational corporation, Lobengula was also overawed by his own fearful perceptions of the white man's military technology. He had heard reports from the frontiers of South Africa of the overwhelming firepower of white armies. The Ndebele king allowed himself to be faced down and let the bristling columns of the Pioneers roll over the veld to establish the Company state in Mashonaland. Its tenuous links with the outside world were guarded by a string of tiny forts, but its greatest security was Lobengula's chronic and ultimately fatal vacillation.

The settlers' dreams of finding an African Eldorado were shattered in the lean years which followed the invasion, but there were still stories of gold deposits just beyond reach, within the borders of the Ndebele heartland. In 1893 the Trojan horse reluctantly accepted by Lobengula into his domains – which he refused to destroy despite the demands of a hot-blooded Ndebele war party – fulfilled his worst fears. The Company cleverly engineered a war in which the Ndebele were marked as the aggressors. Columns of settler volunteers, tempted with promises of farms and mining claims, converged on Gubulawayo, the Ndebele capital, and on the way fought two encounter battles with Lobengula's brave but outgunned regiments. Shortly before his capital was captured and sacked, the defeated king fled north and died in the bush beyond the grasp of pursuing settler patrols. The victors carved the defeated kingdom into farms and mines, seized and distributed the Ndebele national herd as war booty, and built a new frontier town, Bulawayo, on the site of Lobengula's razed capital.

Rhodes's successes stoked the fires of his megalomania. As well as controlling vast financial operations in southern Africa, he was prime minister of the Cape Colony. He was concerned about the growth of Afrikaner nationalism in South Africa and sought to exploit the grievances of the English-speaking mining community in Johannesburg to engineer the overthrow of Paul Kruger's South African Republic. Rhodesia was to be used as a springboard for Rhodes's illegal conspiracy, which was planned in deep secrecy to prevent the intervention of the Imperial government.

In late 1895, BSA Company forces struck south to precipitate a coup against the Afrikaner republic in the Transvaal. But the Jameson Raid was a humiliating fiasco for the Company and its soldiers. It also invited catastrophe in the colony. The Ndebele and Shona, chafing under the Company's regime of forced labour, cattle and land seizures, as well as its arrogant administration, and suffering from the natural afflictions of cattle disease and locusts, rose against the settlers while the country was denuded of its armed forces.

The Company had not completely shattered the Ndebele and Shona political systems, and these, aided by the religious structures of the two peoples, organized countrywide insurrections which decimated the settler population. Ndebele warriors dug up the rifles and assegais they had cached after the war of 1893. The Shona had never been disarmed. The resistance, called *Chimurenga* by the Shona, raged for 18 months. The settler forces, bolstered by contingents of British troops, were hampered by poor logistics and shortage of horses. The insurgents made good use of their superior bushcraft and intelligence network, and avoided the sort of set-piece confrontations which had bloodied Lobengula's regiments in 1893. The Company forces eventually adopted scorched-earth tactics to starve out the rebels, who then retreated to hilltop strongholds and into caves from which they were systematically dynamited.

Rhodes's hubris cost him the premiership of the Cape Colony, although his influence was strong enough to save him from gaol for illegally launching the Jameson Raid. Only the British government's reluctance to administer Rhodesia prevented the abrogation of the Royal Charter to punish the Company for its abuses of power. As well as leaving the Company's powers largely intact (though more closely supervised by Imperial officials), the events of the later 1890s bequeathed a legacy of bitterness to both racial groups. The settlers suffered from a 'risings psychosis', a morbid fear of another unexpected storm of violence. Africans were characterized as treacherous and barbaric, for in the first days of the insurgency hundreds of near-defenceless homesteaders living on lonely farms were taken by surprise and brutally murdered. Africans saw their hopes of throwing off the yoke of Company rule disappear in the smoke of Maxim and Gatling guns and the blasts of dynamite, and the death and destruction they suffered passed into their folklore.

Although Rhodesian forces fought alongside British and Imperial units against the white Afrikaners during the Boer War, the settlers remained mesmerized by the spectre of an African rebellion. The defence system of the first decade of the twentieth century was geared solely towards securing the settlers against the vastly more numerous black population. Imperial supervision forced the Company to develop more subtle ways of controlling the African masses. Forced labour was no longer possible, but increasing taxation compelled African men to seek work in the labour-hungry settler economy to meet their obligations to the tax-man. Registration certificates and pass laws controlled the movements of Africans, and the boundaries of their reserves were strictly defined. African peasant farmers were moved off their land to make way for Europeans, and armed police patrols crisscrossed the territory to display the power of the Company and to nip in the bud any thoughts of insurrection.

The white man's war of 1914-18 resurrected fears of an opportunistic African rising. Internal defence remained a top priority throughout the war against the Germans. Ironically, while the traditions of African tribal life were breaking down and lessening the likelihood of a rising, the Afrikaner rebellion of 1914 in South Africa had its echoes in Rhodesia. Embittered Boers took advantage of Britain's withdrawal of its garrisons to France to stage a rising aimed at regaining their independence. The settler armed forces were alerted to the possibility of a sympathetic rising by Boer settlers in Rhodesia, and Afrikaner passive resistance to the British war effort and recruiting drives kept suspicions smouldering until the armistice.

Ironically, while large numbers of white Afrikaner settlers refused to serve in the forces at war with Germany, several thousand Africans enlisted in an all-volunteer force, the Rhodesia Native Regiment. The unit saw action in German East Africa. The settlers swallowed their repugnance at the thought of arming and training the possible core of some future African insurrection, and of undermining the myth of white supremacy by putting Africans into the field against white Germans. The manpower shortage in the colony bred a pragmatism which evaporated with the unit's demobilization in 1919: the several thousand whites who had fought shoulder to shoulder with African troops in East Africa and with working-class Tommies in France returned to the colony with their class and racial prejudices intact.

The Twenties and the Depression years saw a widening of racial divisions in Rhodesia. The Land Apportionment Act of 1930 formally divided the country's land between the races; the whites reserved to themselves the more fertile areas with higher rainfall and 'gave' Africans the poorer, more arid areas. These soon teetered on the brink of ecological disaster as a rapidly growing African population and its expanding herds of livestock crowded on to the overtaxed land. Labour, agricultural, industrial, educational and health legislation of the late Twenties and Thirties was aimed at creating a secure and prosperous society for the whites at the expense of blacks, and largely succeeded, despite the hard times of the Depression.

Discriminatory policies were more easily introduced after the handover of power to the settlers in 1923. Settler opposition to the policies of the Company had begun almost as soon as the Union Jack was raised at Fort Salisbury in September 1890, but this had grown more vociferous in the first decade of the twentieth century. As the constitution was periodically changed to give the settlers greater power in the Legislative Council, the Company's stranglehold on the country's resources and its monopoly of power came under intensifying attack. The Responsible Government Association, formed in 1917 and later led by a prominent lawyer, Sir Charles Coghlan, welded together a polyglot collection of local interests to defeat those which favoured incorporation with the Union of South Africa. The referendum of 1922 delivered self-government into the hands of the settlers, and the African population's welfare with it.

Although the British government retained supervisory powers, these were never effective, and the settlers were able to create the sort of economy and society they wanted. The Africans' response was slow in gathering momentum, for they were denied the vote and their tribal political systems were losing cohesion under the impact of a changing economy. While a few small political groups tried unsuccessfully to voice African needs and aspirations, the broad masses remained inarticulate and passive.

Although the settlers' defence system was still concentrated on internal security, there were some concessions to the colony's history of warfare against other whites. In 1926 compulsory service for young white males was introduced, in the face of fierce opposition from the white Southern Rhodesia Labour Party, which accused the ruling Rhodesia Party of fascism. The new defence force was organized on a regimental basis and was headed by a Staff Corps. This was the skeleton of the future Rhodesian army, although in the lean Thirties it remained poorly fleshed. The phenomenally high proportion of white settlers who were commissioned during the Great War disposed the Imperial military authorities to view Rhodesia as a training ground for future NCOs and officers should the Empire ever go to war again.

The rearmament of Britain's forces in the face of deteriorating international relations in the 1930s brought closer liaison between the British and Rhodesian armed forces. From 1938 onwards new units, such as a reconnaissance company and a light artillery battery, were formed with the specific aim of taking part in British expeditionary forces. A fledgling air force, attached to the army, had been created in the early Thirties. For the first time, defence policy became consciously outward-looking, planning for eventualities beyond the protection of laagered white women and children against waves of assegai-wielding black insurgents.

The outbreak of war in 1939 saw the Rhodesian forces geared for a world-wide conflict. Rhodesian squadrons of the Royal Air Force (44, 237 and 266) served in Europe, North Africa and the Middle East. Rhodesian soldiers fought with British and South African formations in North Africa and Italy. The high rate of casualties suffered by Rhodesian units during the Great War prompted a policy of dispersal of the colony's treasured white manpower to avoid the possibility of some latter-day Passchendaele causing a national tragedy.

Paradoxically, the largest homogeneous unit representing the colony was the

Rhodesian African Rifles. Raised in 1940-1 to counter the perennial shortage of white manpower, the unit adopted the East African battle honours of its predecessor, the Rhodesia Native Regiment, and fought with Field Marshal William Slim's 'Forgotten Army' in Burma. But there was more widespread resistance to recruiting among Africans than during the Great War. African perceptions of the racial lopsidedness of the Rhodesian economy and the exclusivity of white society had crystallized in the 1930s. The RAR and a labour battalion, the Rhodesian Air Askari Corps, had difficulties drumming up recruits. Grandiose plans for an 'Africanization' of the armed forces around a core of white officers and NCOs had to be drastically revised. Yet some 2,500 Africans did enlist in the RAR, and 13,000 in the Air Askari Corps.

While African society remained largely undisturbed by the world upheaval, white society was more profoundly affected. Not only did 6,500 men (out of an estimated 30,000) serve abroad in all the major theatres of war, but 10,000 airmen were trained in the colony under the Empire Air Training Scheme, arguably Rhodesia's most effective contribution to the Allied war effort. The scope of the fighting and the influx of trainees developed Rhodesian contacts with the wider world. The Air Training Scheme provided valuable immigration publicity for the small white community. Officers and men built contacts with the British armed forces which were to be of great practical and emotional value in the future. In the 1950s and 1960s the settlers constantly played on their contributions to the British war effort to retain British sympathy in the struggle against African nationalism. The colony emerged from the war more confident and less introverted than it had been in the inter-war years.

Under the stewardship of Godfrey Huggins and in the favourable conditions of the post-war world economy, the colony grew more prosperous and, according to the politicians' rosy speeches, promised to become the jewel of Africa. The armed forces were demobilized, though the RAR was almost immediately resuscitated in 1947, and the Defence Acts of the 1950s reaffirmed the principle of compulsory national service in the Cold War era. The armed forces immediately after the war comprised a Permanent Staff of European officers and NCOs to command and administer the Rhodesian African Rifles as the regular core, the 1st and 2nd Battalions of the Royal Rhodesian Regiment as the European reserve component, and the Royal Rhodesian Air Force, which became a unit of the Permanent Force from 1947.

Huggins steered Southern Rhodesia into federation with Northern Rhodesia and Nyasaland in 1953. The southern colony's more powerful economy and larger white population were telling factors in the negotiations over the conditions of federation, and Southern Rhodesia soon dominated this regional political structure. The colony's white population had been almost doubled in the years 1945-53 by Huggins's strenuous efforts to promote white immigration, even at the cost of virtually bankrupting the national exchequer.

The units of the Rhodesian armed forces were absorbed by the federal defence structure, which fitted into Britain's Imperial defence policy under the umbrella of the Central African Military Command. The Southern Rhodesia forces tended to dominate the federal defence system in the same way as federal politics and the economy were dominated by the Southern Rhodesian political structure. This was encouraged by an undeclared reliance by the British government on Southern Rhodesia as a cornerstone of regional defence policy. Detachments of the police force, which had never lost its paramilitary functions, were sent to help to quell disturbances in Bechuanaland in 1950-2, and to Kenya and Nyasaland in 1953. A Rhodesian Far East Volunteer Unit served in Malaya in the early 1950s, and the RAR was deployed there during the Emergency in 1956-8. The Royal Rhodesian Air Force, which was based mainly in Southern Rhodesia, was expanded in the Federation years and acquired jet fighter and strike aircraft in the late Fifties. From 1958-61 detachments served in Kuwait and at Aden in support of British operations in the Middle East.

Yet this period of Rhodesian history was full of paradoxes. As the defence system broadened the scope of its operations and its horizons, the threat to internal security again grew prominent. As early as the 1920s there was a great deal of talk about 'Bolshevik' influence among Rhodesian blacks. Units of the settler defence forces had exercised against mock attacks by columns of African insurgents led by white Bolshevik agitators. In 1927 the Shamva miners' strike pointed to a new era of protracted political struggle in the territory. African nationalism had been given a boost by the service of thousands of Africans alongside whites all over the world during the Second World War and by the democratic idealism of the Atlantic Declaration. The Bulawayo general strike by Africans in 1948 firmly launched the rise of post-war African nationalism in Rhodesia. Legislation such as the Native Land Husbandry Act of 1951, which introduced specific restrictions on African land use and compulsory de-stocking of overgrazed pastures, merely provided a focus for African discontent in the colony. The Federation was supposed to bring the emergence of racial 'partnership', with blacks rising to an ill-defined position of quasi-equality at some undetermined date in the future. But Africans had little faith in the Federation and its professed prescriptions for racial harmony. Huggins unintentionally parodied the whole idea with his description of partnership as that of 'horse and rider', with Africans being supervised and guided by paternalistic whites.

In common with those in other British colonies, Rhodesian blacks followed their own path, and the first modern African nationalist party, the Southern Rhodesia African National Congress, was formed in 1957 and passed into the leadership of Joshua Nkomo. Rather like the irresistible meeting the immovable, the powerful welling of African discontent clashed head-on with the intransigence of the whites, and the result was an explosion of violence. The white response was to eliminate those elements in their own political structure which favoured reform (symbolized by the deposition of the liberal prime minister, Garfield Todd, in 1957), and to curb African political activity. At first the whites held the whip hand, but the mushrooming of nationalism throughout Africa and the rest of the colonized world, and in particular nationalist eruptions in Northern Rhodesia and Nyasaland, forced the whites into beleaguered isolation. British will to contain the spread of nationalist movements and the demands for decolonization had evaporated, and the nationalist parties north of the Zambezi called for the dismemberment of the Federation as part of their own demands for independence.

Faced with a looming internal and external crisis, the white response was to resort to greater coercion and to expand the armed forces. Counter-insurgency (COIN) training had already begun in the early 1950s when members of the Far East Volunteer Unit returned home after their combat tour in Malaya. More emphasis was placed on internal security training for all units, though as late as 1956 an official report commented that the experience of jungle warfare in Malaya was an excellent preparation for nuclear warfare as it developed the potential of junior leaders! But it became increasingly clear that Rhodesians would not be facing Soviet A-bombs – stones and petrol bombs hurled by frustrated African nationalists were the weapons of the growing conflict in the country. The emphasis on COIN training continued to grow in the late Fifties. Sir Roy Welensky, the federal prime minister, commissioned a federal government study in late 1958 to survey the strategic situation south of the Sahara. Welensky drew apocalyptic conclusions from the report. He pointed to 'the stark fact that the battle for Africa was already on', and that 'a vast power vacuum was created, which the communists were only too willing to fill.' His alarm at 'the communist menace' was to be the keynote of Rhodesian perceptions of African nationalism for the next two decades.

The Royal Rhodesian Air Force acquired more sophisticated aircraft: Canberra light bombers were delivered in 1959 and Hawker Hunters and Alouette III helicopters in 1962-4. Three additional European Territorial battalions were formed. In 1961 all European males aged 18 to 50 were registered for emergency call-up into the Territorial Force if necessary. The political and financial neglect of the armed forces of the 1950s was swept away by the winds of change in Africa, and rearmament was stepped up to a feverish pace.

A symbol of the nature of the conflict was the creation in 1961 of an all-white component of the regular forces 'to strike the balance between the European and African units'. In an era of African nationalism the white settlers were no longer prepared to entrust their security to black (and conceivably disloyal) regular troops and a weak European Territorial force. Recruits into 'No. 1 Training Unit' were formed into the Rhodesian Light Infantry, a squadron of the Special Air Service and an armoured car unit, the Selous Scouts.

Rhodesian units continued their links with the British armed forces – Rhodesian officers were trained at Sandhurst, RRAF units flew with the RAF in the Middle East, Canberras trained with the carrier HMS *Victorious* in the Indian Ocean, and the SAS went to Aden in July 1962. But the final parting of the ways with Britain was coming. Sir Roy Welensky believed that Britain was preparing to invade Northern Rhodesia in 1961 to force a majority rule solution in that country. In a portent of Rhodesia's future political alignments, elements of the RRAF exercised with the South African Air Force in the Republic of South Africa in 1962. The Sharpeville incident of 1960 and the growing apparatus of apartheid had made

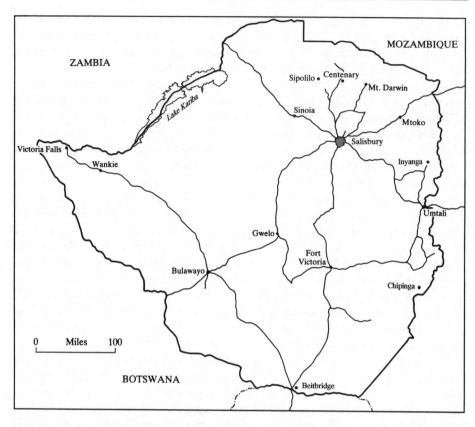

South Africa an international pariah. Rhodesia was on its way to joining it.

Welensky and the prime minister of Southern Rhodesia, Sir Edgar Whitehead, both realised that they were running a race against time. Nkomo's ANC survived repeated bannings to re-emerge under different names (as the National Democratic Party, and later as the Zimbabwe African People's Union and People's Caretaker Council), and the collapse of the Federation would clearly not be far behind the imminent achievement of independence by Nyasaland and Northern Rhodesia. The rejection by African nationalists of the proposed 1961 constitution, which for the first time offered a significant degree of African participation in national politics, was followed by further bannings and eruptions of violence in Southern Rhodesia's urban areas. Africans called the outbreaks *Zhii*, an emotive word implying desperate and frustrated violence. But the victims were mainly blacks, and the European response was to stiffen their own resistance to political reform.

Legislation like the Law and Order Maintenance Act (1960), which gave the government sweeping powers for the control of political opposition and laid down draconian penalties for politically motivated crimes, and the election of the Rhodesian Front – which was committed to white supremacy – in Southern Rhodesia in December 1962, symbolized white determination to resist African political aspirations. The Congo debacle further stiffened white resolve.

When the Federation was dissolved at the close of 1963 and Zambia joined Malawi as independent majority-ruled nations, the federal defence structure was also demolished. African nationalists tried to persuade Britain to take command of the Southern Rhodesian forces to deprive the settlers of the means of resisting a possible Whitehall imposition of majority rule in the country. But Britain allowed the Rhodesian armed forces to become autonomous once again. Most of the Royal Rhodesian Air Force remained in Southern Rhodesian hands, and much other military equipment was grabbed by them. The dissolution also brought a weakening of the Rhodesian forces, for many officers and men took advantage of generous federal golden handshakes to leave the forces.

Rhodesian whites entered 1964 in an isolated and defiant mood, beleaguered from within, their confidence shaken by the dissolution of the Federation and the depletion of their armed forces and population by emigration. The election in Britain of a Labour government, determined to complete the process of decolonization of Central Africa with the achievement of majority rule in Rhodesia, exacerbated the tensions. The independence of Malawi and Zambia and the successful scuttling of the 1961 constitution and the Federation were powerful spurs to African nationalism. A Unilateral Declaration of Independence, contemplated as early as 1961, seemed inevitable. White intransigence and African determination created the conditions for a major racial confrontation in southern Africa.

In 1964 the African nationalist parties, in the tradition of fission in African politics, split into two factions: the Zimbabwe African National Union (led by the Reverend Ndabaningi Sithole) and the Zimbabwe African People's Union (led by Nkomo). Both took the fateful decision to go into exile and to wage a campaign of violence against the whites. Extra-constitutional means had been considered as early as 1960, when a small number of Africans had gone abroad for training in guerrilla warfare. But it was in 1964 that both races felt they had reached the end of the constitutional path to political change. The African nationalists sought their salvation in mobilizing world opinion and fomenting armed insurrection against the white-dominated state. The Europeans sought theirs in a declaration of independence from Britain which would supposedly leave them free to deal as they saw fit with what they felt were their own internal affairs.

In the days before the declaration of UDI on 11 November 1965, units of the Rhodesian army and the Royal Rhodesian Air Force were placed on alert and deployed against a possible internal insurrection. The willingness of the Rhodesian forces to resist a possible British invasion was less clear cut. In 1961 Sir Roy Welensky had accused Harold Macmillan of preparing an armed intervention in Northern Rhodesia. Macmillan had reportedly protested to the federal prime minister: 'Do you really believe that I, who have seen the horror of two world wars, would have tolerated a situation in which Britishers would have been shooting down Britishers, their brothers, alongside whom they had fought on many a battlefield?' But Harold Wilson, egged on by the African nationalist parties and a large bloc in the United Nations, might have countenanced such a scenario.

Although the Rhodesian forces prepared to face it, most senior officers hoped that their oaths of loyalty to the Crown would not be tested. In late 1964 the General Officer Commanding the army, Major General 'Jock' Anderson, had spoken out against talk of the 'unconstitutional' act of UDI. He had been 'retired' on the grounds of age. In 1965 only the Commissioner of Police was strongly for UDI; senior officers of the army and air force opposed the idea of resisting an armed British intervention. Rhodesian intelligence reported that only some middle-ranking officers of the RLI could be relied on to resist the British and that their (mainly South African) troops would follow suit. UDI was a gigantic bluff. While there is no doubt that an African rising would have been crushed, an invading British expeditionary force could have brought the swift collapse of the rebellion.

In the event, the British government rejected the option of an invasion. Ian Smith's Rhodesian Front government had deliberately set the date for 11 November 1965, Armistice Day, to rally the ghosts of Rhodesia's past war efforts for the crisis. And in that there was no British invasion, the ploy worked. But the Unilateral Declaration of Independence was more than an attempt by the Smith government to grasp an illusory freedom of political action – it was an unintentional declaration of civil war.

Sanctions on Rhodesia soon followed. Rhodesian Hunter and Canberra engines inside Britain and those in transit for servicing by Rolls Royce were impounded, thereby creating a serious and immediate problem for the small Royal Rhodesian Air Force. But Rhodesian technical ingenuity, French sanctions-busting and South African largesse became the countervailing template for the imminent conflict.

Chapter Two

THE OPENING ROUND
1965-1972

'The ability to run away is the very characteristic of the guerrilla,' asserted Mao Zedong. Throughout the 1960s the Zimbabwean guerrillas found themselves running far more often than fighting. Until 1966 their nationalist leaders appeared to be more concerned with jet-set diplomacy than with preparing for a bush war. Most of the violence that did erupt was faction fighting between ZAPU and ZANU in the sprawling black townships. Occasionally whites were attacked: in July 1964, Petrus Oberholzer was fatally wounded when a group calling itself the 'Crocodile Gang' stopped him and his family at a crude roadblock in the Melsetter area. From the early 1960s small numbers of Zimbabwean blacks were sent for training in Tanzania, China and Eastern Europe, but their practical impact on pre-UDI Rhodesia was insignificant.

When UDI was declared the nationalists could do little except beseech Britain to act for them. This was a fatal flaw in the nationalist strategy: until the early 1970s they still believed that Britain would take up arms on their behalf. They were completely wrong; they would have to do the job themselves.

In April 1966, a group of 21 ZANU insurgents infiltrated from Zambia into Rhodesia and they split up into three teams. Their aim was to cut power lines and attack white farmsteads. One group, dubbed the Armageddon group, was surrounded by police on Hunyani farm, near Sinoia. This seven-man squad, some trained at Nanking Military College, was wiped out by the Rhodesian forces, who suffered no casualties. It was the first real 'contact', the Rhodesian term for a military encounter. ZANU leaders grossly exaggerated the incident at the time, but the 'Battle of Sinoia' now occupies pride of place in the nationalist hagiography. Although ZANLA leaders today may admit that the battle was a fiasco, they stress its significance as the first day of the war. The date, 28 April, is now commemorated as Chimurenga Day.

The ruling ZANU-PF party in today's Zimbabwe has apotheosized this event, partly to emphasize that it began the war before its old rival, ZAPU. In fact, all seven 'heroes of the revolution' involved in the debacle were being fed by police Special Branch and the political commissar, according to Central Intelligence Organisation sources, was a Rhodesian agent. The tame guerrillas were supposed to lead the security forces to arms caches and nationalist sympathizers. Instead, because of an

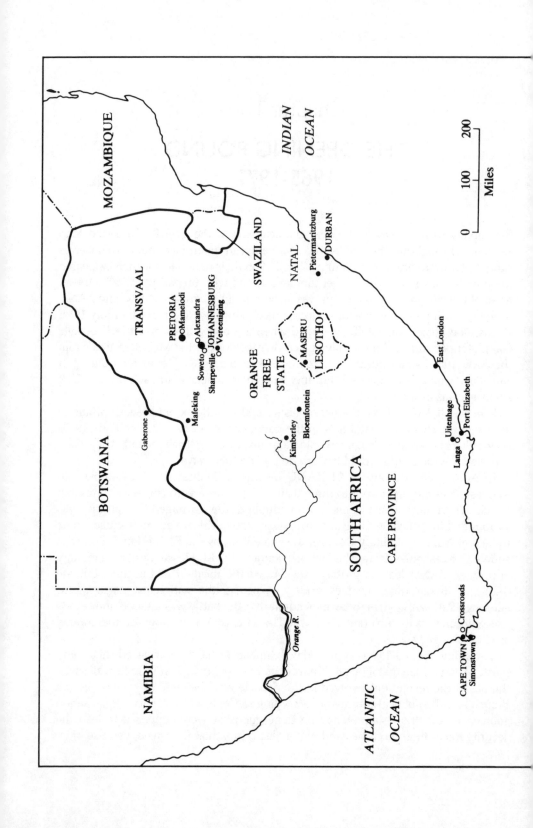

administrative cock-up, they were all killed, inefficiently. An air force gunner in an Alouette expended 168 rounds, from a hastily rigged MAG 7.62mm, to shoot dead one guerrilla running across open ground in daylight. The regular and reserve policemen involved in the hunt were mostly armed with World War One-vintage rifles and Second World War revolvers. According to one eyewitness, 'It was nothing more than a baboon shoot, the police reservists congregating like farmers (which most of them were) around every kill and exposing themselves unbelievably to enemy fire.' A history of the Rhodesian air force commented thus on its first 'kill' in the war: 'It was a very unconvincing and unprofessional action. Fortunately for the police, the guerrillas were too confused to take advantage of the inexperience of the hunters.' Another Rhodesian commander described the response as 'a shambles'. Racially arrogant, the Rhodesians always overplayed guerrilla incompetence, terming it disparagingly the 'K factor' ('kaffir' factor). Indeed, the military performance of the guerrillas, particularly in the early part of the war, was appalling. Both sides, however, learned from their mistakes. In the end the Rhodesians often met fierce resistance and came to repent their initial underestimation of the enemy.

Shortly after the Sinoia 'battle', on the night of 16/17 May, another one of the three sections killed Johannes Viljoen and his wife on their Nevada Farm, near Hartley. The Viljoens' two young children were spared. ZANU immediately claimed responsibility for the Viljoen killings and warned: 'For every one of our sons and daughters killed by the settlers, we shall kill settlers with compound interest.' The guerrillas who shot the Viljoens were eventually captured, but that incident, on top of the Sinoia contact, sent ripples of anxiety through the Rhodesian white community.

In 1967 and 1968 the pace of guerrilla activity quickened. The nationalists dabbled in urban warfare. Explosives were smuggled in through the borders in cars and lorries. Usually they were discovered. ZANU sent a white woman activist to leave bombs in Salisbury's major hotels, but the plot failed. At the same time, a small number of white nationalist sympathizers at the University College of Rhodesia were active in encouraging grenade attacks. A café in Salisbury was damaged; so too was a suburban house. There were no serious casualties and the group of university lecturers was caught. One of them, an Italian lecturer in economics, Dr Giovanni Arrighi, was deported. Another, Pretoria-born John Conradie, was jailed for 20 years. Academics rarely succeed in practical revolutionary tactics, but the grenades on campus sent the Rhodesian Front into paroxysms of anger: the university just managed to retain its shaky independence of government. (The RF government allowed the university some leeway as it was one of the few Rhodesian institutions exempted from the application of sanctions. Because it was technically multiracial, it was allowed to work within the Commonwealth Universities programme.)

But far more important than academics' activities were the conventional incursions. In August 1967 a combined force of 90 guerrillas from ZAPU and the South African African National Congress (ANC) entered Rhodesia near the Victoria Falls. They intended to move into Tjolotjo Tribal Trust Land (TTL), to establish recruiting bases. Later the ANC forces planned to infiltrate through Botswana and head for Soweto township in Johannesburg. But the guerrillas were on a suicide mission. They had been told they would be welcomed by the local people, but the tribesmen in the sparsely populated shrubland of north-western Rhodesia were suspicious of the insurgents. Soon the bush telegraph brought the news to Rhodesian intelligence. In the first major operations of the war, 47 of the insurgents were killed by the security forces in three weeks. More than 20 were captured and the survivors, many of them wounded, escaped into Botswana, where they were imprisoned but subsequently released into the care of Zambian authorities.

The failure of this joint ZAPU/ANC sortie had many consequences. The involvement of South African insurgents prompted Pretoria to send police units to aid Rhodesian COIN operations in the Zambezi valley. (A number of army and air force units were included; the 'police' label was used to discourage international accusations that South Africa had intervened militarily in a British colony.) The initial South African contingent amounted to about 2,000 men, though by 1969 it reached 2,700, only a thousand short of the Rhodesian regular army. In the beginning Rhodesian troops regarded their South African allies with near contempt and disparagingly dubbed them 'clumpies' because of their clumsy bushcraft. 'Ropes' – thick, hairy and twisted – was another impolite epithet. Rhodesian commanders thought that the South Africans were more of a liability than a help, and so were reluctant to allow South African troops to join in the fray. But the government insisted that Rhodesia had to accept the help for political rather than security reasons. Pretoria initially gained much more than the Rhodesians. The South African troops acquired valuable experience, while Rhodesian units had to operate behind them to fill in the gaps created by their allies' inefficiency and inexperience. For the following seven years Pretoria provided vital manpower support for Rhodesia's anti-guerrilla campaign. John Vorster, the South African premier, explained that he had sent his men in order 'to pull our own chestnuts out of the fire'. He also included his own 18-year-old son in the contingent. Later on in the war, Salisbury was to become totally dependent upon South African military largesse, particularly the loan of helicopters and their crews. At the outset of the war, the Rhodesians had just eight military helicopters. Equally vital was South African economic subvention, which eventually amounted to approximately half of the annual Rhodesian defence budget.

A second manifestation of the ZAPU/ANC joint forays was the scope of the southern African planning by the insurgents. It was not merely a series of guerrilla pinpricks, but a concerted strategy. In the long run, the strategy of forming an alliance with other guerrilla groups was valid, but in the short term the tactics were disastrous. Large-scale conventional incursions proved futile against highly trained, mobile troops, backed by total air supremacy. But it was not exactly a turkey-shoot. In the fighting of August and September 1967 the Rhodesian security forces lost their first man killed in action in the country since the Shona and Ndebele uprisings of the 1890s. But the guerrillas suffered severe casualties. Even worse were the ensuing splits in the nationalist movements, already strained by tribal, ideological and personality clashes. ZANU praised the courage of the insurgents, but castigated the alliance with the ANC as a 'gross blunder'. The ANC, said ZANU, should be pinning down its enemy in South Africa, not encouraging Pretoria to bolster the northern frontier of white rule to the detriment of the Zimbabwean nationalists. Besides, the ANC, argued ZANU, was superfluous: the four million Zimbabweans without external aid could easily overcome the 200,000 whites. The ANC's South African rival, the Pan-Africanist Congress, condemned the conventional tactics as 'a criminal act of manslaughter'. ZAPU retaliated against the rebuffs from ZANU and the PAC and hinted darkly that ZANU agents had tipped off Rhodesian intelligence.

Despite the recriminations within the nationalist ranks, the guerrillas kept coming. In early 1968, 123 guerrillas of both ZAPU and the SAANC crossed the Zambezi near the Chewore river. During a three-month period they set up Viet Cong-style base camps containing considerable amounts of medical equipment, food and arms. Because of the heavy rains Rhodesian security force patrolling was light. A game ranger, however, stumbled upon the guerrilla presence, and on 18 March the security forces went in and destroyed the guerrillas' six base camps. In a running battle lasting nearly a month more than 69 insurgents were killed for the loss of six of the Rhodesian forces. The remaining guerrillas were either captured or chased across the Zambezi back to Zambia.

In July a ZAPU/SAANC tandem force tried again. Three groups totalling 91 men slipped across the Zambezi. Once more they were spotted by Rhodesian security force patrols. Despite their sometimes fierce resistance the guerrillas were routed, although in one contact a South African policeman was killed. He was the first South African policeman to die in a direct contact with guerrillas in the war in Rhodesia. By the end of 1968 more than 160 insurgents and 12 security force members had been killed.

The 1967-8 incursions had failed. Instead of large formations, lone guerrillas were subsequently sent into Rhodesia to acquire intelligence and to prepare for a more thorough process of infiltration. The slackening tempo of the war lulled the Rhodesian government into a false sense of complacency and lazy assumptions of military supremacy. Indeed some Rhodesians even believed the war was over. But Rhodesian intelligence had accurately assessed the growing guerrilla strength. What they did not know was where the insurgents would strike and when. It was not the end of the war; instead it was the prelude to the coming *Chimurenga*. Although ZAPU forces were slow to revise their strategy, the leaders of ZANU and its military wing, the Zimbabwe African National Liberation Army (ZANLA), moved quickly to reappraise the conduct of the war. They argued that the ANC and ZAPU had ignored the first two stages of classic Maoist guerrilla warfare. By jumping to the third conventional phase they inevitably handed the tactical advantage to the well-equipped units of the security forces. ZANU turned to the obvious source of help to remedy its deficiencies: Chinese instructors. ZANU had sent its first contingent of five men, led by Emmerson Mnangagwa, to China for training in September 1963, but the first instructors at ZANLA's training camp at

Itumbi in southern Tanzania did not arrive until 1969. Initially a few chosen ZANLA cadres were sent to China or Cuba; later the majority were trained in Mozambique or Tanzania. In the latter stages of the war, basic training for some recruits was provided inside Rhodesia. Training was divided into two phases. The first consisted of physical education, political indoctrination and training on basic infantry weapons. The second phase involved tactics (ambushes, patrol formations, and so on). Further specialized instruction was then given to the more able students.

The administration of the war was also improved. In April 1969, exiled ZANU leaders in Lusaka set up an eight-member war council, the *Dare re Chimurenga*. One of the *Dare's* first moves was to try to persuade the Front for the Liberation of Mozambique (FRELIMO) forces operating against the Portuguese to allow ZANLA to operate from their territory. As the 1966-8 incursions had proved, the inhospitable terrain and the Rhodesian *cordon sanitaire* along the Zambezi had made guerrilla transit from Zambia hazardous. FRELIMO leaders, however, were reluctant to accede to ZANU's requests because of FRELIMO's special relationship with ZAPU, which it regarded as the lead Zimbabwean nationalist movement.

For the white Rhodesians, things looked decidedly rosy by the end of the 1960s. In economic and military terms UDI seemed a success. The new confidence encouraged an upswing in the influx of white immigrants. In stark contrast, morale in the guerrilla movements was low and manpower was in short supply. ZAPU and ZANU began to 'conscript' black Rhodesians living in Zambia. Sometimes Zambians were also press-ganged, much to the annoyance of the Zambian government. But what really angered the Zambian president, Kenneth Kaunda, was the constant squabbling between ZANU and ZAPU. Foiled by the Rhodesian army, the guerrillas began to turn their guns on each other. ZANU and ZAPU, in the camps in Zambia and Tanzania, quarrelled over strategy and tribal affiliations. Occasionally the bickering erupted into pitched battles.

Political and tribal animosity was exacerbated by poor administration in the guerrilla camps. In 1970 James Chikerema, a ZAPU leader, described the ZAPU camps as representing 'the depth and height of decay, corruption, nepotism, tribalism, selfishness and gross irresponsibility on the part of the military administration from top to bottom'. In October 1971 Chikerema tried to reconcile the ZANU-ZAPU splits by forming the Front for the Liberation of Zimbabwe (FROLIZI). But the Front was short-lived and ineffectual. In March 1972, Kaunda and other OAU leaders compelled the rival nationalists to unite under the banner of a 'Joint Military Command'. But there was little to command. And, like most shot-gun unions, the marriage was brief and acrimonious.

From 1969 to 1972, isolated guerrilla attacks caused Salisbury only occasional concern. In January 1970, for example, guerrillas attacked Victoria Falls airport and a nearby South African military camp. Infrequent sabotage attempts and sporadic landmine blasts scarcely dented an assertive white nationalism that believed its rule would last 1,000 years.

ZANU was actively ensuring that it would be a short 1,000 years. Despite the failures to unite with ZAPU, ZANU was determined to set its own house in order.

One of the weaknesses had been the lack of military expertise on the *Dare re Chimurenga*. Often a political decision would be made to satisfy the pressures from the OAU, and the guerrillas in the field would suffer. The combat commanders did their best to modify rash political strategies and instead concentrated on laying the foundations of a classic Maoist protracted struggle. (In 1973 Josiah Tongogara, the able ZANLA commander, joined the *Dare* and injected a stiff dose of military pragmatism.) The key to the successful infiltration was FRELIMO support. FRELIMO had consistently urged ZAPU to operate from Mozambique, but had met with evasion. ZANLA eventually prevailed upon FRELIMO to be allowed to operate from bases in Mozambique and to use FRELIMO weapons supplies. (ZANLA guerrillas, however, had to pretend to be acting as a part of FRELIMO.) From their new logistic base, weapons were transported into north-east Rhodesia and then cached. ZANLA skilfully enlisted the support of local spirit mediums who assisted in the politicization of the local people. The guerrillas constantly hammered home the theme that the liberation war of the 1970s was a continuation of the *Chimurenga* struggle of the 1890s. In the north-east, government administration had always been poor, and the tribal population, especially the KoreKore people, had a tradition of sullen non-cooperation with the authorities. Soon large columns of guerrillas with tribesmen acting as porters were winding their way into Rhodesia from Mozambique's Tete province. Rhodesian intelligence had got wind of the ZANLA build-up, although not its extent. Although Smith may have given some credence to the comforting (and totally erroneous) reports from the Ministry of Internal Affairs, his Cabinet received regular, and accurate, briefings from the top intelligence advisers. Although Rhodesian intelligence chiefs tended to ignore Internal Affairs sources – maligning it as 'Infernal Affairs' – hardliners in the Cabinet, such as Desmond Lardner-Burke, took them seriously. When intelligence men warned of the impending strikes, Lardner-Burke would complain of repetition of security lectures that were 'all gloom and doom that never materialized'. Thus Salisbury failed to mobilize its troops against a ZANLA force which had expanded its politicization programme and strengthened its logistic links with FRELIMO.

Rhodesian intelligence was also aware of the deteriorating grip of the Portuguese on Mozambique. Ken Flower, head of the Central Intelligence Organisation, visited the Portuguese premier, Marcello Caetano, twice in Lisbon. The permanent Rhodesian representative in Portugal, however, was feeding Salisbury with all sorts of poor intelligence; he chose to believe the confident propaganda put out by the Portuguese generals. When Salisbury finally voiced its concern, Lisbon rebuked the Rhodesians for undue alarmism. Since UDI, Rhodesia and Portugal had co-ordinated their strategies to include joint cross-border sweeps. (South Africa was included soon after, under the codename 'Alcora'.) When the Rhodesian authorities expressed their dismay at the FRELIMO successes in Tete, Caetano rapped Salisbury over the knuckles: 'Some of our neighbours with less experience than we have, do not conceal their fears and in this way play the game of the enemy. They have been told more than once there is no reason for their great fright.' Rhodesian forces operated regularly with the Portuguese both on the ground and in the air. At the tactical level, the Rhodesians generally thought that there was little wrong with the average Portuguese soldier's fighting spirit, but he often lacked the necessary fire discipline, creating unnecessary noise and expenditure of ammunition. Portuguese troops appreciated working with Rhodesian officers, because they led from the front. The few Portuguese officers born in Mozambique were usually admired for the same reason. Most metropolitan officers commanded from the rear. Co-ordination between the Portuguese air force and army was also very poor. Despite this, even as late as 1973, the Portuguese were inflicting military reverses on FRELIMO, but politically the metropolitan base for the war was crumbling. FRELIMO would soon be able to augment its logistic support for ZANLA.

The Rhodesians were also gradually building up the size of the regular army. (The length of national service had been increased in 1966 from 4½ months to nine months.) They were taking extra precautions, but their mood was one of complete confidence. In 1972 they were unaware of the scope of the ZANLA infiltration from Mozambique in the east. To the north along the Zambezi, the Rhodesians had totally outclassed their opponents in direct combat. It was to take six years for ZAPU to recover from the defeat of its conventional sorties. The ZAPU/ANC alliance had been knocked out in round one. In round two the Rhodesian army was taken by surprise. In December 1972 ZANU launched its offensive.

Chapter Three

ROUND TWO: 1972-1976

'The enemy's rear is the guerrillas' front.' This was particularly true of South African pressure on Rhodesia from 1972 to 1976. John Vorster undermined Rhodesia almost as much as the combined efforts of the insurgents and the OAU did. Pretoria's leverage, however, was not applied until the second part of round two. The guerrillas struck the first blows.

ZANLA troops had built a widespread underground infrastructure in the northeast of Rhodesia; the local spirit mediums had been won over and the peasants politicized. In November 1972, security forces intercepted a large ZANLA column in the Mzarabani Tribal Trust Land, which stood between the white farming area of Centenary and Mozambique. Suddenly the scope of the infiltration began to dawn on the politicians in Salisbury. In December it was announced that national service would be increased from nine months to one year. But the expansion of the armed forces could not avert the first wave of the new offensive.

On 21 December 1972, ZANLA attacked the isolated Altena farm in the Centenary district. An eight-year-old white girl was wounded in the foot. (According to Rhodesian sources, this attack was meant to be part of a simultaneous assault against five farms, but the Altena group misread their instructions and struck 24 hours prematurely. The ZANLA version is different: Rex Nhongo was the operational commander in charge of 21 men in the Nehanda sector – the ZANLA name for the area. He ordered the Altena attack in order to divert the security forces which were closing in on other guerrilla groups in the Mtoko region.) The de Borchgrave family, who lived at Altena, moved to the adjoining homestead, Whistlefield farm. Two nights later ZANLA launched a rocket and grenade raid, which wounded de Borchgrave and his daughter. In the morning a relieving security force vehicle detonated a landmine. A white corporal was mortally wounded and three other soldiers were injured. On 28 December another three Rhodesian soldiers were killed in a landmine blast. Other attacks on farms followed. The guerrillas had infiltrated into a wide arc from Sipolilo, west of Centenary, to Mtoko in the east, and southwards towards the Chiweshe and Madziwa TTLs. The real war had started. Operation Hurricane was set up to repulse the guerrilla drive. But the response was slow and unsure; the Rhodesian war machine had grown soft with complacency.

Guerrillas were filtering in from Mozambique and Zambia. Rhodesia mounted raids into Portuguese territory (though they had been working alongside the

Portuguese army since 1967). The Zambians should also be taught a lesson, argued Ian Smith, and on 9 January 1973 Rhodesia closed its borders with Zambia, except for copper shipments, which brought large revenues to Rhodesia Railways. Kaunda was unmoved. Although Smith rescinded the order, the border stayed closed from the Zambian side. Portugal and South Africa were incensed; both governments wanted to use Zambian exports via Beira and South African ports as leverage to induce Zambian moderation. Now that incentive was removed, and Rhodesia had to contend with another front along the entire Zambian border.

External diplomacy had failed. So the Rhodesian government tried to wipe out internal support for the guerrillas. Collective fines were imposed on the affected areas. Tribesmen were hit where it hurt most: their cattle were impounded. In February 1973, all facilities – shops, clinics, schools, churches, businesses and mills – were shut down in the Chiweshe TTL. Other areas were also 'closed' while the Rhodesian army swept them. 'Inform on the guerrillas or your schools and shops will stay shut' was the message. Although intelligence began to improve, these collective measures embittered the peasant farmers.

Even more counter-productive in psychological terms was the establishment of protected villages. Whole communities were uprooted and put behind the wire. Although militarily effective, it was a propaganda gift to the insurgents. So were the 'no-go areas' and the 'free-fire' zones along the Mozambique border. As the curfews were extended, the inevitable increase in innocent civilian deaths made guerrilla recruitment easier.

Still, guerrilla movement was seriously hampered by these measures and in some cases ZANLA had to resort to abduction. On 5 July 1973 the first large-scale exodus of schoolchildren took place. Two hundred and ninety-five pupils and staff were marched from St Albert's Mission in the Centenary area. Rhodesian security forces intercepted the column and all but eight were returned. Although many young men left schools to join the guerrillas voluntarily, the abduction attempts increased in the following years. But the insurgents' manpower problem was minor compared with the Rhodesian government's limited resources of combat soldiers. White draft-dodgers were hounded. Coloureds (the term for mixed-race Rhodesians) and Asians (who had previously been exempt) were conscripted. Call-ups were extended to include more age groups; pay and conditions were improved for the regulars in the police and the army. Inevitably the drain of white skilled labour from the economy and the accelerating pace of emigration diluted the efficacy of the war-strained economy. Some RF MPs and businessmen argued that a large permanent standing army would be more cost-effective. The consensus in the Operations Co-ordinating Committee (a joint war council) was against building up a large standing army. It felt that the rural police reserve, which knew its own areas, was more effective. The expansion of local COIN groups had been advocated by Allan Savory, the maverick RF MP, but his views were ridiculed by his party, especially when he became an outcast from the RF. The government still maintained publicly that the insurgency was a 'temporary emergency'. It was not necessary to plan for a protracted war, a long war of attrition which would bleed Rhodesia dry.

While insisting that there was not really a war, the government began to mobilize its full resources. From 1974 the regular army was expanded, partly by encouraging foreign recruitment. A second battalion of the RAR was formed. The haphazard call-up system was improved. At the same time a serious attempt was made to wage a psychological counter-offensive. The government scorned the advice of Allan Savory when he warned that the guerrillas 'only require the mass of the population to be passive. We, to win, require the mass of the population to be actively in support of us and not passive. We are at a severe disadvantage here.' But something had to be done about winning 'the masses'. As in Vietnam, the carrot and the stick were tried. The Ministry of Internal Affairs rushed through a programme of rural development schemes. Tribespeople were offered large rewards for pointing out guerrilla hideouts or the location of weapons caches. Then there was the stick. The augmented security forces were concentrated to clear areas where guerrilla support was widespread. From mid-1974 the PV (protected village) programme was put into top gear. In the following two years about 240,000 Africans were dumped into protected or 'consolidated villages'. Like the experiments in Mozambique, Angola, Algeria and Vietnam, the system produced only patchy results. Sometimes the rural population benefited from the amenities in the villages and felt relieved that they had been removed from intimidation by both sides in the war. Often, however, the conditions in the PVs were deplorable. In 1974 Operation Overload removed tens of thousands of tribesmen from the Chiweshe and Madziwa areas and placed them in PVs where conditions were primitive and disease-ridden. The Rhodesians, like the Americans in Vietnam, forgot that hearts and minds also live in bodies.

Yet the short-term gains were impressive from the Rhodesian point of view. By the end of 1974, Rhodesian intelligence estimated that only 70 to 100 hardcore guerrillas remained operative inside the country. The insurgents could perhaps have faced total elimination within a few months, if the security forces had kept up the pressure. But then the international factor ruptured Salisbury's COIN campaign. It went by the name of detente.

Detente was precipitated by South African reactions to events in Portugal. In April 1974 an army-inspired coup toppled the ultra-conservative government in Lisbon and the Portuguese forces became the only European army to revolt against the retention of colonial rule. (In Algeria the French army had rebelled in order to *retain* the French possession.) Like the Russian army in 1917, the Portuguese army became a debating society, not a fighting force. The war effort in the three African 'provinces' collapsed. A month after the coup the revolutionary junta in Lisbon asked Salisbury to halt all pursuit raids into Mozambique. A few days before Mozambican independence, according to the CIO agents running the operation, six former Portuguese air force pilots flew six Alouette III helicopters into Rhodesia, and were handsomely rewarded in US dollars.

Nevertheless, the *cordon sanitaire* around white-ruled Southern Africa was disintegrating; the sinews of white supremacy were raw and exposed. The new Mozambique and South Africa were groping towards an accord – Vorster did not want to disrupt his 'outward policy' of detente with black Africa. But Smith's

Rhodesia was getting in Pretoria's way. South Africa wanted a moderate and pliant black regime to replace Smith and a long war in Rhodesia would produce a hardline Marxist regime inimical to South Africa. Mark Chona, Kaunda's top aide, and Hendrik van den Bergh, South Africa's intelligence chief, had been working secretly to force a compromise in Rhodesia. The war was destroying Zambia's economy, and Kaunda was tired of the rival Zimbabwean nationalists fighting in his country. Peace would suit both Kaunda and Vorster. As a result of tremendous pressure on Smith from Pretoria and equally blunt tactics by Kaunda and Julius Nyerere, a hurried and uneasy coalition of nationalists agreed to accept a ceasefire starting on 11 December 1974. A number of senior black political detainees were released and constitutional talks without preconditions were scheduled. As a quid pro quo for Kaunda's arm-twisting of the nationalists, Vorster promised to remove South African forces from Rhodesia.

The ceasefire did not work: the Rhodesians pulled back only some of their forward groups and failed to release all the detainees; the guerrillas continued to infiltrate. For example, on 16 December 1974 a group of guerrillas led by Herbert Shungu sent an emissary to a South African police camp with an invitation to discuss surrender terms. The South Africans walked blithely into a trap and were ambushed on the high-level Mazoe bridge. Six of them were killed.

Despite the failure of the ceasefire, Pretoria was determined to keep up the pressure. Disregarding the anger in Salisbury, the South African foreign minister, Dr Hilgard Muller, announced on 11 February 1975 that the SAP had been removed from their forward positions. On 1 August the remaining '200' SAP were ordered out of Rhodesia. (Secretly, under the code name Operation Polo, more than 50 helicopter pilots and mechanics remained to run the Rhodesians' vital chopper force.) Vorster had played his part by leaning on Smith. Now Kaunda nudged the nationalists to agree to a conference at the Victoria Falls bridge in August. The talks proved abortive, except for the unexpectedly good personal accord reached between Vorster and Kaunda. Black and white Rhodesians seemed light years away from settling their differences.

The ceasefire had been a major psychological setback for Salisbury. The nationalists spread the message on the bush telegraph that the whites had been defeated and were surrendering. Ian Smith's comments on the ceasefire were:

> We were on the brink of dealing a knock-out blow. We had them on the run; of this there is no doubt... In a sense we dropped our guard and as a result we lost a bit of ground. This not only affected us militarily but, more important, psychologically.

The nationalists, however, were not in a position to take advantage of their propaganda success. The year 1975 was a bad one for their liberation struggle. In the previous December the 'Nhari rebellion' had erupted within ZANLA. Thomas Nhari, a senior member of the general staff, kidnapped senior ZANU men in Lusaka as well as taking over the Chifombo camp on the Mozambique-Zambian border. Tongogara's wife and children were also held captive and tortured. Nhari, as an ex-ZAPU man, had been trained in Russia. One of his complaints was the lack of sophisticated weapons reaching ZANLA. The disgruntled cadres that followed him also complained about the lack of supplies and poor administration. Eventually Nhari's men were brought to heel and the leaders, including Nhari and Dakarai Badza, were executed, but only after the deaths of between 50 and 60 ZANLA personnel. Then in March 1975 the charismatic leader, Herbert Chitepo, was assassinated in Lusaka. In a Zambian-sponsored 'international' inquiry that followed, the blame was placed upon ZANLA; and a number of leaders, including the unfortunate Tongogara, were tortured and imprisoned in Zambia. Chitepo's death was a major setback for ZANLA and the war effort was forced into low gear for a year. (Who killed Chitepo? Although much of the initial evidence pointed to ZANLA infighting, the Zambians had a major axe to grind. They were embarrassed by Chitepo's outspoken criticism of their policy of detente with South Africa. Salisbury also gained from Chitepo's death. Years later, former agents in the Rhodesian CIO admitted to organizing the murder. Two former British SAS men, Alan 'Taffy' Brice and Hugh 'Chuck' Hind, set up the operation in Lusaka. The Welshman planted an explosive device in the wheel arch of Chitepo's blue VW Beetle. The CIO also sent Brice to London in late 1979 to assassinate Mugabe at the Lancaster House talks.)

Zambian pressures forced the remaining members of ZANLA to flee to Mozambique. Zambia became the sole stamping ground of Nkomo's ZIPRA troops, the military wing of ZAPU. The emasculation of the ZANU leadership disrupted the logistic network to the men in the field; food and supplies ran short. The gaolings and the deaths in the Nhari rebellion had diluted the efficiency and the numbers of ZANLA's combat commanders. The less experienced replacements soon fell victim to increased security force activity in Rhodesia and the expansion of the PV programme. ZANLA morale sagged and the casualty rate rocketed. According to Rhodesian intelligence, 'in December 1975 there were only three groups of 10 terrorists each operating in Rhodesia'. That was only a slight exaggeration.

ZANU was also short of funds. The OAU had insisted on funnelling its financial support to the African National Council, the nationalist umbrella organization headed by Bishop Abel Muzorewa. Zambia had removed its diplomatic backing for ZANU after Chitepo's death. ZAPU, on the other hand, was given Kaunda's total endorsement; and ZIPRA continued to get a cornucopia of Russian arms through Lusaka. ZANLA had only a shaky base in Mozambique. Samora Machel, the Mozambican president, personally distrusted Mugabe; Machel still viewed ZANU as a fractious offshoot of ZAPU and questioned ZANLA's support in the eastern parts of Rhodesia. Although Machel kept Mugabe and his colleague, Edgar Tekere, under loose house arrest, he grew to respect Mugabe's commitment to the armed struggle and to appreciate his support both among the fighting cadres and the 'masses' in the countryside.

Gaining the total support of FRELIMO was only one of Mugabe's problems. Some sections of ZANLA had grown tired of the infighting between ZANU and ZAPU and the mismanagement which grew to alarming proportions in 1975. The idea of a 'third force' evolved to try to heal the nationalists' splits by coordinating the military wings, thus bypassing the fractious politicians. The Zimbabwe People's Army (ZIPA) was formed, led by Rex Nhongo from ZANLA and Alfred 'Nikita' Mangena of ZIPRA. The OAU and the frontline states initially welcomed this merger. Soon ZIPA began to act as an independent force. ZIPA wanted to separate from ZANU to form a revolutionary political party which would represent a total commitment to the armed struggle; a separate ZIPA delegation turned up at the Geneva conference, held later in 1976. FRELIMO, however, locked up some of the ZIPA leaders and others returned to the ZANLA fold. The ZIPRA elements left Mozambique to try to rejoin their comrades in Zambia and Matabeleland.

Although ZIPA's influence was temporary, it did launch a fresh offensive into Rhodesia. In Tete, ZIPA concentrated on mobilizing the masses; in Manicaland it adopted a strategy of sabotage, and in the south the guerrillas tried to destroy part of the new rail line to South Africa via Rutenga. The fresh onslaught began on 21 January 1976 when a group of 90 ZIPA guerrillas crossed the border south of Nyamapanda. The following morning four were killed and one was captured. Like so many captured guerrillas, he provided the Rhodesians with a wealth of information. He explained that this unit was part of a three-pronged assault. But the second wave, against the Melsetter area abutting the Mozambique border, did not take place until five weeks later and the third assault in the south-east did not occur until seven weeks later – three months after the planned 'simultaneous' incursions. This delay gave the security forces time to deploy more troops. Extra call-ups stretched the numbers to about 20,000 on active service. In February 1976, Operation Thrasher, based at Umtali, was established to monitor the eastern border, and in May 1976, Operation Repulse, with its HQ at Fort Victoria, was set up to counter guerrilla infiltration in the south-eastern lowveld.

In March 1976, the Rhodesian government appeared to be on top of the war. Ian Smith was conducting a cosy series of talks with Joshua Nkomo about a settlement – a settlement which as far as Smith was concerned would never include black majority rule. To most whites the war seemed restricted to the border areas. In the towns and cities, where the vast majority of whites relaxed in comfortable suburban cocoons, life seemed perfectly normal. The army was doing well; the police informer network was flushing out guerrilla sympathizers; the blacks in the armed forces and the police (who outnumbered the white members) were loyal. Salisbury clearly felt able to fight a long war, with blacks and whites fighting side by side against what it called 'international communism'. It was only a question of time before the West came to its senses, or so the argument ran.

Indeed, international factors were about to influence the course of the war, but not in the way Rhodesian whites expected. The power most immediately concerned was South Africa. When the Nkomo-Smith talks broke down at the end of March 1976, Pretoria was determined to push Salisbury towards an urgent settlement. The reason? Despite military successes in the Angolan civil war, the South African army had been forced by political constraints to retreat. The Cuban-backed People's Movement for the Liberation of Angola (MPLA) had claimed a huge victory. For

Pretoria the long-dreaded nightmare had become a reality. More than 20,000 Cuban combat troops were positioned in Angola. They would be bound to aid the attacks by the South West Africa People's Organization (SWAPO) into South African-ruled Namibia/South West Africa. Pretoria did not want any escalation of the Rhodesian war into Mozambique which might suck Castro's men into another country contiguous to South Africa.

FRELIMO-ruled Mozambique was totally absorbed in consolidating its independence. The almost total exodus of Portuguese whites had left the country in chaos. Mozambique was dependent upon Rhodesian tourists and food and transport revenues. Although Samora Machel was anxious to avoid all-out war with Rhodesia, his commitment to the guerrilla struggle was unequivocal. But the escalation of hostilities made war between Rhodesia and Mozambique inevitable. On 23 February 1976 the Rhodesian air force strafed the village of Pafuri, a mile beyond the south-eastern tip of Rhodesia. Four days later Mozambique seized two Rhodesian train crews. Then Smith repeated his errors of 1973 when the Zambian border was closed. He halted all Rhodesian rail traffic through Maputo (formerly Lourenço Marques). In retaliation, on 3 March, Machel cut all links and put his country on a war footing. One-sixth of Rhodesia's rolling stock, as well as massive amounts of sanctions-busting exports, were caught inside Mozambique. Rhodesia was now completely dependent upon the two rail lines to South Africa. This was a leverage Pretoria would soon employ.

The war began to creep towards the centre of the country. At Easter 1976, three South African tourists were killed when travelling on the main road to South Africa. Convoys on the main routes south were then inaugurated. The rail line via Beit Bridge was sabotaged. Then the other rail artery, the Bulawayo-Botswana line, came under attack. Some ZIPRA members of ZIPA who had fled from Mozambique rejoined their comrades operating from Botswana and Zambia. Under intense OAU pressure from mid-1976, ZIPRA forces began to infiltrate across the north-western Zambezi and the north-east of Botswana. In August 1976, Operation Tangent was opened to counter the new ZIPRA moves. The previous month, guerrillas had also attacked a restaurant and a nightclub in Salisbury with Chinese stick grenades, injuring two whites.

The Rhodesian government was more concerned about FRELIMO support for ZANLA incursions from Mozambique. Between February and June 1976 the Mozambique government estimated that 40 Rhodesian raids had been launched across the border. Rhodesian intelligence reported that about 900 guerrillas were preparing to cross into Rhodesia in August from the Nyadzonya camp. Smith's commanders wanted to launch an Entebbe-style raid and wipe out the guerrilla concentration. This would also bolster sagging white morale. Smith was wary; Vorster had warned him not to raise the tempo of the conflict and thus risk the entry of Cubans into the Rhodesian war. On 5 August a group of about 60 guerrillas attacked a security force base at Ruda, north of Umtali. No casualties were caused, but it was unusual for the guerrillas to hit a base in such numbers. Three days later four territorial soldiers from Umtali were killed in a mortar attack in the Burmah valley, south of Umtali. A fifth Umtali man died in pursuit operations. For a small, close-knit community such as Umtali the loss of five local men was a major blow. The townspeople demanded action against the guerrillas ensconced across the border only a few miles away.

Smith had the support of the other hawks on his war council. The target would be Nyadzonya about 40 km north-east of Umtali. On 9 August Operation Eland comprising a convoy of vehicles containing 84 Selous Scouts crossed the border. The column was made up of seven armoured Unimogs and four Ferret armoured cars (pre-UDI donations from the British). Two of the Unimogs were armed with Hispano 20mm cannon scavenged from retired Vampire aircraft. The Selous Scouts, including many blacks, particularly a turned ZANLA commissar, Morrison Nyathi, and an attached SAS member who spoke Portuguese, were dressed as FRELIMO soldiers. The vehicles, too, were disguised as Mozambican. After deploying some of the force along the route, 72 men led by a South African, Captain Rob Warraker, drove coolly into a major ZANLA base containing over 5,000 personnel. The SAS man ordered, in abusive Portuguese, the gate to be opened. It was 8.25 am. Dropping off a mortar unit at the entrance, the Scouts drove onto the parade ground, where excellent intelligence had accurately predicted that the inhabitants would be assembled. While the SAS man and a Shona-speaking Scout harangued the assembly with revolutionary clichés, the ZANLA cadres began to swarm around the Rhodesian vehicles. Eventually, as those pressed right against the vehicles realized that whites were inside, Warraker gave the order to fire. Initially at point-blank range, three twin MAG machine guns, one .50 Browning machine gun, one 12.7mm heavy machine gun, two Hispano-Suiza 20mm cannons, three .30 Brownings on the Ferret armoured cars and the personal weapons of the Scouts opened up. Carnage ensued. Hundreds were shot, burnt or drowned while trying to escape in the nearby Nyadzonya river. The commander of the Selous Scouts later wrote that the raid was 'the classic operation of the whole war…carried out by only seventy-two soldiers…without air support…and without reserves of any kind'. ZANLA, however, insisted that Nyadzonya was a refugee camp and later held up the raid as the worst atrocity of the war. It seems that, although nearly all the personnel in the camp were unarmed, many were trained guerrillas or undergoing instruction. According to ZANLA documents captured later, 1,028 were killed (without a single security force fatality). ZANLA had been totally surprised.

So was Vorster when he heard the news. He immediately terminated Operation Polo, the code-name for the South Africans who had secretly stayed on in Rhodesia after the official withdrawal in August 1975. Helicopter pilots, mechanics, and liaison officers were summarily withdrawn. The Rhodesian air force's strike capacity was cut in half. Worse followed. Although the closure of the Mozambique border had caused genuine congestion on the two railways to South Africa, artificial choke points soon developed, particularly when it came to vital supplies such as arms and oil. Vorster was angry; the cutbacks in pilots, petrol and bullets made sure Smith knew it. And there was more. On Vorster's instructions, Dr Muller, the foreign minister, declared that South Africa supported the principle of majority rule in

Rhodesia. The unsayable had been said. Politically Vorster had pulled the rug from under Smith.

The Soweto disturbances, which began in June 1976, had prompted Vorster to compromise over Rhodesia and Namibia. Henry Kissinger, the American secretary of state, knew that the key to compromise in Rhodesia lay in Vorster's hands. He was the only one who could nail Smith to the ground once he was down. Kissinger promised Vorster concessions on American anti-apartheid policy if he delivered Smith's head on a platter. During a series of talks in Pretoria in September Vorster did just that. In an angry encounter, Vorster read the riot act to the Rhodesian premier: agree to majority rule or we will cut off your supplies. On 24 September, on Rhodesian television, Smith conceded the principle of majority rule. He announced that in return for majority rule (which he did not define) the war and sanctions would end and a 'trust fund' would be established for development. This was all part of the Kissinger package. Smith added: 'The alternatives to acceptance of the proposals were explained to us in the clearest terms which left no room for misunderstanding.'

There was certainly room for misunderstanding in the Geneva conference which followed Smith's surrender. The nationalists were supposed to discuss the mechanics of the rapid transition to majority rule. But the various parties, the United African National Council (UANC), ZANU (Sithole), as well as Mugabe's ZANU and Nkomo's ZAPU (which had coalesced to form the Patriotic Front), all claimed to be the sole leaders of the African masses.

Smith expected the conference to fail. The moderates within his party realized that unfettered white rule was ending and that the best game plan would be to compromise with the most conservative of the black nationalist groups. Other RF MPs went around their constituencies explaining that the Kissinger package would buy time. Even if the two-year transition was accepted, the whites would still control the security apparatus. And if things did not work out in two years' time, then after that period of grace from sanctions and war Rhodesia would be in a much stronger position to finish off the guerrillas for good – with South African backing and perhaps even a wink from the West.

But all the nods and winks in the world could not hide the fact that Smith had reversed the original war aim of the whites: to prevent black rule. Morale in the army slumped. Some of the younger army officers began to mumble about a military coup and Special Branch was kept busy monitoring these white right-wing radicals, as well as trying to keep tabs on the black guerrillas.

The guerrillas had planned to launch an offensive to coincide with the Geneva conference; it did not come off. Three days before the conference started, the Rhodesians hit bases in Mozambique. In the north-east, in Tete province, six camps were destroyed. Eighty tons of war material were captured. Most of it was destroyed but eight tons, mainly anti-aircraft guns, anti-tank guns, mortars and heavy machine guns, were brought back to Rhodesia. In the south of Mozambique, camps in Gaza were hit and the main railway to Maputo was sabotaged. The guerrillas, however, suffered few casualties. The camps had received advance warning and so they had been evacuated. This became a frequent pattern which angered military commanders in Salisbury. They conjectured that a senior Rhodesian intelligence source was leaking information, either to the South Africans (who, they suggested, might be tipping off ZANLA), or directly to Mozambique. Nonetheless, the raids in August and November had pre-empted the offensive planned for the rainy season of 1976/7.

When the Geneva conference ended without any result, South Africa loosened its armlock on Rhodesia. Salisbury would get enough arms to hold off the guerrillas until a settlement could be reached, but not enough to obliterate them, which would have brought in the Russians and their East German and Cuban proxies. Smith had clearly dispensed with international diplomacy and moved towards an 'internal settlement'. When the chairman of the Geneva conference, Ivor Richard, tried to resuscitate the talks in early 1977, the idea of involving the guerrillas in the transitional security arrangements shocked Smith and his commanders. To them the internal route to black rule looked much safer.

Most of the whites backed Smith's rejections of the British modifications of the Kissinger package. As P K van der Byl, the defence and later the foreign minister, said so dramatically: 'If this new proposal was to be imposed on us, it is better to fight to the last man and the last cartridge and anyway die with some honour than die in front of one of Mugabe's people's courts.'

The easing of South African pressure had ensured that the security forces were not down to the last cartridge, but nonetheless the full-scale war was about to begin. From 1965 to 1972, the guerrillas had managed to apply pinpricks to white rule. In the second phase, from 1972 to 1976, there had been a large degree of African political mobilization, particularly in Mashonaland, but the government had managed to contain the burgeoning conflict with the reluctant and erratic support of South Africa. In the following three years, 1977-79, the war would grow to engulf the whole country and to destroy the Rhodesian government's resolve to fight on.

Chapter Four

THE RHODESIAN SECURITY FORCES

THE STRUCTURE

The armed forces of Rhodesia won virtually every battle and skirmish they ever fought against the guerrilla armies, yet they lost the war. In July 1977, Foreign Minister P K van der Byl said of white Rhodesians' resolve never to live under a guerrilla regime: 'We will contest every hill and every river, every village and every town, every crossroad and every bridge.' Van der Byl's penchant for Churchillian rhetoric was renowned, but his declaration epitomized the objectives of the Rhodesians' war against the nationalists: never to surrender their political, social and economic power to black majority rule. Yet the war was lost, and in April 1980 the guerrillas grasped the reins of power for which they had fought so long.

The story of the Rhodesian armed forces during the civil war is one of tactical brilliance and strategic ineptitude. Rarely in military history have such thinly stretched troops, hampered by chronic manpower, training, equipment and financial constraints achieved such consistent successes against enemy forces which enjoyed the tactical and strategic initiative for most of the war, and often reached numerical parity in the field. But the Rhodesian obsession with successful tactics created a fatal blindness to the strategic imperatives of a protracted revolutionary war such as the guerrillas were waging.

The early stages of the war were fought with the armed forces much the same as they had been at the break-up of Federation. The rashness of the guerrillas' early strategy and tactics required no expansion of the armed forces or mobilization of reserves much beyond peace-time levels. Until 1972 the brunt of the counter-insurgency operations was borne by the British South Africa Police, the RAR, the Rhodesian Light Infantry and the Royal Rhodesian Air Force (the 'Royal' was dropped in 1970 when Rhodesia became a republic). Reserve forces assisted from time to time, but did not assume the importance of later years.

The counter-insurgency operations were originally conceived of as a 'police action', with the army aiding the civil power against what were characterized as politically motivated criminals. Guerrillas were tried and convicted through the civil courts and were imprisoned or executed through the same machinery as common criminals. This preserved the fiction that the government was waging a campaign against violent criminal elements rather than an incipient civil war, but despite its

RHODESIA UNDER SIEGE 1979

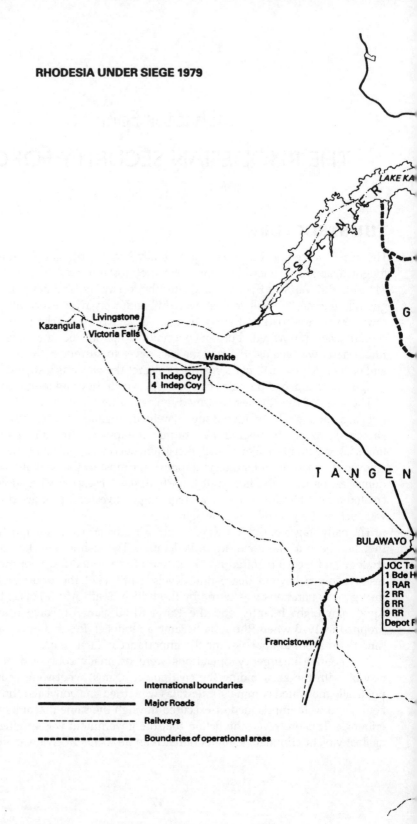

Livingstone
Kazangula
Victoria Falls
Wankie

1 Indep Coy
4 Indep Coy

TANGEN

BULAWAYO

JOC Ta
1 Bde H
1 RAR
2 RR
6 RR
9 RR
Depot F

Francistown

----------------- International boundaries
——————— Major Roads
- - - - - - - - - - - Railways
==================== Boundaries of operational areas

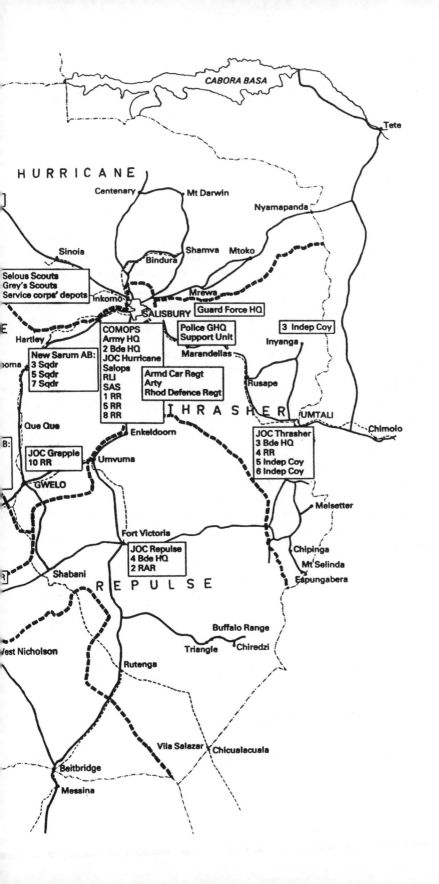

political usefulness this attitude ignored the realities of the conflict. The police were responsible for the painstaking collection of evidence and the preparation of criminal dockets. It was only in 1978-9 that disaffected areas were placed under martial law and tribunals empowered to deal with captured guerrillas.

REGULAR FORCES

Police

In a sense it was natural that the BSAP should be involved in counter-insurgency operations from the start. The unit (formed partly from the earlier British South Africa Company police) was raised in 1896 to combat the Shona and Ndebele insurgents, and in 1897 was almost solely responsible for mopping up the final stubborn pockets of resistance. The Rhodesian authorities liked to boast that, after 1897, the police did not shoot and kill a single African until 26 July 1960, during serious rioting in Bulawayo. The force was structured as a cavalry regiment and its military ethos remained with it until the 1980s. Although its functions became increasingly civil in succeeding decades after its foundation, it never entirely lost its paramilitary role nor its military spirit, signified by the force's nickname, 'The Regiment', and its status as the 'senior service'.

The regular police, numbering about 2,000 whites and 6,000 blacks at the height of the war, received long periods of counter-insurgency training during their recruit courses. Although most active policemen served in a civil capacity, most white junior ranks were required to serve periodic tours in the Police Anti-Terrorist Unit (PATU), otherwise essentially a reserve element.

As the war intensified, so the combat role of the regular police expanded. The Support Unit, nicknamed the 'Black Boots', was formed as a regular counter-insurgency unit and eventually expanded into a light infantry battalion of black constables officered by whites. The unit was highly successful and at times scored a higher kill rate than regular army formations. A widening war encouraged the proliferation of other specialist police units. The Special Branch, initially responsible for the investigation of political crime and undercover surveillance, diversified into the collection of field intelligence when it absorbed the police 'Ground Coverage' network of operatives and informers. A Special Branch section, the SB-Scouts, was a small unit of Special Branch agents, Selous Scouts and captured guerrillas which carried out more dangerous and esoteric intelligence-gathering, as well as conducting clandestine operations against the enemy's political and military infrastructure. A Police Mounted Unit, formed in 1976, was an attempt to increase the mobility of police COIN forces, but it was a gimmicky formation which remained limited in size. The explosion of stock theft, which was part of the guerrilla strategy of undermining the white economy and its logistics system, brought the creation of specialized anti-stock theft teams. Their high mobility and ruthlessness in dealing with stock thieves, as well as a mandatory nine-year gaol sentence for cattle theft, were only partly successful in controlling this chronic problem for the white farming community. The spread of the war to the urban areas in the latter stages of the conflict was countered by the Urban Emergency unit, a 'special weapons and tactics' (SWAT) group, which was highly successful in rooting out and deterring urban terrorism.

Like all the armed forces, the police suffered from a shortage of quality manpower. This was partly alleviated by the allocation of part of the national service intakes for each year from 1973, and the greater responsibility of reserve units to assist in preventing and detecting crime in urban areas and the safer rural districts. Increasing reliance was also placed on black recruits, who made up the rank and file, and the stretching of white officers' responsibilities.

Army

The cutting edge of the Rhodesian security forces was provided by the regular units of the army, and they assumed the status of a strategic reserve-cum-shock force in the late 1970s. All the regular units expanded considerably during the war and came to absorb portions of the periodic national service intakes of white youths. In time these national servicemen formed the reserve elements of the regular units and were called up for tours of duty with them.

The Rhodesian African Rifles (which received white national service officers, but no other ranks) expanded from a pre-UDI strength of one battalion to four. The second was formed in 1974, the third in 1977 and the fourth began recruiting in 1978. Only the second enjoyed anything like the training and respect that white officers accorded the first, veteran battalion. The fourth battalion never really functioned properly, and by the end of the war the RAR training establishment was simply churning out vast numbers of black soldiers to meet the insatiable demands of the armed forces for some sort of trained manpower to plug the gaps in the security forces' disintegrating control of the countryside. Raw black troops were integrated with white reserve units, which were dwindling through emigration, to bolster their strength and assimilate combat experience as quickly as possible. At that time some officers envisaged a future Rhodesian army in which virtually every white soldier was an officer or an NCO commanding vast numbers of black rank-and-file, but this did not come about before the war's end.

The Rhodesian Light Infantry finally reached full battalion strength in the early Seventies after years of inadequate recruitment. It was boosted by foreign enlistment and national service conscripts in its commando (company-sized units) structure. The RLI achieved notoriety as a sort of southern African Foreign Legion to which mercenaries flocked from all over the world. Estimates of the total numbers of foreigners who had served in the Rhodesian forces ranged up to 2,000, but a figure of 1,400 is more likely. A large proportion of them was concentrated in No. 3 Commando of the RLI. Although the guerrillas were able to make a great deal of propaganda out of foreign recruitment as a measure of the moral, political and military depravity of the Rhodesian government, these men were more ideological soldiers of fortune than true mercenaries. Most enlisted out of political and racial conviction or purely for high adventure, since their pay and conditions of service were the same as those of white recruits of Rhodesian origin.

The Special Air Service also attracted foreigners, though its tough selection course kept the unit relatively small, with a high proportion of white Rhodesians in its ranks. Although Peter McAleese records that at one stage in the late 1970s, in 'A' Squadron, most of the 33 regulars were foreigners, this tally excluded the Rhodesians in the Territorial SAS. On external operations, the SAS often wore enemy uniforms, so that if an operator was killed, especially if he were a foreigner, he could officially be disowned by the authorities. The formation had languished after the dissolution of the Federation, its strength dropping to as low as 20, but by 1978 volunteers (including national servicemen) took it up to three-squadron strength. Rhodesia's 'C' Squadron SAS had been formed to serve in Malaya alongside the British 'A' and 'B' Squadrons. (To this day, in the British SAS orbat, the 'C' Squadron remains vacant in honour of the lost Rhodesian element.) The Rhodesian SAS squadron later became 1 (Rhodesia) Special Air Service Regiment. A secret component was 'D' Squadron, made up of South African special forces Reconnaissance Commandos. Generally, the 40 South African operators preferred to work as a distinct unit, sometimes commanded by an SADF colonel, though they also fought alongside the Selous Scouts and Rhodesian SAS in external raids. They would sometimes fly to Salisbury on scheduled flights in civilian clothes, be met at the airport and then change into Rhodesian uniform. They were there to learn, as much as to help.

Two new units to emerge during the war were the Selous Scouts, which adopted the name relinquished by the Armoured Car Regiment, and the Grey's Scouts. The Selous Scouts took its name from the well-known nineteenth-century hunter, Frederick Courteney Selous; Henry Rider Haggard is said to have based the character of Allan Quatermain on the same adventurer. The Selous Scouts were originally formed as a small specialist tracking unit (called the Tracker Combat Unit) to provide support for other units on COIN operations. Initially there were two groups, under 2 Brigade, based at Kariba and Bindura. But the unit's functions multiplied, as did its size, to three troops, then a full battalion of 1,000 officers and men, most of whom were black. Selous Scouts conducted clandestine operations both inside and outside Rhodesia's borders. Individuals were attached to the Rhodesian intelligence service to gather information from as far afield as Tanzania and Angola. One Selous Scout became the most distinguished, and decorated, Rhodesian soldier. Captain Chris Schulenburg, a South African known as Schulie, usually with just one black Scout, performed feats of long-range ground reconnaissance unparalleled in modern counter-insurgency. (The full story of this modest officer was told in *The Selous Scouts: Top Secret War*.) The Scouts' Support Troop acted as assault infantry in raids into neighbouring countries, though it was never as effective as the SAS. (Most of the blunders of the Rhodesians on raids into Zambia were attributable to this formation acting on its own initiative or with too much licence granted by General Walls himself.) The unit's notoriety for treachery and brutality was only partly deserved, for the bulk of its members were engaged on routine military tasks. But the Selous Scouts did field 'pseudo-gangs' to deceive the guerrillas and their supporters, and to carry out punitive atrocities against villages which collaborated with the guerrillas. Selous Scout pseudo operators were paid a Rh$100 bounty for every guerrilla killed or captured along with their weapons. This rose to Rh$150 a head if there were more than ten guerrillas. The formation's penchant for secrecy (despite the wide publicity given to its existence and to its stringent selection tests), and the bogus cloak-and-dagger attitude of some of its ranks, helped the guerrillas to paint a picture of the battalion as a latter-day Waffen-SS. The undoubted efficiency and bravery of the soldiers in the unit, many of whom were national servicemen or reservists, and the extreme conditions under which they often operated, contributed to the images of ruthless shock troops promoted by the mass media around the world.

The Grey's Scouts were a mounted infantry unit formed to exploit the mobility of horses for COIN operations. The formation had mixed success, but they attracted high quality volunteers, again including many foreigners, and established a reputation for aggressiveness. At times they operated purely as foot-soldiers, depending on operational conditions.

Apart from the Grey's Scouts and the third and fourth battalions of the RAR, the regular units were increasingly deployed as military fire brigades within the country, and on external operations after 1976. The trend was to hand over routine, ground-covering patrols to reserve forces. Fire Force duties (see chapter on weapons and tactics) were allocated to the RLI, the RAR, the Support Company of the Selous Scouts and, less frequently, the SAS. Formations served two- to three-week tours as Fire Forces before being allocated to other operations. In consequence, most of their ranks received parachute training.

External operations were carried out almost exclusively by these regular formations. The SAS spent most of its time across the border. The Squadrons were deployed for months at a time in Mozambique, Zambia or Botswana on regular operations to harass guerrilla camps and lines of communication and to gather intelligence. Full-scale assaults on guerrilla bases, some involving combat paradrops from as low as 300 feet, were also a part of the unit's responsibilities. The RAR, RLI and Selous Scouts deployed detachments of up to company strength into neighbouring states, though most operations were on a smaller scale.

Other combat formations were the Independent Companies made up of national servicemen, the Artillery and the Armoured Car Regiment. The Independent Companies had specific areas of responsibility (for example, 2 Indep. Coy was based at Kariba, 3 Indep. Coy at Inyanga) in which they constantly operated. Occasionally they were deployed on Fire Force duties and on external raids. Their quality was never very high as they were the residue of national service intakes after officer training, the regular units, the specialized arms and police had taken their pick of conscripts. One such unit, 7 Indep. Coy, was a cover for a unit of French recruits into the Rhodesian forces. Some were veterans of the Foreign Legion, but they were not successful in Rhodesian conditions and were disbanded.

The service corps were largely staffed by regular troops, though their deficiencies were also made up by drafts of national servicemen and reservists. The corps divisions of responsibility were roughly similar to those of the British army: the Corps of Engineers, the Corps of Signals, Army Services Corps, Army Medical Corps, Military Police, Army Pay Corps, Army Educational Corps and the Corps of Chaplains. There were also miscellaneous departments such as the Psychological Action Group (Psyac) and Military Intelligence to co-ordinate field and external intelligence data. The Military Intelligence department performed poorly partly because of the small size of its staff, of whom nearly all were reservists. A big exception, however, was the signallers in Military Intelligence who operated the Radio Intercept Services. A great deal of vital information was gleaned from radio interception of guerrillas and regular troops based in Mozambique and Zambia. A Special Investigations Branch was created to ensure the internal security of the army and to root out subversion and dissidence among troops.

The army's 'tail' was remarkably lean, and the usual imbalance between combat and support units in modern armies was not a severe problem for the Rhodesian forces. Many functions of the 'tail' were carried out by cheap black auxiliary labour, so that little white manpower was allocated to trivial, but necessary, support functions. The emigration of skilled artisans from the country had serious repercussions for the armed forces. Motor vehicle mechanics were in chronically short supply, especially when the number of landmine and traffic incidents escalated alarmingly from 1976. The gaps in the security forces' maintenance capabilities were filled to a great extent by private contractors and by calling up skilled personnel to serve in security forces' workshops.

Air Force

The Rhodesian Air Force was a vital component of the war machine. Air force officers continued the traditions of the 'Brylcreem Boys' by claiming that they were responsible for the largest number of kills among the security forces, and that their operations made the bulk of other formations' successes possible. There was more than a grain of truth in this, for the air force allowed the most efficient deployment of the strategic reserve, and carried out photo-reconnaissance and air strikes on guerrilla concentrations in and outside Rhodesia.

The RAF's strike capability was based on a squadron of Hawker Hunter FGA9 fighter-bombers, one of Canberra B2 and T4 light bombers, one of Vampire RB9s, and Cessna 0-2 (Lynx) and Siai-Marchetti SF 260 (Genet) propeller-driven strike aircraft. Provost T52s and Vampire T55s were used in a strike capacity in the early years of the war, but were later relegated to training roles. The jet aircraft were used mainly for external operations, though the Hunter was a maid-of-all-work, since it carried out cross-border strikes, supported Fire Force operations and protected Rhodesian airspace. The Cessnas, which were brought through the sanctions barrier in red and white civilian livery, were converted to a military role and armed with machine guns, antipersonnel rocket pods and bomb racks in Rhodesia. They formed the backbone of Fire Force support throughout the country, since their slower speed and excellent maneuverability made them more suitable for the pinpoint accuracy often required in counter-guerrilla operations in close or broken terrain.

But it was in the transport of troops that the RAF played its most important role. Helicopters gave the Rhodesian forces the tactical flexibility they needed to control vast swathes of rugged countryside. The basic Rhodesian tactical element, the 'stick' of four or five men, was designed around the seating capacity of the mainstay of the helicopter capability of the Air Force, the Aerospatiale Alouette III. This machine was used not only for the rapid development of tracker and fighting teams, but was later the basis of Fire Force operations in the transport, command chopper and gunship roles, as well as being important for the evacuation (casevac) of the wounded. The force of 50-plus Alouettes, many on loan with their pilots and technicians from South Africa, was supplemented by a handful of Alouette II utility craft. Earlier in the war, the RAF had tried to acquire Pumas. Unlike the Alouettes which had been designed for civilian use, the Puma was specifically a military aircraft. As one senior Rhodesian air force officer lamented, 'The UN mandatory sanctions made the sale of such equipment to Rhodesia impossible – even for the French.' French technicians from Sud Aviation were nevertheless regular visitors to Rhodesia to advise on helicopter technology. A considerable boost to the airlift capability of the Rhodesian forces was the acquisition in 1978 of seven Bell 205s, the 'Huey' of Vietnam War fame, from Israel via the Comoro Islands. With a capacity of 12 to 16 men, each Bell could carry the equivalent of a former Fire Force of three to four Alouette IIIs. Cheetah was the name given to the Bells, which arrived in an appalling state. Without any manuals, they were completely overhauled, after 'removing tons of sand', according to a technician who worked on them.

As the scale of encounters between guerrilla detachments and units of the security forces increased, and before the acquisition of the Bells, paradrops from Dakotas were made an integral part of Fire Forces after September 1976. This necessitated large-scale parachute training of regular units which were routinely deployed as Fire Forces.

The transport squadrons of the RAF, which included Aermacchi AL60s, dubbed 'Trojans' by the Rhodesians, and Britten-Norman Islanders, also supplied remote base camps of the security forces and the network of airfields from which combat aircraft operated.

The squadron bases were at New Sarum, near Salisbury (home of the Canberra bomber, DC-3 and helicopter squadrons), and Thornhill, at Gwelo (home base of the Hunters, Trojans, Genets and Vampires). The operational areas were served by a network of Forward Airfields (FAFs), which ranged from large facilities like those at Grand Reef (Umtali) and Wankie, to airstrips attached to JOCs like that at Mtoko. A FAF was any airfield out of which aircraft operated in support of security forces' operations, and from time to time would accommodate Fire Forces as well.

Late in the war a new base was built near Hartley. The project was kept out of the public eye, but the facility was capable of supporting the most sophisticated jet fighter aircraft, and may have been planned as a base for operations by the South African Air Force. As it was remote from large population centres, operations could be mounted from it with considerably more secrecy than from Thornhill and New Sarum, which used the civil runways serving Salisbury international airport. The SAAF did provide much support and training, especially for external raids. Dakotas, Canberras and Alouettes on loan, or in support, were relatively easy to disguise but the Puma and Super Frelon choppers were not. Pretoria also provided ammunition, bombs, avionics and electronic surveillance for the Rhodesian air war. In a secret exchange (Operation Sand), Rhodesian instructors, technicians and student pilots were sent to South African bases. Flying training on Impala jets was conducted at Langebaan air base and also in Durban. The Rhodesians also manned one entire SAAF Mirage III squadron for a short period.

The RAF was supported by a large fleet of civilian aircraft operated by the Police Reserve Air Wing. These aircraft, most of them propeller-driven, carried out routine supply and administrative functions, although some were armed with Browning machine guns for a ground support role. Some PRAW pilots developed considerable expertise in tracking guerrillas from the air.

Airfield and installation defence was provided by an armoured car unit comprising national servicemen and members of the air force reserve, around a regular core, and by an all-black General Service Unit.

Reserves

If the regular army, police and the RAF were the mainstays of the Rhodesian security forces, the bulk of military manpower was engaged in less spectacular roles. It is a rule of thumb that the larger the formation the blunter the instrument. The major source of manpower for the Rhodesian armed forces was mobilization of reserves. The call-up net eventually encompassed all able-bodied white men between 18 and 60. All white youths between 18 and 25 were liable to conscription. The commitment eventually rose to 18 months, though those who would go on to universities had to serve 24 months since they would enjoy exemption from reserve duties while they were students. Men in the 25 to 38 age bracket were liable to reserve duty in the army, but were increasingly posted to other formations and services. Those who had missed national service conscription were first called up for training. Men over 38 were liable to serve in the Rhodesia Defence Regiment or the Police Reserve structure. The commitments of various groups differed. The most heavily pressed group were men in the 25 to 38 age bracket, who at the height of the war were liable to serve six months a year with their units. The pattern of tours became 'six weeks in, six weeks out', but even that was changed to 'four weeks in, four weeks out' in periods of acute manpower shortage, such as the traditional guerrilla rainy season offensives.

In the pre-UDI period there were two reserve formations, the Territorial Force based on white battalions of the Royal Rhodesia Regiment (the Royal was dropped when Rhodesia declared itself a republic), and the Police Reserve. The Rhodesia Regiment trained national servicemen who were conscripted for six weeks' basic training under the 1957 Defence Act. In the early 1960s the number of battalions was increased and the length of basic training rose to 4½ months. Conscripts had a reserve commitment in the battalions of the Rhodesia Regiment on release from basic training. Police Reservists were volunteers who supported the normal operations of the BSAP, and played an important role in suppressing urban disorders in the early 1960s.

Both forces changed considerably in the war years. The Territorial Battalions lost their training role and became exclusively reserve units once national servicemen were allocated to Independent Companies, the regular units, the specialist arms, the police and other supporting parts of the armed forces' structure. Servicemen who had completed their initial period of active service were transferred to the TF battalions until they were 38. The TF battalions, which were city- and district-based, eventually numbered eight (designated 1, 2, 4, 5, 6, 8, 9 and 10 RR) and with a total nominal strength of 15,000.

As national servicemen began to pass through a diversity of units from 1973, so each formation built up a TF, reserve element which was called up for periodic tours of duty. Even the SAS, Grey's Scouts and Selous Scouts had reserve components of part-time soldiers. The Rhodesian Intelligence Corps was commanded by a territorial officer and was staffed almost completely by reservists. It collected and collated field intelligence and provided up-to-date maps for all arms of the security forces.

The Police Reserve became a repository for less able and older conscripts. Men in the 38 to 60 age bracket were automatically conscripted into its ranks, although PATU contained considerable numbers of active, younger men, exempted from army service for occupational reasons, police regulars and national servicemen who had passed on to a reserve commitment, and large numbers of farmers. Sections of PATU conducted highly successful operations, but their main function was to cover ground aggressively and act in a reconnaissance role. Other elements of the Police Reserve were the 'A' Reserve, which assisted the duty branches of the BSAP in crime prevention, and the Field Reserve. The latter was used mainly for protection duties on farms, bridges, convoys, radio relay stations and other installations. The International Institute for Strategic Studies estimated a peak strength for the Police Reserve of 35,000 in 1978, but this is probably too high a figure. In 1979, Police Reserve strength in Salisbury, the country's biggest reservoir of white manpower, stood at only 4,500, and it is unlikely that there were more than 30,000 reservists in the rest of the country. The standard of training, equipment, leadership and organization of the Field Reserve was not impressive and it was only the low calibre of the guerrillas which saved periodic slaughtering of these poorly trained reservists.

Africans were not liable to conscription until 1978, when a very limited and cautious programme was introduced to conscript black youths aged 18 to 25. The potential problems of conscripting the vast numbers available, many of whom were reluctant or disaffected, were so great that the programme never really got off the ground before the ceasefire in December 1979.

Asian and Coloured youths were liable to conscription, and in due course these communities were also brought into the reserve structure. Low morale and inefficiency were caused by discrimination in terms of service, pay and conditions, but these were equalized with white conditions of service towards the end of the war. Most Asians and Coloureds were drafted into the Protection Companies for defensive duties and as drivers in the early days of the war, but later formed the bulk of the Rhodesia Defence Regiment (nicknamed the Rhodesian Dagga [marijuana] Regiment because of its poor discipline). Many also served in the Police Reserve.

Training was a headache for the military authorities throughout the war. The elite units received elite training. The Selous Scouts and SAS were trained for periods of up to eight months before taking the field, and their pre- and post-deployment retraining programmes were excellent. The training of Territorial Force battalions was gradually improved, but a chronic shortage of instructors persisted, whose skills were also badly needed in the field. This deficiency was exacerbated by the armed forces' poor use of the skills and qualifications of reserve manpower. General Walls spoke of fitting round pegs into round holes, but a great deal of valuable manpower was wasted on the performance of military tasks which could have been carried out by far less-qualified soldiers. The Police Reserve in particular suffered from low-calibre instructors.

Once the armed forces began to mushroom, low-quality troops became a chronic weakness of the Rhodesian forces. The Guard Force was created in 1975 as a 'Fourth Arm' with the responsibility for manning protected villages, the Rhodesian version of the strategic hamlets of Malaya and Vietnam. The Rhodesia Defence Regiment was created in 1978. One battalion was attached to each brigade headquarters to protect military installations and lines of communication. Because large numbers were required for these units at short notice, training was superficial. The tedious nature of their static tasks made the units poorly disciplined and Guard Force details often committed crimes against the populations they were charged with protecting. Had they stood against a determined, well-trained enemy they would have had little chance. Both these units received drafts of white national servicemen and (often elderly) reservists, but these were usually of low calibre and suffered from poor morale because of their attachment to notoriously inefficient units. Towards the end of the war, when the Ministry of Internal Affairs and Security Force Auxiliaries took greater responsibility for defending PVs, Guard Force received better training and sometimes fought in an infantry role. But their primary task remained defensive, including the protection of white farms, ranches and communications links.

One unsuccessful expedient adopted was that of integrating inexperienced troops with battle-hardened units. The RAR's battalions were used to try to give a quick patina of combat experience to large numbers of recruits who were given shorter than usual periods of basic training from 1978. This experiment had limited success, but the attempt to integrate the previously all-white Rhodesia Regiment battalions was a disastrous failure. The racial prejudices of the territorial soldiers and the inexperience and unreliability of the African recruits caused morale among the whites to plummet. The white territorials alleged that the Africans displayed cowardice under fire, and resentment against this invasion of a former white preserve was reflected in lower combat effectiveness.

Two other formations should be mentioned. The Ministry of Internal Affairs, responsible for the administration of the country's African population and the TTLs, where most guerrilla activity occurred, increased its military role as Rhodesia became a garrison state. By 1978-9 administration of large areas of the country was possible only in the presence of armed force. Internal Affairs personnel in the districts were invariably armed. The rank and file, made up mainly of District Security Assistants (DSAs), was generally low-calibre manpower, poorly trained, led and equipped (initially with .303 bolt-operated rifles, though they later received LMGs). The DSAs were in close contact with the African population of the TTLs, which meant that they were in close contact with guerrilla operations, with consequently high, morale-sapping casualty rates. The quality of the District Assistants (DAs) and paramilitary DSAs depended largely upon the quality of the District Commissioners who led them. As one police officer who worked closely with Internal Affairs, noted of the DAs and DSAs, 'They died well and died en masse.'To try to counter insurgency in districts where leadership was poor, Internal Affairs set up the Administrative Reinforcement Unit (ARU). Despite its apparently innocuous name, this white-led force was 'full of hard men', according to one Rhodesian military historian. 'Despite sounding like they checked paperclips, the ARU was very gung-ho and well-equipped.'

A late appearance was the auxiliary army, grandly titled *Pfumo reVanhu* ('the Spear of the People'; *Umkonto wa Bantu* in Matabeleland) which emerged from the internal political settlement of 3 March 1978. Under code name Operation Favour, the auxiliaries were boosted in number to try to match the size of ZANLA. About US$10 million was raised with money coming from Saudi Arabia, and especially from the Sultan of Oman, a good friend of Rhodesia and a fervent anti-communist. Ostensibly comprising guerrillas who surrendered under an amnesty similar to the *Chieu Hoi* programme in Vietnam, a large number (about 90 per cent, according to one Rhodesian officer who worked with them) were in fact raw recruits, some merely boys, lured or press-ganged into its ranks from urban townships. Some units fought well, especially in the Urungwe TTL, but others were merely an armed rabble. Originally liaison between the Rhodesian military authorities and the SFAs was carried out by Special Branch agents, but towards the end of the war many auxiliaries protecting PVs came under Internal Affairs control and the rest under a new unit, the Special Forces. Their political alignment to Sithole's ZANU and Muzorewa's UANC was more a hindrance than a help, for this made ideal propaganda for the guerrillas. Any military value they may have had was offset by the political costs of periodic rampages and reigns of terror inflicted on African populations in their areas of responsibility, called 'frozen zones' (distinct from zones reserved for Selous Scout operations) because other Rhodesian units were not permitted to operate there. The Rhodesian government's verdict on this generally unsuccessful experiment was revealed when, in 1979, it felt forced to wipe out two ill-disciplined and disaffected groups of auxiliaries loyal to Sithole.

COMMAND AND CO-ORDINATION

The orchestration of this war machine became increasingly difficult as the conflict progressed. Not only was there a proliferation of military units and an increase in the numbers deployed on COIN operations, but a large number of civil ministries both took part in the war effort and required co-operation with the security forces to continue functioning in areas infiltrated and subverted by guerrillas. Internal Affairs was in the forefront of the war, but the Ministries of Transport and Roads, of Water Development and of Manpower, Health and Social Services all played mundane but vital roles in the counter-insurgency campaigns. The army was administered by four brigades, the police by provinces, the air force by squadrons, Internal Affairs by province and district, and other participating forces and ministries on different criteria. Initially the war effort was co-ordinated mainly through the Operations Co-ordinating Committee (OCC) and inter-ministerial contact in a 'War Council' (formed in 1964). In the field, co-operation between the services was provided by Joint Operations Commands (JOCs), on which representatives of each of the armed services sat with liaison officials of Internal Affairs (and other civilian ministries where required). In this way the total resources of the operational area could be most efficiently deployed. The informal atmosphere at JOC meetings usually made them a smooth conduit for the issue of orders to combat units and the supporting infrastructure, though sometimes inter-service rivalry (mainly between the police and the army) bedevilled individual JOCs and sub-JOCs.

But the dramatic widening of the war from 1976 impelled the creation of a more complex organization. The country was divided into 'operational areas'. The first, and only one until 1976, was Operation Hurricane, which covered the north-east of the country. Mozambique's decision to allow complete freedom of movement to ZANLA guerrillas and to assist their operations brought the creation of Operation Thrasher in the eastern districts and Operation Repulse along the south-eastern border in 1976. Operation Tangent was created later, in August 1977, to cover the western part of the country, where ZIPRA guerrillas began to operate after Zambia and Botswana decided to step up their assistance to the armed nationalists. Operation Splinter came to cover Lake Kariba, Operation Grapple the Midlands, and Salops the city of Salisbury and its immediate hinterland.

The JOCs were located in major centres: JOC Hurricane was at Centenary and Bindura until it moved to Salisbury in the closing stages of the war, JOC Thrasher at Umtali, JOC Repulse at Fort Victoria, JOC Tangent at Bulawayo and JOC Grapple at

Gwelo. Salops was primarily a police operation which required no formal JOC, while Splinter was controlled by a sub-JOC. There were 17 sub-JOCs in all by the end of the war. In late 1978 it was decided to make JOCs potentially mobile so that they could be deployed in the field at the centre of large-scale operations if required, but this ambitious concept did not catch on and most JOCs remained static. At JOCs, local operations were conducted within the framework of national strategy and operational policies. The JOC, usually under the chairmanship of an army brigadier, set priorities for deploying combat troops and Fire Forces, co-ordinated the protection of installations, the movement of Africans into strategic hamlets, and repair and maintenance of damaged roads, bridges, telephone lines and railways.

JOCs also issued situation reports (sitreps) for the operational areas under their control. These catalogued all incidents in which guerrillas or *mujibas*, their youth wing, played a part, from store robberies and assaults to large-scale skirmishes between the security forces and guerrilla groups. The sitreps were an essential tool in setting priorities at JOC level for deploying forces, and provided an important gauge of guerrilla intentions.

At the national level, the War Council was revived after a period of relative inactivity. A Ministry of Combined Operations (ComOps) was created in March 1977. The War Council comprised the prime minister, the minister of Combined Operations and Defence, perhaps a few other ministers invited for specific reasons, and the commanders of the army, police and air force. The services of the popular and highly regarded army commander, Lieutenant General G P Walls, whose retirement was imminent in terms of army regulations, were retained by creating the post of Commander of Combined Operations. This 'super-JOC' had, as its deputy commander, former Air Marshal M J McLaren, and was responsible for translating the government's political decisions into a military strategy.

But instead of formulating strategy, ComOps involved itself largely in the day-to-day administration of operations, occasionally even instructing JOCs where to move small units. Sometimes this would help, when ComOps interfered to order reluctant JOCs to move their Fire Force to adjacent JOCs when the situation demanded. The rather pompous Director General of Operations, Brigadier Bert Barnard, tended to by-pass Army HQ in his instructions to army personnel. ComOps also assumed complete operational control of both the SAS and the Selous Scouts, leaving Army HQ to deal with just the administrative needs of the special forces. In consequence, a deep rift emerged between the amiable Walls and the head of the army, Major General John Hickman, who had the finest military mind in the country, according to many officers who served with him.

Under the Transitional Government set up at the end of the war, effective control of the military was retained in white hands by pruning the War Council to the prime minister and service commanders, separating the ministries of Defence and Combined Operations, and relying on ad hoc liaison between white ministers and military chiefs. After June 1979, the conduct of operations was left almost entirely to Combined Operations Headquarters so that Muzorewa was consequently able to state with conviction that when raids were launched across Rhodesia's borders in 1979 (while he was in the United States) he was unaware of the decision.

STRATEGY

Until 1976, Rhodesian strategy was totally defensive in conception. The objectives of the military machine were to defend Rhodesian territory against guerrilla incursion, and to isolate and destroy successful infiltrations. Until 1972, the war was essentially a border conflict, with Rhodesian forces able quickly to locate and eliminate those guerrilla groups which infiltrated through the security cordon along the northern borders.

The pattern of search-and-destroy operations, based on reconnaissance and sweep patrols, remained unchanged when the war took on a new complexion with the far more successful guerrilla infiltrations from the north-east, which began in 1972 and erupted in attacks on farms. Military operations were confined to defending farmsteads and installations and locating and destroying guerrilla detachments.

Eventually the realization came that the guerrillas' resurgent strength lay in their close contact with the African population, and that the armed nationalists had moved from cross-border commando operations, in which there was little or no contact with local African populations, to a Maoist strategy of guerrilla warfare. The guerrillas had deftly seized the strategic initiative during 1972 when they infiltrated the north-eastern border regions, and without firing a shot had established arms caches and a political and logistic infrastructure among the African people in this remote region. Straws in the wind were ignored by a complacent military and administrative machine which had not kept abreast of the development of military thinking among the guerrillas.

The response to the shock of the new incursions was to develop a 'hearts and minds' political strategy similar to the American pacification programme in Vietnam. This revolved around the concentration of Africans in disaffected areas in protected villages in an effort to drain Mao's 'sea' away from the guerrilla 'fishes'. By denying the guerrillas succour among the African populations it was hoped that their operations would either wither away, or that they would be forced into the sort of disastrous commando operations they had mounted in the late 1960s. Several hundred thousand people were moved, some by force, into these strategic hamlets. But the 'fishes' stubbornly survived and expanded their operations, particularly after 1976, when the guerrillas once again seized the strategic initiative in the eastern, south-eastern and western areas. The protected villages strategy was extended to encompass the new operational areas, though the sheer geographic and demographic scale of the Rhodesians' problem meant that large areas could not be controlled. Until late 1976 this 'hearts and minds' approach did not include political reform to increase African participation in local and national politics.

In August 1976, the Rhodesians seized the strategic initiative for the first time by carrying the war into the guerrilla hinterland across the Mozambique border. This strategy was further developed, in 1977 and subsequent years, with daring raids and air strikes on guerrilla camps in Mozambique, Zambia, Botswana and even Angola. At one point units of the SAS were already airborne to attack camps in Tanzania, but these were recalled at the last moment. Eventually Rhodesian forces mounted small-scale operations outside their borders on a daily basis, and carried out frequent large-scale operations against increasingly heavily defended guerrilla camps.

Yet Rhodesia's strategic position continued to deteriorate until by 1979 the guerrillas had effectively denied real control of much of the countryside to the Rhodesian government. General Walls had given up the conception of simply holding territory as early as 1974, and his strategy became more concerned with human beings (killing guerrillas and controlling the African population). Until the very end of the war, 'body counts' and 'kill ratios' continued to preoccupy Rhodesian officers and public opinion. They had learned little from the American experience in Vietnam. By 1979, civil administration outside the cities was possible only if government employees were armed or protected by soldiers. The African population increased its support for the guerrillas despite the blandishments and punishments of the Rhodesian government.

The fundamental weakness of Rhodesian strategy was political. Rhodesian soldiers prided themselves on being apolitical in the modern democratic tradition. The President of Rhodesia, John Wrathall, said in 1977: 'The Rhodesian Army has always, quite properly, remained aloof from any involvement in politics', but the acceptance by the armed forces of UDI and the declaration of a republic in 1970 were definite political statements. Events in 1980, especially the reluctance to stage a military coup, did show that the Rhodesian armed forces were obedient to their political masters. Even if the armed forces could claim something of an *apolitical* nature, it was the *unpolitical* thinking of Rhodesian military strategists which proved fatal. Rhodesian officers were trained at the School of Infantry at Gwelo. The staff there trained regular and national service candidates for commissions, provided courses for NCO instructors, and gave advanced training to senior officers. The school was modelled on Sandhurst, where many senior officers had received their first officer training in the 1950s and early 1960s, but it lacked the British institution's intellectual tradition. One academic researcher commented that he looked through editions of the army magazine, *Assegai*, spanning 20 years, in search of some intellectual spark among Rhodesian officers, but found none. A strong anti-intellectual tradition pervaded white society, which called the University of Rhodesia the 'Kremlin-on-the-hill', and this was reflected in the thinking of the armed forces. There was no discernible philosophical basis to the Rhodesian counter-insurgency war, and Rhodesian officers would have been surprised at the suggestion that there should be one. This playing down of politics within the armed forces was a crippling deficiency in waging a campaign against the revolutionary war strategy of the guerrillas after 1972. While the guerrilla soldier spent much of his daily training routine attending political lectures which endlessly hammered on a few simple revolutionary themes, the Rhodesian soldier received virtually no professional political indoctrination. At no stage did a school of political warfare exist. The guerrilla leadership was infused with a sense of historical mission, and successfully turned a significant proportion of its soldiers into political animals, but Rhodesia's military leadership strove to project the image of the 'simple soldier'.

The political immaturity of the high command was reflected in its perceptions of guerrilla politics and strategy. Although there was much speed-reading of the works of Mao and other guerrilla theorists after 1972, little rational, dispassionate study of guerrilla aims and methods ensued. Until the late 1970s few white Rhodesians would accept that they were fighting a civil war. Before then the guerrillas were perceived as some sort of communist-inspired gang of stateless criminals. Until the last days of the war, sitreps denoted guerrillas as 'Communist Trained Terrorists' (CTTs). Although this was a change from the earlier use of 'Communist Terrorist', it was a chronic misconception of the Rhodesian forces that they saw the guerrillas as Marxist agents of Eastern-bloc imperialism rather than armed black nationalists who had become beholden to the Eastern Bloc because the Western powers rejected their demands for arms. Socialist revolutionary ideology was a convenient vehicle and compatible model for their specific objectives and organization. It was these same people, who, until 1968-9, hoped that Britain would intervene militarily to end UDI. Although foreign media observers tended to underplay the guerrillas' commitment to the Eastern Bloc and to some sort of socialist order in a future Zimbabwe, the Rhodesians tended to veer the other way.

Central to a sound strategy is an honest perception of the aims of those devising that strategy. Mao's maxim that one must know one's enemy, but above all one must know oneself, was lost on the Rhodesians. Ian Smith and many others sincerely believed that Rhodesia had 'the happiest Africans in the world'. P K van der Byl was convinced that: 'This is not a racial war, but black terrorists and white-skinned communists on one side and a multiracial army of black and white soldiers fighting shoulder to shoulder on the other side.' Politicians proved more adept at explaining why Africans should not support the guerrillas than at explaining why they did.

But the initial aim of the war was to prevent power passing to any black government, no matter how moderate. An admission of racism, even if only within the high command and Cabinet, might have produced a more coherent strategy, but no clearly articulated political ideology emerged among white Rhodesians. No driving vision evolved, like Hitler's racially pure Aryan world, or socialists' dreams of an egalitarian society purged of misery, or democrats' hopes for a truly free society, or even South Africa's preservation of the Volk. The Rhodesians' vague conservatism, hole-in-the-corner racism and defence of a life-style were no substitutes for a sense of mission. Government propagandists tried to preach a crusade against Soviet imperialism and the excesses of communism, but this never became deeply rooted in a white community with a relatively high standard of education.

This failure of any sense of mission was compounded by the intellectual tradition of the white community. Though some hotheads dreamed of 'final solutions' and 'scorched earth' as an answer to African political aspirations, and may have done something towards this in the field, these were rarely the sentiments of conviction. Most Rhodesians had been educated to believe that the French and Russian revolutionaries had had just cause to revolt, even if it was emphasized that the new regimes were little better than those they had toppled. White society was remarkably egalitarian and democratic, and most Rhodesians had difficulty in reconciling their justifications of the political, social and economic disadvantages of the African population with the sense of outrage they would have felt had they been subjected to these themselves.

A further factor weakening Rhodesian defence was emigration. Despite the Smith government's attempts to make emigration unattractive by controlling the conditions under which whites could leave the country, particularly the amount of money they could take with them, this loophole was never closed. Some whites claimed that they had nowhere else to live, but wags commented that the definition of a loyal Rhodesian was someone who could not sell his house nor get his money out of the country. Despite P K van der Byl's rallying cries for Rhodesians to fight to the last round, white society was still largely settler in outlook. More than half the white population of the late 1970s had arrived in Rhodesia since UDI. Most Rhodesians argued that if they did not like the way things were going, or would go under a black government, they could always leave for greener pastures. The war became a race between the white community's increasing emigration rate and the high command's ability to maintain the life-styles to which Rhodesians had become accustomed.

Robert Taber, in his *The War of the Flea*, points to a fundamental weakness in most counter-insurgency campaigns:

> The purpose of the counter-revolutionary is negative and defensive. It is to restore order, to protect property, to preserve existing forms and interests by force of arms, *where persuasion has already failed*. His means may be political in so far as they involve the use of still more persuasion – the promise of social and economic reforms, bribes of a more localised sort, counter-propaganda of various kinds. But primarily the counter-insurgents' task must be *to destroy the revolution by destroying its promise* – that means by proving, militarily, that it cannot and will not succeed.

Rhodesian strategy was shot through with a fatal negativism. There was little real faith in positive political reform as a war-winner. In any event, this undermined the very reasons for the war being fought. White Rhodesians had struggled hard and long against the only thing that could have avoided a war: African participation in national politics. To change horses in mid-stream was extremely difficult, but the Rhodesian government did try it. The war shifted from a war against the principle of black majority rule government to a war for the sort of black government white Rhodesians were prepared to live under. The secret hope was for an ultimately 'white' solution, or, at worst, a pliant black government. But once the principle of having any sort of majority rule government at all was conceded, white Rhodesians' war aims became increasingly confused, and their strategy consequently weaker.

The gradual and grudging surrender of power to Africans and the acceptance of the principle of majority rule was a painful process. General Walls might claim that: 'I made it clear when I became Commander of the Army in 1972 that one cannot win this war by purely military means', but attempts to win the war through political means were hesitant and half-hearted. It was only in 1977 that blacks were first commissioned in the army and given opportunities for promotion in the police. Black soldiers and other members of the security forces were not permitted to vote in the country for which they risked their lives. Too many officers believed cynically that Africans respected only force, and followed the American military dictum that 'when you have them by the balls their hearts and minds will follow'. A Psychological Action section was formed, but it was mesmerized by gimmicks and produced flashy, poorly informed propaganda.

Official disclaimers to the contrary, most officers realized that Africans loathed the protected villages even when the physical conditions in them were satisfactory. The system of PVs could have been the linchpin of a successful strategy, but generally the poorest quality manpower was allocated to their administration and protection.

A further fatal flaw was the tendency to underestimate the enemy. The tactical ineptitude of the guerrillas encouraged a belief that the 'K-factor' (a cryptonym for 'Kaffir-factor') would ultimately prevent the defeat of the Rhodesian forces. Rhodesians might point proudly to their consistent tactical successes and the ever-mounting body counts, but they failed to realize that the guerrillas were waging a successful protracted war. It was futile to conjecture that in a straight fight the Rhodesians could annihilate the entire guerrilla armies, and to rail against the refusal of guerrillas to stand and fight like men, when so little was done to undermine the massive popular support they had built up through a skilful manipulation of the poverty and the disadvantaged existence of the bulk of Africans, and through the use of selective brutality. Rhodesian officers would boast that the guerrillas controlled only the ground they stood on at any one moment, but by 1978-9 this was true also of the Rhodesian government's grip on vast areas of the country.

Faced with the inner weakness of their strategy, the Rhodesians resorted to more and more desperate measures. The policy of winning hearts and minds was largely abandoned in the field just when the first moves towards a political strategy were coming to fruition. Perversely, it was considered that black participation in the political process would permit tougher, war-winning policies. Martial law was introduced, the punitive destruction of the villages and livestock of those who aided the guerrillas became routine and a more aggressive external strategy was adopted.

In 1978 and 1979, efforts were made not only to harass guerrillas across Rhodesia's borders but also to destabilize those states sheltering them. Like the Israelis in the closing stages of the Yom Kippur War, the Rhodesians sought to 'break the bones' of Zambia and Mozambique to force them to cease their assistance to the guerrillas. Dredges were sunk in Beira harbour, bridges were blown up in Zambia and other military and civilian installations were attacked. The highly efficient regular Rhodesian forces turned large swathes of these two countries into a devastated no man's land. Zambia was a deserted wasteland for up to 30 km from the Rhodesian border, and Mozambican towns such as Espungabera and Malvernia became heaps of rubble.

The original 'total war' strategy was devised in 1976 by Group Captain Norman Walsh (who later headed the Zimbabwean air force). This had two phases: the destruction of Mozambican and Zambian infrastructure, particularly bridges taken out by the SAS, and, secondly, all guerrilla concentrations in those countries. Air force planners argued that this could effectively destroy the opposition. The CIO vetoed these plans because of the possible political repercussions, though parts of the strategy were implemented in the last months of the war, but by then it was too late.

The Rhodesians also fomented and aided internal revolts inside Mozambique. The *Resistançia Naçional Moçambicana* (RNM, also MNR, later called RENAMO) was created, supplied and trained by the Rhodesian forces. Its training camp at Odzi, in Rhodesia, was evacuated by South African Air Force Puma helicopters and Hercules transports a few days after the election victory of ZANU (PF) in 1980. RENAMO, like Frankenstein's monster, took on a life of its own, capturing large tracts of Mozambique, partly because of genuine disaffection with FRELIMO rule, not least among dispossessed traditional chiefs and alienated religious groups in the large Catholic and Muslim communities. Created by the Rhodesian CIO, and nourished by apartheid South Africa, to the outside world RENAMO was tainted with double original sin. The movement destabilized Mozambique with civil war from 1977 to 1992, which served the short-term interests of the crumbling white regimes. RENAMO claimed some spectacular attacks in Mozambique, including major installations in Maputo, but most of these were SAS or joint SAS-RENAMO operations. As early as 1973 the Rhodesians had recruited assistance among Zambian civilians for laying mines, and Zambian nationals aided later cross-border raids. But the Zambian strategy was counter-productive and once again underestimated international reactions and the emotional commitment of Africans to the achievement of majority rule in Rhodesia. Although considerable war-weariness had undermined the guerrillas and their allies by 1979, their reserves of strength were just that much greater than those of the isolated Rhodesians and their war-torn economy.

In *World Armies*, L L Mathews observed: 'Provided with only relatively small forces and equipment sometimes both obsolescent and elderly, General Walls, first as Army Commander and then as Commander Combined Operations, has waged a campaign of extreme professional competence that will deserve a place in the world's Staff College courses for many years to come.' Yet this undoubted professional skill and tactical superiority did not stop the guerrillas from achieving their objective, the toppling of white supremacy, thereby winning the war.

Chapter Five

THE GUERRILLA ARMIES

STRUCTURE AND TRAINING

While the Rhodesians became increasingly confused in their war aims, the guerrillas had a clear vision of their purpose. Their goal was to break the back of white supremacy and establish a state based on black majority rule. This gave the guerrilla armies and their leadership remarkable stamina, and their cause the strength to weather many political crises and recurrent military defeat in the field. But the apparent simplicity of the guerrilla objective masked enormous confusion and bitter conflict over how that objective was to be attained. At times dissension among the guerrillas was far more potent in delaying the achievement of majority rule than the firepower of the Rhodesian armed forces. Clashes of ideology, partly exacerbated by different foreign patrons, played a part, but the over-riding factor was the persistent tribal antagonism between the Shona majority who tended to support ZANU, and the Ndebele support base for ZAPU. Within each tribally based guerrilla army, clan politics, as well as clashes of personality, also undermined unity.

The diversity of experience and training of the first groups of guerrillas further retarded the emergence of a clear strategy for defeating the Rhodesian state. Small groups were trained variously in Ghana, Cuba, Egypt, Algeria, Tanzania, China, Russia and other Eastern bloc states. There was little uniformity in the type of training given, but the emphasis was on sabotage and commando tactics. In the early 1960s the guerrilla forces were too small to have a coherent military strategy; their role was more that of demonstrating a high level of commitment among nationalists and of trying to intimidate white politicians into making political concessions, or towards the negotiating table.

Guerrillas loyal to ZAPU were trained all over Africa, and beyond, and then concentrated in camps in Zambia. ZANU guerrillas were trained in many parts of the world as well, but in 1965 ZANLA, the military wing of the party, established a training base at Itumbi, in Tanzania. Basic military training was given by instructors of the Tanzanian army, but there were a number of ZANLA instructors whose primary function was the political education of incoming recruits. In 1971, ZANLA moved from Itumbi and set up its major training camp at Mgagao, also in Tanzania. Under pressure from the OAU and sympathetic African states, ZANLA guerrillas and recruits into ZIPRA, the military wing of ZAPU, trained together in Tanzania, at Mgagao and Kingolwira, to try to forge some unity between the nationalist forces.

GUERRILLA INFILTRATION ROUTES

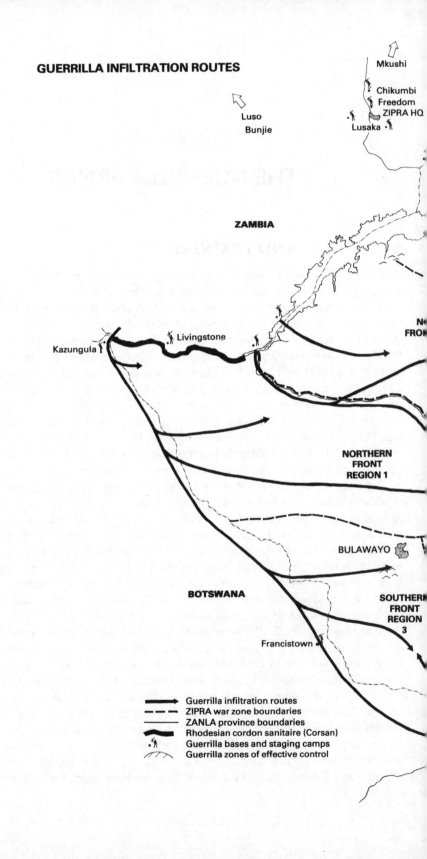

Mkushi

Chikumbi
Freedom
ZIPRA HQ
Luso
Bunjie
Lusaka

ZAMBIA

Livingstone

Kazungula

N
FRO

NORTHERN
FRONT
REGION 1

BULAWAYO

BOTSWANA

SOUTHER
FRONT
REGION
3

Francistown

Guerrilla infiltration routes
ZIPRA war zone boundaries
ZANLA province boundaries
Rhodesian cordon sanitaire (Corsan)
Guerrilla bases and staging camps
Guerrilla zones of effective control

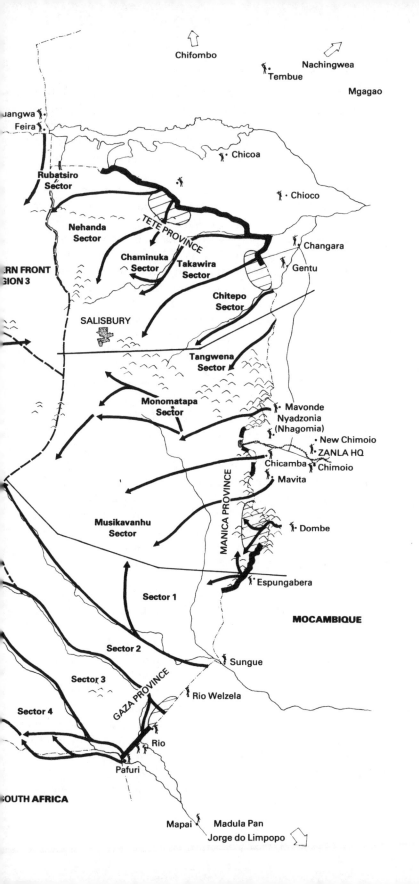

ZIPRA, however, maintained covert training camps in Zambia and in the mid-1970s training once more became fragmented. In defiance of the OAU Liberation Committee instruction that all guerrilla training was to be at a joint camp at Nachingwea, in Tanzania, from 1976, ZIPRA trained its guerrillas in Zambia and Angola, and once Mozambique had fallen to FRELIMO the main ZANLA training effort moved to that country. From 1977 the insurgents made no pretence of joint training, though the idea of military co-operation survived somewhat longer. Towards the end of the war ZANLA was giving rudimentary training to some recruits inside Rhodesia, though this was often of extremely short duration and was used more for political and propaganda purposes than for its military usefulness.

The size of the guerrilla armies mushroomed after 1975, when Portugal lost Mozambique. Until then the guerrillas were numbered in the hundreds, but most of them were not committed to combat and remained in training or holding camps. In 1972 there were about 300 trained ZANLA guerrillas and the offensive in the north-east in December that year was mounted by 60 of them. ZIPRA had been larger for some time (there were 400 ZIPRA guerrillas in early 1970), but in the years 1975-6 was rapidly outstripped by ZANLA. By the end of 1975, ZANLA had almost 6,000 trained guerrillas or recruits undergoing training; of the 700 guerrillas sent into action in the renewed onslaught of January 1976 more than 500 were ZANLA troops and the rest ZIPRA.

The widening of the war to cover almost the whole of Rhodesia in 1976-7 drew many thousands of Africans into the guerrilla recruiting net. At some peak periods as many as 1,000 recruits a week were crossing Rhodesia's borders into Mozambique and Botswana. As the guerrillas developed their political infrastructures, their systems of recruiting and conscription became more systematic. So great was the flow that by 1979 ZANLA was able to suspend recruiting across the borders of Rhodesia; potential recruits were advised to stay with guerrilla groups operating in the country. ZIPRA had hoped to catch up with ZANLA in numbers by 1977, but always lagged behind. Intensive ZIPRA recruiting drives, conscription and abductions continued at an escalating rate during 1978 and 1979.

In mid-1977, ZANLA had 3,000 guerrillas operating in Rhodesia and ZIPRA not many more than 100 to 200. A year later, ZANLA had 10,000, and at the ceasefire in December 1979, 17,000 ZANLA guerrillas reported to assembly points. By that stage ZIPRA guerrillas numbered about 20,000, according to ZIPRA intelligence sources disclosed after the war, though many were still scattered for training all over the world. As late as June 1981, 900 ZIPRA cadres were still in Libya.

But the guerrilla armies were in effect far larger than this. The *mujiba* system, which was crucial to the survival of combat guerrillas, encompassed tens of thousands of young people throughout the country. *Mujibas* (the females were called *chimbwidos*) acted as intelligence scouts and messengers for the guerrillas, and in some areas as enforcers of guerrilla discipline meted out to civilians. Towards the end of the war their organization was highly developed. ZANLA *mujibas* had a hierarchy which paralleled that of the ZANU parent party (with the president and the treasurer the most important officials) in most villages in eastern Rhodesia. ZANLA claimed 50,000 *mujibas* by 1979, and this was not an unrealistic figure. That number could probably be multiplied several times if the men, women and children who gave occasional but vital assistance to the guerrillas are counted for their contribution to the guerrillas' military effort.

The nature of training changed considerably in the course of the war. The early emphasis on commando tactics was replaced by a more thoroughgoing programme of training in revolutionary warfare. One of the most significant turning points in the war was the arrival at Itumbi base of a team of Chinese instructors in 1969. Their presence grew in the following years (there were 20 at Mgagao by 1971), and their influence on the guerrillas was profound, particularly on ZANLA. Although there was some joint training under the Chinese, ZAPU's political connections with the Soviet Union prompted ZIPRA objections to the Chinese programme. Nachingwea camp in Tanzania, which had been the major FRELIMO base until 1975 when they left to occupy Mozambique, was given to the guerrillas for joint training in 1976. It could hold up to 5,000 trainees, but ZIPRA hung back from participation in this joint exercise, and preferred to train its guerrillas under Soviet influence in Angola and Zambia.

Guerrilla armies are usually young armies. Despite official rules stating that fighters, as distinct from *mujibas*, had to be over 18, ZANLA records for the post-1980 demobilization and ZNA integration showed that the majority of combatants were in the 16-21 age bracket. Most of these guerrillas were of peasant stock, which fitted the Maoist philosophy of the movement. ZIPRA attracted a much higher percentage of volunteers, often from a more urban background. Over half had been employed before joining the insurgents. At least ten per cent were recruited from South Africa, where they had been working as migrant labourers. Though the ZIPRA army was young, the majority were in their early twenties, and most had not come straight from school. The older and often better educated ZIPRA cadres could more easily match the technical requirements of the conventional elements of the army. Ten per cent of ZIPRA soldiers were women, and most were incorporated into one unit, the ZIPRA Women's Brigade. This was a conventionally trained infantry brigade, with its own engineers, communications and other support services, with female commanders.

IDEOLOGY

ZIPRA training was dominated by the revolutionary theories of the Soviet Union and its satellites. It was the Russians who supplied, with some reservations about its use, ZIPRA's conventional war capability. Rex Nhongo, who became ZANLA's commander on the death of Josiah Tongogara in December 1979, had originally trained under ZAPU auspices. In an interview with a British journalist, David Martin, he contrasted his training in the Soviet Union with that under Chinese instructors: 'In the Soviet Union they had told us that the decisive factor of the war is weapons. When I got to Itumbi, where there were Chinese instructors, I was told that the decisive factor was the people.' It is interesting to note how the Soviets had become mesmerized by weapons technology, even in guerrilla warfare, rather like the Americans in Vietnam. The industrial superpower which had emerged from the Russian revolution of 1917 was clearly suffering from a hardening of its revolutionary arteries.

Still, ZIPRA did wage a guerrilla campaign in western Rhodesia which was not dissimilar to the 'people's war' fought by ZANLA. One difference which did stand out was the use of terror in mobilizing mass support; ZIPRA tended to be more selective in its targets and used far fewer of the spectacular disciplinary massacres ZANLA carried out in the eastern part of the country. ZIPRA did not practise the mass politicization and night-time *pungwes* because it claimed that it had sufficient local support, nourished by the more extensive branch structure of the older ZAPU organization, although much of it had been driven underground.

ZANLA training emphasized the political indoctrination of recruits. This was not only to entrench their commitment to ZANU and ZANLA but also to equip them for politicizing the African populations among whom they were to operate. Perhaps the most highly politicized group ZANLA ever deployed was the detachment of 60 which started the war in the north-east in late 1972. Tongogara later described them as being more political commissars than combat cadres. This group had had an unusually protracted period of training because of the difficulties of mounting operations into Rhodesia. Thereafter the political content of training fluctuated with the conditions of the war. When ZANLA was trying to push large numbers of guerrillas into Rhodesia for specific offensives, training was shortened and political education had to be skimped. At times other factors intervened. In 1977, ZANLA commissars were prevented from giving political education in Tanzanian camps as a result of the conflicts between rival factions within the guerrilla movement and Tanzanian attempts to gain some sort of leverage over ZANLA.

The Marxist orientation of the guerrilla armies was the subject of considerable debate during the war years. The Rhodesians were unequivocal – to them the guerrillas were either 'Communist Terrorists' or, at the very least, 'communist trained terrorists'. Western observers sympathetic to the guerrillas tended to see them as Marxists only for the purpose of gaining from the Eastern bloc the military and other assistance denied by Western governments. The guerrillas themselves added to the confusion in their practice of revolutionary warfare and with some of their ideas.

The works of Marx, Lenin and Mao were the staple fare of guerrilla political education. ZIPRA paid little attention to Maoist doctrine, but did in practice use some Chinese revolutionary tactics. The Soviet connection meant that Castro's Cuban experience was more important to them. But ZIPRA training throughout the war tended to remain more diverse than ZANLA's, and its theory of guerrilla warfare less precisely formulated. ZANLA's doctrine was dominated by Chinese theory and FRELIMO practice. As early as 1970, ZANLA guerrillas fought alongside FRELIMO troops in Mozambique to temper the theoretical training given at Itumbi. By 1978 the works of Mao were ZANLA's bible of guerrilla warfare.

But if the Marxist basis of the guerrillas' struggle was more than skin-deep, nationalist objectives tended to dominate all political thinking. ZANLA recruits were educated in the 'National Grievances'. Issues such as land alienation, education, health and welfare discrimination, political oppression, low wages and social inequalities were the staples of the recruits' political diet. ZIPRA guerrillas were steeped in the chicanery used by the British South Africa Company to destroy the Ndebele state in the 1890s. ZANLA guerrillas learnt of their ancestors' risings of 1896-7, the 'first *Chimurenga'*. A ZANLA document of 1976 which outlined the overall war aims of the guerrillas claimed that 'the principal objective of our revolution is the seizure of power by means of destruction of the racist political-military machine and its replacement by the people in arms in order to change the existing economic and social order.' Significantly, it made no specific reference to socialist objectives.

While much guerrilla propaganda was heavily larded with the jargon of 'scientific socialism' and spoke of the 'inner contradictions' of the capitalist system in Rhodesia, some bizarre contradictions in the guerrillas' organization and thinking were evident. Multi-coloured *'Chimurenga* cloth' was worn by ZANLA guerrillas as scarves. The red in it signified blood, the black was to make the guerrillas invisible to Rhodesian forces, and the white was to intensify the guerrillas' vision so that they could more easily evade enemy patrols. Items of clothing of these colours were worn for the same purposes. The constant linking of the 'first *Chimurenga'* of the 1890s and the second of the 1970s was somewhat bogus in that the risings and resistance of the early colonial period were backward-looking reactions, not progressive movements for social reform.

The most glaring contradiction was the embracing of traditional religion by the guerrillas. A spirit medium, Mbuya Nehanda, became a heroine of the guerrillas' struggle.

In the early stages of the 'people's war' launched by ZANLA in 1972 she was consulted on a wide range of military and political matters. The names used by spirit mediums could be confusing, especially when rival mediums claimed to be the reincarnation of the same traditional Shona spirits. In 1898 an old woman, who was reputed to be the medium for the Shona spirit known as Nehanda, was executed by the settlers for incitement to murder during the troubles of the 1890s. This medium became a martyr of the first *Chimurenga* and hence the significance of her reputed reincarnation, Mbuya Nehanda, for the second *Chimurenga.* While Marx exposed religion as 'the opium of the people', the Zimbabwean guerrillas saw it not only as an important functional factor in their struggle but personally believed in it. Josiah Tungamirai, who became ZANLA's chief political commissar, the very guardian of the army's political education, was a staunch believer in the powers of mediums. He said to journalist David Martin: 'Personally I didn't believe in that because I was brought up in the church.' But in time he changed his beliefs and he reported: 'When we wanted to go and open a new operational zone we would have to approach the mediums first.' Similarly, for ZIPRA the autocratic ruler, Lobengula, deposed by the settlers in 1893, became a folk hero, and the importance of ancestral spirits and Ndebele deities in the 1896 rising was linked with the struggle of the late twentieth century.

These contradictions were exposed by some radical party elements and left-wing critics of the guerrillas' politics. International Trotskyites criticized the *petit bourgeois* origins and attitudes of many of ZANU's leaders, including Mugabe. Nkomo was mistrusted for his intimate links with Lonrho, the capitalist multinational corporation. In 1977, adherents of more radical, socialist ideologies in ZANU attempted a coup against the party leadership. They were branded as 'ultra-leftists' – a Marxist code-word for Trotskyites – by the ZANU leadership.

The early history of the ZANU regime established in April 1980 provided few clues as to the real convictions of the guerrillas and their political leaders. The radical socialist Edgar Tekere was purged from his Cabinet post as an embarrassment to the party and Mugabe's government. The capitalist economic system and much of its social infrastructure remained intact. Initially, Mugabe seemed intent on creating a Western-style social welfare state rather than a typical communist economy. By and large it seems that Marxist doctrine had a strong emotional attraction for the guerrillas, that it offered them a straightforward explanation of what had happened historically in Rhodesia, and provided a model for a solution to their struggle. But the guerrillas' adherence to anti-capitalist, anti-Western dogma was pragmatic. They were forced to look to the communist bloc states for guiding principles in the same way as they were compelled to look to them for arms.

STRATEGY

Guerrilla military strategy was in a constant state of flux until the late 1970s. The nationalist politicians and their military wings wrestled with the problems of translating their fluid political ideas, even within the framework of a clear war aim, into a military strategy that would bring about the defeat of the well-armed and motivated Rhodesian armed forces.

The disastrous first phase of conventional, commando-type operations of both ZAPU and ZANU was important in the evolution of the guerrilla strategy which eventually threatened the defeat of the Rhodesians in the field. The post-independence regime now marks 28 April as Chimurenga Day to commemorate the 'Battle of Sinoia', which was nothing more than a minor skirmish in 1966 in which a small guerrilla group was annihilated by Rhodesian forces. The propaganda importance of the battle was far greater than its military impact, but it has since become the subject of a great deal of historical distortion. It was to be some years before the guerrillas absorbed the lessons of 1966, and similar incursions took place in 1967 and through 1970. The victorious guerrillas later emphasized the symbolic importance of Sinoia for their armed struggle, but they did expect military gains at the same time. Some nationalists have tried to deny this. One has commented: 'In purely military terms it must be seen for what it was – a defeat... That particular battle could in any case not have been won by as small a group of guerrillas surprised and subjected to superior ground and air bombardment.'

What then did the guerrillas hope to achieve? Was this a stage in which the nationalist politicians deliberately sent in suicide squads of guerrillas merely to raise the political temperature of the conflict? It appears that they did not make this sort of cool deliberation and that the group killed near Sinoia was instructed (before being subverted by the CIO) to seize the town and precipitate an insurrection against the Rhodesian government. This was consistent with the diplomacy of the nationalist political exiles who at that time sought to force a British military intervention in the rebel colony. It was also attuned to the dominant influences in the guerrillas' training. The emphasis in Soviet satellites was on the coup type of revolution and on the subsequent consolidation of power. In the 1950s and early 1960s this was bolstered by the success of Castro's revolution. But Rhodesia was very far from being as rotten an apple as Batista's Cuba, and Che Guevara's romantic but unsuccessful and fatal attempt to reproduce a Fidelist revolution in Bolivia was perhaps a better illustration of the potential of that strategy.

The conventional strategy of the 1960s has been dismissed by observers of the war, and by the guerrillas themselves, as impractical and futile in the face of Rhodesian conventional superiority. But had the 10 years following the debacles of 1966-8 been spent in building up a conventional army equipped with more of the weapons the guerrilla armies deployed in 1978-9 (automatic anti-aircraft weapons, SAM-7 missiles, tanks and field artillery), there might have been a chance of a conventional victory. ZIPRA and the Soviets clearly believed that there would come a time when conventional weapons would be vital in the armed struggle and built up a conventional brigade for that decisive stage. (And the Rhodesians, aware of this threat, also trained for conventional war.)

ZIPRA was vitiated by a long-standing debate on military strategy. It was not a sudden Moscow diktat which created the most secret ZIPRA plan: Operation Zero Hour. This envisaged a co-ordinated conventional offensive on several fronts simultaneously. Five regular battalions with artillery support were to seize bridgeheads in the northern front at Kanyemba, Chirundu and Kariba to enable ZIPRA troops to cross with armour and artillery. At the same time attacks were to be mounted on the airfields at Kariba, Victoria Falls and Wankie, which would be secured to enable the transfer of ZIPRA MiGs from Angola. The principal objective was to enable regular troops to seize and hold the strategic rear bases along the border in support of the offensive to be launched from within Rhodesia. As the offensive moved in-country, guerrilla units already in place would sabotage transport links to undermine the Rhodesian counter-offensive, which would be further slowed by urban warfare. Zero Hour was planned for the start of the 1979 rainy season, October or November. Far from encouraging this plan, the Soviets refused to release ZIPRA pilots in training in the USSR. Rhodesian raids on the army being assembled on the Zambian border delayed Zero Hour, which was ultimately aborted by the Lancaster House talks.

Looked at historically, the guerrillas were probably right in opting for the guerrilla/revolutionary war strategy, but the myth and mystique of the guerrilla should not obscure the alternatives. When it is remembered that North Vietnam conquered South Vietnam only through the conventional invasion of 1975, guerrilla warfare is placed in its proper perspective. And if the Lancaster House settlement had not intervened, would ZANU(PF) or ZIPRA have won power through military means in 1980-1?

But rather than building up their conventional capability the guerrillas turned to 'people's war'. In January 1970 James Chikerema of ZAPU said:

> We do not intend to finish in a matter of two, three, four or five years... this is a protracted struggle. The type of war we fight depends on changes of tactics and I can tell you that we've changed our tactics. We will combine both – where they meet us and intercept us, we will stand and fight; where they don't see us, we will go to our own areas and infiltrate into the population and our masses.

Chikerema was later to advocate sabotage and 'Fidelist' tactics in a confusing change of heart, but there was a strong drift towards 'revolutionary war' among the guerrillas, particularly in ZANLA. In 1970-1, ZAPU was undergoing an internal crisis and had no real plans to fight in the immediate future. But, under Chinese instruction, ZANLA prepared in that period to mount a Maoist offensive.

In the aftermath of the Geneva conference in 1976, the concept of protracted war became more than a way of reconciling the militarily weaker guerrillas to a long haul. At that time the guerrillas did not want a swift handover of power by the whites. Not only did they need to set their own houses in order and build their armies, but they hoped that a protracted war would sweep away rival nationalist groups which relied on internal political support in Rhodesia. A swift white collapse at that time would have caught the guerrillas unprepared to take control of the whole country or win an election.

The initial and vital preparatory phase of the new strategy, beginning in early 1971, was facilitated by the spread of FRELIMO's operations in the Tete province of Mozambique from 1968. As early as 1969, ZANLA sought FRELIMO co-operation and the use of Tete as an infiltration route into Rhodesia. The Zambezi river was too formidable a barrier across which to mount sustained guerrilla operations. Although groups infiltrated across it throughout the war, the major invasion routes into Rhodesia had to develop around the flanks of the river, through Mozambique for ZANLA, and through Botswana for ZIPRA.

There were political obstacles to such co-operation. FRELIMO, like ZAPU, was one of a cluster of 'legitimate' or 'authentic' liberation movements recognized by the Soviet Union in 1969. The price of Soviet recognition and assistance was strict adherence to Soviet policies, and the Russians refused to aid ZANU throughout the war, looking on it as a Chinese-dominated 'splinter group' even though it bore the brunt of the fighting. FRELIMO aid was therefore correspondingly reluctant at first, but in time a close relationship developed between FRELIMO and ZANU, and even more so between their military wings, the FPLM and ZANLA. The turning point came in 1972 when FRELIMO encouraged ZAPU to mount operations into

Rhodesia through Tete. ZAPU had to decline because of the tribal affiliations of ZIPRA. ZAPU had little support among the Shona peoples of the north-east, and the predominantly Ndebele guerrillas would not have survived long there. Despite constant guerrilla claims that their support was not tribally based, the 'fishes' were of the wrong tribal background to operate in the Shona 'sea'.

From the opening of the guerrilla offensive in the north-east in December 1972 ZANLA presence inside Rhodesia was continuous until the ceasefire seven years later. This marked the transition from the earlier commando war of externally based incursions to guerrilla, revolutionary warfare. The ZANLA objective was to carry out at first as many military actions as possible without jeopardizing the continuity of their presence in the remote region. A year's supply of munitions had been cached in the months preceding the offensive, and nearly all this was consumed before large-scale re-supply became possible again in late 1973.

The first attacks were on white-owned farms, but operations extended to other targets such as government buildings, to assassinations of officials, ambushes on roads and fleeting contacts with Rhodesian forces. Most of these actions were pinpricks in military terms, but their wide geographical spread and their persistence marked a new stage of the war. Previously Rhodesians had been used to a short cycle of operations: an incursion followed swiftly by disintegration of the guerrilla groups under heavy attacks and then mopping up. Before 1972 frequent periods intervened when no combat guerrillas operated in Rhodesia. After 1972 at times as few as 30 to 100 were operational, but never again were there no guerrillas in the country.

A new cycle of violence emerged. The guerrillas reinforced surviving cadres inside Rhodesia or mounted new offensives at the height of the rainy season (December to February), when covering foliage was at its lushest and water supplies plentiful. Thereafter conditions for guerrilla operations deteriorated, and this was reflected in mounting casualties inflicted by Rhodesian forces. September and October were murderous months for the guerrillas because of the lack of cover and scarcity of water. It was also a highly dangerous period at guerrilla bases outside Rhodesia, for then the guerrilla forces had to be concentrated for the offensives to be mounted with the coming of the rains, and they presented vulnerable targets for enemy raids.

The guerrillas used an 'oil-patch' approach to their campaigns. From 1972 the fringes of ZANLA political influence and organization spread slowly through the TTLs of the north-east, filtering towards the capital down the Chiweshe and Mount Darwin-Mtoko-Mrewa complex of TTLs. Once safe havens had been established among co-operative civilians, military operations were launched against the government infrastructure in the TTLs or against neighbouring white farmlands.

But the potential of the north-east for the guerrillas was limited. The area was remote from the heartland of white power. White Rhodesians spoke initially of the war 'on the border' or in 'the Zambezi valley'. As FRELIMO worked southwards inside Mozambique so the invasion front widened, but the Rhodesian security forces were able to seal off the north-east with Operation Hurricane. A three-year stalemate developed, with the guerrillas unable to break out from the arc of TTLs in the north-east and the Rhodesians unable to eradicate the guerrillas and their political network.

In 1974, Herbert Chitepo, one of the major forces behind ZANLA's adoption of a 'people's war' strategy, wrote:

> The strategical aim ... is to attenuate the enemy forces by causing their deployment over the whole country. The subsequent mobilisation of a large number of civilians from industry, business and agriculture would cause serious economic problems. This would have a psychologically devastating effect on the morale of the Whites ...

But while the guerrillas were confined to the north-east by the containment strategy of the Rhodesian security forces, ZANLA's capacity to stretch the white economy to breaking point was illusory.

The collapse of Portuguese power in Mozambique instantly revolutionized the strategic positions of the opposing armies in the Rhodesian war. The ripping open of Rhodesia's entire eastern flank with the withdrawal of the screen of Portuguese troops was made more catastrophic by the renewal of ZIPRA operations against the country through Botswana. Rarely has the strategic initiative passed so swiftly and so decisively to guerrilla forces.

The international detente exercise of 1975 and the transition period from Portuguese to FRELIMO rule in Mozambique delayed ZANLA's capitalizing on its new advantage. But in early 1976 attacks were launched all along the eastern border of Rhodesia. There were minor differences of emphasis in the different parts of the guerrilla front, but the overall strategy was to suck the Rhodesians into overstretching their resources to the point where they could no longer hold the entire country. Economic targets and communications links were priorities for attack. Where no permanent interdiction of routes was possible there would be attacks to create a climate of psychological isolation in the white community. The rail line to Beira was a target until FRELIMO rendered it redundant by closing the border in March 1976. The main road to the south, from Salisbury to Beit Bridge, was ambushed, forcing the Rhodesians to mount convoys. The Rutenga-Beit Bridge rail link was a primary target as a symbol of Rhodesian self-sufficiency. Frequent sabotage of the line compelled the Rhodesians to guard virtually every culvert and bridge along its length and eventually to protect trains with 'nanny wagons' – flatbed trucks mounted with 20mm cannon. Throughout the country 'mobilization of the masses' went on ceaselessly, encompassing more and more districts. Spurred on by the sudden explosion of the ZANLA sphere of influence and by the OAU Liberation Committee, ZIPRA mounted an offensive into western Rhodesia in mid-1976. The primary aim was to build up the sort of popular support enjoyed by ZANLA to the east and to scoop up recruits for training. By 1977 the Rhodesians' establishment of Operation Grapple, covering the Midlands, marked the saturation of the entire country by guerrillas.

Once the initial preparatory phase had been completed, the guerrillas were able to develop more sophisticated strategic concepts. ZANLA worked out a rolling strategic plan – 1977 was the 'Year of the Party', during which ZANU's house was set in order and unity achieved; 1978 was the 'Year of the People', in which the party was to become firmly entrenched among the black population; 1979 was the 'Year of the People's Storm', during which the white state and its black allies would become engulfed by the revolutionary struggle; and 1980 would be the 'Year of the People's Power', bringing the collapse of the white-led resistance, the strategic capstone.

In 1978 there was increasing emphasis on economic targets, in particular white farmlands and communications links. As the guerrillas became more entrenched within the African population, and Rhodesian government control of rural areas began to break down, so the opportunity to seal off the urban areas presented itself. One guerrilla leader commented: 'Our purpose was to isolate the cities and cut them off, not to attack them. A few well-planned strikes to frighten the white population.' For ZANLA it was the classic Maoist strategy. ZIPRA, because of its Russian influence, paid greater attention to the role of the cities, and in late 1978 announced an urban guerrilla campaign. It was ZANLA, however, which scored the most spectacular urban successes with the blasting of a Woolworth's store in Salisbury and the destruction of the fuel depot in the city's industrial sites.

The urban guerrillas were generally sent in from outside the cities, and their inability to survive the Rhodesians' informer networks and intelligence work was a constant problem for the development of a sustained urban campaign. The two teachers who planted the Woolworth's bomb were able to escape to Mozambique, but the guerrillas who planted letter bombs in Salisbury postboxes were captured at a roadblock on the road to Umtali and hanged under martial law. The guerrillas who destroyed the Salisbury oil depot were killed by Rhodesian forces in the Mtoko area. On the whole, urban guerrilla warfare was of greater psychological value than military or economic. As one security forces officer said: 'Salisbury was the safest place in the country, but ironically it was the biggest morale headache we had during the war.'

PROPAGANDA

The guerrillas waged a far more effective psychological and propaganda war than the white Rhodesians. While the Rhodesians viewed these vital elements of guerrilla warfare as adjuncts to the more important business of killing guerrillas, the nationalists placed a major emphasis on them. The propaganda effort was crucial to, and a natural outgrowth of, the struggle for the political allegiance of the black population. Guerrilla propaganda was simple but effective. White Rhodesians were generally contemptuous of African culture and, although there were training courses on 'African customs' for most soldiers and policemen, an unbridgeable gulf of misunderstanding persisted.

The guerrillas were in close touch with the aspirations of blacks in white-dominated Rhodesia, and their closeness was skilfully exploited in spreading their propaganda throughout the population. Although they disseminated widely printed material, including dramatic 'Socialist Realist' posters, the major medium of information was the spoken word. The following are the rough notes *(verbatim)* for a guerrilla political commissar's speech to villagers in the 'Gaza Province' of south-east Rhodesia:

Topic to be carried on

1. Speak politely to the masses and each other/no rebuke in public/no demand on shortage/no harrassment/to teach/ no strict speaking or beating/no refusal of poor food offered by the masses/'Deal with ZANU'

2. Its police/we are our own liberator. 'Its objectives and realities'.

3. Deal with ZANU/ZANLA with their relationships.

4. The past and present stages and future stages.

5. The hardships and encounter/'ZANU as opposed to its opponents' such as ZAPU/ZIPRA and its leader 'Joshua Nkomo' 'UANC Muzorewa' 'ZUPO Chirau''ANC Sithole' which meanseroncally ZANU and its Selous Scouts.

6. Denounce in strongest terms Internal Settlement.

7. How they want to hijack the ZANU revolution with Smith plans to stooges.

8. The formation of ZANU 'When it was formed''Why it was formed''What is its role''Who are the enemy'

9. ZANU idealogy Political objectives, exonomical objectives, land policy, welfare and liberators objectives.

This guerrilla was poorly educated and his speech must have been confused, but he had one overwhelming advantage over the advertising executives who supervised the Rhodesian propaganda campaign – he came from and knew the people to whom he spoke. He was unsophisticated, but the impoverished peasants among whom he operated were usually illiterate and even more unsophisticated. They would never know that the photographs of 'Rhodesian Mirages' in guerrilla propaganda magazines were really shots of Boeing 737 civil airliners, or that guerrilla claims to have shot down an average of three Rhodesian aircraft a month throughout the war, or to have destroyed Kariba, were ridiculous. While such strong emotional and kinship ties connected the guerrillas with their 'sea' such propaganda was highly effective.

On the international propaganda front the guerrillas were in an even more privileged position. The entire Eastern bloc, and virtually all Third World nations and their propaganda machines, strongly supported the guerrillas' cause. In the West the media (with a few exceptions such as the London *Daily Telegraph*) was strongly sympathetic to the guerrillas' struggle against the discriminatory Rhodesian regime, though it had reservations about some of the guerrilla tactics and links with the Eastern bloc. The Western liberal tradition precluded broad sympathy for the white Rhodesians. As a former British High Commissioner to Uganda noted: 'Most people feel admiration for the Rhodesians' bravery and staying power, but a moral revulsion at why they're fighting at all.' For the influential liberal and radical chic sections of Western opinion the guerrillas had a romantic, Che Guevara mystique far removed from the dirty little war in the bush. The guerrillas managed to create the impression that atrocities, especially against 'refugee camps', were a Rhodesian monopoly. Another brilliant propaganda ploy was the treatment of white captives. Given the conditions in which the guerrillas themselves lived and fought, they were treated well, and the freed captives testified to this. But not many observers asked why there were so few live captives in guerrilla hands and what had happened to those prisoners who never reached Mozambique or Zambia. But while the Rhodesians pressed on with mass hangings of captured guerrillas after secret judicial proceedings, the guerrillas were able to appear more humane in the eyes of the world.

Ultimately it was on the propaganda fronts, both internal and international, that the guerrillas created the conditions of their victory. At the crucial point of their struggle, in mid-1979, no nation, not even South Africa, was able to recognize the Muzorewa government. The Conservative administration in Britain could not bring itself to fulfil its promise to recognize a reasonably legitimate black government in Rhodesia. The way was clear for a guerrilla triumph.

STRATEGIC ACHIEVEMENTS

ZANLA set itself ambitious strategic tasks for 1979. These included the creation of true 'liberated zones', some of them to be defended by a 'people's militia', the establishment of more areas with a low level of security forces' activity as potential 'liberated zones', to intensify attacks on the Rhodesian forces, and to continue to tear apart the social and economic bases of white power. A specific objective was to drive as many white farmers off the land as possible and to establish complexes of *povo* (people's) villages (see chapter on weapons and tactics) on the abandoned estates. There was an added dimension to the politicization programme for 1978-9, for the guerrillas had to discredit those nationalists who had joined the internal settlement. ZIPRA held back the bulk of its forces, but recruiting went on at a feverish pace in 1979, and their guerrilla operations seeped eastwards. One of ZIPRA's objectives was to establish a presence over as wide an area as possible, given expectations of some sort of imminent collapse of white resistance and a more confused and open political situation in the aftermath. As early as 1977, Rhodesian intelligence reported that ZIPRA was establishing in western Rhodesia arms caches which were earmarked for a *post-Chimurenga* political struggle with ZANLA.

One initiative contemplated by ZANU which would have had spectacular consequences was the Cuban plan to set up a guerrilla government on Rhodesian soil and thus to pre-empt any international moves to recognize the Muzorewa government elected in April 1979. The guerrillas' limited military capacity to mount and protect such a political coup, even with the backing of substantial FPLM forces, meant that it would have been little more than a media event of short duration, with the leaders immediately returning to exile and their 'representatives' living a precarious existence in some of the safer areas.

The guerrilla programme was impressive, but it had been only partly achieved by the time of the ceasefire. The internal nationalists were discredited, principally because they could not stop the war, and, indeed, had intensified it. The Patriotic Front parties had a political network, which could be backed with force, right across the face of Rhodesia. There were more, and more ferocious, attacks on the security forces, civilians, economic and communications targets. No true 'liberated zones' had been achieved, although there were areas, such as Headlands and Mtoko, in which highly developed systems of '*povo* camps' had been established. Some areas of Rhodesia were a no man's land. By late 1979 a quarter of a million acres of the vast Nuanetsi ranch in south-east Rhodesia had been abandoned by its management. Guerrilla bands and security forces' patrols roamed across an empty landscape. The guerrillas also hoped to cut the road to Beit Bridge from Salisbury continuously. This was to be done by intensive sowing of landmines, but the supply of these was inadequate to achieve this strategic task. Guerrilla groups were firmly established in the Chinamora TTL near the northern suburbs of Salisbury and had worked west through the Wedza area and into the Seki TTL south of Salisbury, but the capital was isolated only in a psychological sense and not in effective military terms.

MILITARY ORGANIZATION

ZANLA's military organization was far more highly developed and sophisticated than ZIPRA's. ZANLA initially organized its war effort into 'war zones'. The first was the Zambia-Zimbabwe Zone along the northern border of Rhodesia. The north-east front, opened in 1972, was designated the Mozambique-Zimbabwe Zone (MMZ), and there was another, the Botswana-Zimbabwe Zone (BBZ), which was never really operational. Once the entire border with Mozambique was available to the guerrillas for infiltration into Rhodesia, ZANLA theatre organization was based on Mozambique's administrative structure. The ZANLA operational areas were simply eastward extensions of Mozambique's provinces. 'Tete Province' covered the old MMZ theatre and extended it southwards to the Inyanga North area. 'Manica Province' extended from there to Espungabera, and 'Gaza Province' encompassed operations in the extreme south and south-east of Rhodesia. While these 'provinces' theoretically extended right across Rhodesia to its western border, it was only in 'Gaza Province' that ZANLA infiltrated as far as Botswana. 'Manica Province' in practice extended as far west as Gwelo and Que Que, and 'Tete Province' to the Sinoia region.

ZANLA divided its 'war zones' and 'provinces' into 'sectors'. In the north-east these were named after heroes and spirit mediums important in the folklore of the 1896-7 risings. The first to open up was 'Nehanda' sector, followed southwards in

1973 by the 'Chaminuka' and 'Takawira' sectors. In the other provinces, sectors were designated on a different basis. The sectors in 'Manica Province' were named after heroes of the modern nationalist struggle: 'Tangwena', after chief Rekayi Tangwena, who defied Rhodesian government orders for his people to evacuate their ancestral homelands to make way for white farms, and 'Chitepo', after the slain Herbert Chitepo. 'Gaza Province' was divided into four sectors, starting with Sector IV in the Beit Bridge area and ranging through Sector I in the vicinity of the Fort Victoria-Birchenough Bridge road. Also within that province were two independent 'detachments', the 'Musikhavanhu detachment' and the 'Zimbabwe detachment', which was responsible for operations around the symbol of the nationalist struggle, the Zimbabwe Ruins.

Sectors were broken down into detachments, usually numbering 100 to 200 men operating in 10 to 15 'sections', the smallest administrative and combat unit. The strengths and boundaries of sectors and detachments were fluid. Although boundaries would be drawn along watercourses, main roads and other prominent landmarks, a sector would often mean more in terms of specific guerrilla personnel than any geographical area.

ZIPRA's organization was less developed, particularly with regard to guerrilla operations. Their zone of operations was divided into four provinces. Two, covering Matabeleland North and South, stretched into the interior from the Zambian and Botswana borders. The third covered the area from Urungwe TTL in north-central Rhodesia to Karoi, and the fourth from Belingwe to Vila Salazar. As with ZANLA's provinces, operations in the ZIPRA zones were most intense close to the border. Botswana's commitment to ZIPRA's struggle was less complete than Mozambique's to ZANLA's, and this, combined with Nkomo's holding back of the bulk of his forces, inhibited the growth of a highly structured organization such as ZANLA built.

The ZIPRA army was divided into two components, the guerrillas proper and the conventional war brigade. The latter unit comprised sections, platoons, companies and regiments. The rank structure reflected that of the Soviet army – not that of Trotsky's egalitarian Red Army, but that of Stalin's. There were officers', sergeants' and corporals' messes to cap the conventional hierarchy. The guerrilla component remained small and rarely operated in formations larger than a section or platoon. Their base camps, scattered along the Botswana border, from which most incursions were mounted, tended to be far smaller than ZANLA's big camp complexes in Mozambique, although in Zambia ZIPRA training camps were of a comparable size. ZIPRA's guerrillas have been best described as 'mobile revolutionary vanguards', operating much like Soviet partisans, rather than as Mao's type of guerrilla 'fish'.

The President of ZANU was the commander-in-chief of ZANLA, rather in the way the President of the United States is the commander-in-chief of the American armed forces. He was elected by the party central committee. In ZANU's case, Mugabe emerged from his post as secretary-general to displace Ndabaningi Sithole as president after the internal strife during 1974-6. The party political structure was linked to ZANLA through the *Dare re Chimurenga*, ZANU's 'war council'. This had been appointed in April 1969 by the ZANU central committee, many of whose members were in gaol in Rhodesia, to wage the war against the white state. The same *Dare* was reappointed in 1971. At that stage none of the members had any military experience, nor were they active in field operations. Even the secretary of defence, who automatically headed the ZANLA high command, had no military background. Since the *Dare* was dominated by civilians, the decisions made were those of politicians, not soldiers. The dictates of African or international diplomacy tended to weigh more heavily in military decisions than the military situation in Rhodesia and the capabilities of the guerrilla army.

The change came in 1973 when Josiah Tongogara was appointed to the *Dare* as secretary of defence, and therefore automatically to the chairmanship of the ZANLA high command. Tongogara was a military man first and foremost, and after 1973 no one without military experience sat on the ZANLA high command under his control.

The high command comprised the senior guerrilla officers responsible for translating the *Dare*'s war strategy into a concrete military campaign. It was headed by Tongogara from 1973 until his death in December 1979. His deputy, the chief of operations, was Rex Nhongo, who succeeded Tongogara as ZANLA commander in 1979. Other members of the high command included the ZANLA political commissar, the chief of logistics and other departmental heads. The high command's bureaucratic instrument was the 'general staff', numbering several hundreds by the mid-1970s. This contained the personnel responsible for training, logistics, communications and routine administration.

Each 'province' was controlled by a 'co-ordinating committee' which, by the war's end, was in close contact with FPLM units stationed inside Mozambique. The co-ordinating committee was linked to the provincial field operations commander responsible for operations inside Rhodesia, whose deputy was the provincial political commissar. These commanded the sector commanders and sector political commissars, who in turn controlled detachment and section commanders and commissars. After the Mugabe regime came to power in 1980 the term 'commander' was bandied about as a status symbol by ex-guerrillas, but it was an essentially ubiquitous label covering responsibilities equivalent to those of a sergeant in a Western army (section commander) up to Tongogara's post as commander of ZANLA. In the early 1970s an easy-going camaraderie was deliberately cultivated among the guerrillas, with no saluting or privileges of rank. While this was never completely lost, and ZANLA remained remarkably egalitarian in spirit to the end, the increasing strains of war and the size of the guerrilla army forced a closer definition of the powers and authority of 'commanders'.

ZIPRA had a similar organization. The ZAPU central committees appointed a 'war council', which, in the early 1970s comprised J Z Moyo (later killed by a parcel bomb), James Chikerema (who later split with ZIPRA and then joined the internal nationalists) and a handful of military members. The commander in the crucial stages of the war was Alfred 'Nikita' Mangena, who was killed by a landmine laid by

Rhodesians raiding into Zambia. His deputy, Lookout Masuku, succeeded him as commander. There was also a hierarchical structure of 'commanders' and political commissars extending down to section level.

CO-ORDINATION BETWEEN THE NATIONALISTS

There were several attempts to create organs to unify ZANLA and ZIPRA military operations. These moves were more for political reasons than for any practical military purposes. The first was the Joint Military Command formed in 1972. This body had no practical function. It had been formed primarily to head off Chikerema's sleight-of-hand efforts to promote a new guerrilla body, the Front for the Liberation of Zimbabwe (FROLIZI). This was a ZAPU splinter group under his leadership which tried to gain control of all Zimbabwean guerrillas. Chikerema touted FROLIZI as the authentic liberation movement which united all factions. It was little more than a bold confidence trick, but Chikerema did gain some credence at the OAU and internationally. ZAPU and ZANU formed the Joint Military Command, and in 1973 a Joint Political Council, to quash Chikerema's 'unity' platform based on FROLIZI.

The Zimbabwe Liberation Army (ZLA), like FROLIZI, was an attempt by Bishop Abel Muzorewa to hijack the guerrilla armies. In December 1974 he was promoted by the frontline states and the OAU as a unifying leader. The African National Council (ANC) led by Muzorewa enjoyed the prestige of having defeated the 1971 Smith-Home settlement proposals, and Muzorewa had shown his commitment to armed struggle by going into exile after the subsequent failure of negotiations with the Smith regime. ZAPU and ZANU were more or less forced to accept Muzorewa's umbrella leadership. The more radical elements of ZANU rejected him, however, and in mid-1975 the ANC executive, including Muzorewa, Nkomo, Sithole and Chikerema, formed the Zimbabwe Liberation Council in an attempt to gain control of the whole nationalist struggle. The ZLA was the ZLC's military wing, but it was an empty cipher which had little support among the fighting guerrillas. Muzorewa and Sithole tried to keep the fiction of the ZLA going into 1977 and 1978, though by then it was farcical. The ZLA hoodwinked Rhodesian whites into the 'internal settlement' in the hopes that Sithole and Muzorewa could stop the war, but that was its only real contribution to the achievement of majority rule.

Under frontline pressure, ZANU and ZAPU formed the Zimbabwe People's Army (ZIPA) in 1975-6. This was an operational amalgamation of ZIPRA and ZANLA under an 18-man military committee. There were nine members of each army on the council, but the most important posts were held by ZANLA representatives. Rex Nhongo was its commander (Tongogara was then in detention in Zambia for his alleged implication in the murder of Herbert Chitepo), and the ZIPA political commissar was Alfred Mangena, then commander of ZIPRA. At that point the OAU Liberation Committee and Tanzania were pressing hard for joint training of the guerrillas at Nachingwea, and ZIPA was a similarly natural outgrowth of this pressure for unity.

ZIPA mounted the offensive of early 1976 into eastern Rhodesia. ZIPRA provided about 15 percent of the guerrillas sent into action, but many of them deserted and filtered westwards to Botswana, launching the ZIPRA recruiting campaign in Matabeleland. ZIPRA was in no way committed to a long-term offensive in eastern Rhodesia, for practical and tribal reasons, and the co-operation soon faded away. ZIPA was also a dead letter by the beginning of 1977. But both armies did gain something from ZIPA: ZAPU was better plugged into the OAU Liberation Committee than ZANU, and ZIPA provided a convenient way for ZANLA to make a claim on the committee's supply of arms to the guerrillas. In the past ZIPRA had benefited most from the committee's aid. ZIPRA was able to use the combined offensive as a means of measuring the potential for intensified insurgency in Matabeleland and as a stimulus for a recruiting drive.

The Patriotic Front alliance forged in 1976 for the Geneva constitutional conference produced no effective military unity. Although, in an extremely confused period, ZIPA sent a separate delegation to the conference, with Nhongo unexpectedly appearing in a Swiss hotel, the military reality was that ZANLA and ZIPRA were by then separate armies again.

The last attempt to unify the two armies was made in early 1977 when J Z Moyo of ZAPU went to Maputo (shortly before his assassination) to negotiate the setting up of a 'Military Co-ordinating Committee' with ZANU. This would have given some credence to the claims of unity by the Patriotic Front political alliance. But Moyo's death brought the end of hopes of military unity. From then on ZIPRA and ZANLA fought their own battles, and in 1977 and 1978 there were clashes between the two armies in areas where their operations overlapped.

Just as attempts at unity between the armies and the political parties failed, the political wings were also racked by disunity. The development of guerrilla strategy seems in retrospect to have been a straightforward, almost inevitable process – the commando incursions of the early 1960s failed, giving way to a period of reconsideration, then the emergence of a correct 'people's war' strategy. But the unfolding of this process was far from neat. Considerable internecine wrangling and violence erupted within the parties which was not resolved (and even then not completely) until 1978.

The major struggle within ZANU began in the late 1960s. The problem throughout lay in the split between those who saw a place for negotiations with the Smith regime and those who argued for all-out war as *the* only solution. Sithole had been the firebrand of the Sixties, but in 1969-70 he lost ground to the more radical elements in ZANU. The turning point for him was the declaration he made in the dock at his trial for allegedly plotting the assassination of Smith in 1969: 'I wish publicly to dissociate my name in word, thought or deed from any subversive activities, from any terrorist activities, and from any form of violence.' The other members of the central committee took him at his word, though the whites did not and imprisoned him, but it took the ZANU radicals until 1974 to lever Sithole from the party presidency. He clung on tenaciously, and it was only in 1977 that he lost any hope of regaining his former prominence.

Control of the party passed inexorably into the hands of the more radical party members, and Mugabe emerged in 1978 as the clear and publicly acknowledged leader and as commander-in-chief of ZANLA. This could not have been done without the commitment of the fighting guerrillas to armed struggle. The Mgagao Declaration of 1975, compiled by guerrillas at the training camp in Tanzania, was the clarion call of the irreconcilables. It declared:

> We therefore strongly, unreservedly, categorically and totally condemn any moves to continue talks with the Smith regime in whatever form. We the freedom fighters will do the fighting and nobody under heaven has the power to deny us the right to die for our country.

Mugabe fled Rhodesia during the abortive detente exercise of 1975-6 and took control of the party apparatus and ZANLA in the next 18 months. He began to reconstruct the war effort from Chimoio, and by 1978 was able to direct a far more vigorous and effective campaign than had been fought before. Ironically, it was the radical element which went to the Geneva talks in 1976 and to Lancaster House in 1979. Significantly, in 1979 there were rumblings among the fighting guerrillas that negotiations with the Muzorewa government would rob them of the victory in the field which they felt was imminent. In terms of the party's ideology, the seizure of power by a true socialist party should have been impossible without a revolutionary struggle to the bitter end. But instead of winning that power out of the barrel of the gun in a Chinese-style people's war, ZANU won it through a Western-style ballot.

ZAPU did not lay itself open to such glaring inner contradictions. Nkomo, one of the great political survivors of all time, never rejected the possibility of talks with the Smith government. Nkomo talked to the Rhodesians from December 1975 to March 1976, when the negotiations broke down, and thereafter periodic contact was maintained. It was only the shooting down of the Viscount civilian airliners in 1978 and 1979 by ZIPRA guerrillas which put him beyond the pale from the Rhodesians' point of view. But Nkomo was at Lancaster House, as expected, and he talked with the Rhodesians again. The murder of Jason Moyo in 1977 had considerably weakened the war party within ZAPU, and thereafter Nkomo's influence was unrivalled.

The ideology of people's war should have precluded guerrilla participation in negotiations for a peaceful transition to majority rule in Rhodesia. Tongogara adopted the Vietnamese approach to negotiations – the guerrillas had little to lose from them as long as the armed struggle continued unabated or even intensified. But the guerrillas were not so confident of ultimate victory that they could afford to treat negotiations lightly. Like the Rhodesians and the Muzorewa government, they felt they were in a race against time, a possible Western recognition of the internal settlement, and the lifting of economic sanctions. Time was one of the crucial three dynamics of Maoist warfare (time, space and will), but the guerrillas were not sure enough of their own will and of that of the 'sea' to refuse negotiations. By 1979 considerable war-weariness affected the guerrillas, and the African population inside Rhodesia. The huge turnout of voters in April 1979 was largely a result of

Muzorewa's unfulfillable pledge that he could end the war. The heavy punishment inflicted by the Rhodesian forces on the guerrillas in cross-border raids in mid- and late 1979 increased the attractiveness of the negotiating table, especially for the Mozambican government. But even at Lancaster House, and throughout the ceasefire and election period, the guerrillas kept open the option to resume hostilities if they lost the election, by constantly exposing the duplicity of the British and the intimidation of, and subtler pressures on, voters by the Rhodesian forces and civil administration.

The history of the guerrillas' long struggle and events after the 1980 election showed that the war in Rhodesia was not a classic Asian people's war. Certainly the tactics and much of the strategic framework were borrowed directly from the Asian experience, but the way the struggle was waged and the way the war ended placed the *Chimurenga* war very much in the tradition of Western revolutions. In reality it was what Marxists call a 'bourgeois nationalist' struggle, dressed in the ferocious garb of people's war.

Chapter Six

WEAPONS AND TACTICS

WEAPONS

Generals in modern armies bristling with sophisticated weaponry have had to face the fact that the most cost-effective way to kill a man with a rifle is to use another man with a rifle. Although both sides deployed heavy weapons in the war in Rhodesia, the infantry rifle was the major instrument of death.

The standard rifle of the Rhodesian security forces was the 7.62mm Fabrique Nationale FAL automatic rifle. Large numbers of these had been supplied through the British ministry of defence when the RLI was formed in 1961, and in subsequent years. After UDI the flow of these weapons was maintained by the purchase of the South African version, designated the Rl, which had a less effective muzzle flash shield than the Belgian version, and which could not take the standard NATO rifle grenades. The FN was a temperamental weapon designed for sophisticated armies in Europe. Its precision structure required careful maintenance and the weapon was prone to stoppages when it became worn. The call-up system meant that these rifles were in almost continuous use by different soldiers over many years. It was only in the elite units that weapons were issued to individuals for long periods.

With its long 7.62mm round and high muzzle velocity, the FN was far more effective and longer-ranged than Soviet-designed guerrilla weapons which took the shorter 7.62mm intermediate round. The heavier round inflicted gaping wounds and caused a high mortality rate among those hit, though the weight of the ammunition reduced the quantities which could be carried by patrols. Despite the fact that its length could be a hindrance in close bush, the weapon was universally admired for its stopping power and versatility. One Selous Scout described it as a rifle, light machine gun (in its automatic fire configuration) and mortar (using rifle grenades), all in one.

Later in the war large numbers of Heckler & Koch G3s, also firing the standard 7.62mm NATO round, were supplied by Portugal. These were issued to troops deployed on protective duties, though their light and often flimsy construction and difficult maintenance saw their rapid deterioration in the hands of soldiers with less training.

The Rhodesians' standard light machine gun was the MAG, known in Britain as the GPMG. This was carried at section and 'stick' (squad) level and gave devastating firepower to the small Rhodesian tactical units. Priority in distribution was given to elite and active combat units, as there were never enough to equip every unit with MAGs. When the scandal involving corruption in the procurement of arms broke in 1978, the limited information disclosed publicly was enough for law enforcement agents in Europe to seize a valuable shipment of 500 MAGs destined for Rhodesia.

Other units had to make do with Browning .303 machine guns, heavy-barrelled versions of the FN with 30-round magazines and Second World War-vintage Bren guns converted to take the standard NATO round. Besides FNs, the police force had a large number of different weapons available for its operations, including Greener and Browning automatic shotguns, German PI and Czech CZ 9mm pistols and Lee-Enfield .303 rifles. Personnel of the internal affairs ministry serving in war zones were largely equipped also with .303 rifles. Spread throughout the Rhodesian forces was a great variety of other weapons, including Browning 9mm and CZ 7.65mm pistols, Israeli-supplied Uzis, Sten and Stirling submachine guns and various Rhodesian-made machine pistols of 9mm calibre. From time to time other weapons were tested by the Rhodesian forces, including the American standard infantry rifle, the M-16. In addition, 120,000 privately registered firearms were in the hands of the white population.

Ammunition supplies were secured from and through South Africa. The South Africans produced their own 7.62mm, 9mm and .303 inch ammunition, much of the latter being of inferior quality and causing stoppages, particularly in Browning machine guns.

The FN's adversary was the now famous symbol of revolution in the Third World, the AK-47 and its successor, the AKM. Firing the 7.62mm intermediate round, it had less hitting power than the NATO 7.62mm rifles, but it had certain overriding advantages for guerrilla armies which were largely made up of poorly educated, ill-trained peasants. The AK family was in the tradition of Russian weapons: rugged, dependable and cheap. Instances of AKs firing more than 3,000 rounds without being cleaned or lubricated were recorded during the war. Guerrillas could bury AKs for months, and even when the wooden stocks had been eaten away by termites and the components had become rusty, they would fire on the first shot. Lighter ammunition meant that the guerrillas could carry more rounds in the distinctive 30-round 'banana' magazines. The guerrillas did not discourage ammunition wastage and favoured extravagant automatic fire, so that these larger quantities of ammunition were vital. The AKs could also take a family of rifle grenades, but their most widely used optional fixtures were bayonets. The most common were triangular-section 'pig-stickers' and saw-back bayonets. These were used for the summary executions and mutilations by the guerrillas to maintain discipline and loyalty among their supporters, and to despatch their civilian opponents. The AK was supplied in a number of configurations depending on the supplier. The Soviet Union, Yugoslavia, China and Romania all supplied different versions of the basic rifle.

The AK was supplemented by the SKS semi-automatic rifle and a number of other small arms. In early days the guerrillas were armed with a motley assortment of weapons bought in the international arms bazaar, but even as late as 1979 the security forces captured German-made MG-34 machine guns of World War Two vintage. Most weapons and ammunition were of Soviet origin or design and included the extremely light and highly accurate RPD machine gun, the PKM machine gun with the long 7.62mm round, PPShk submachine guns and Tokarev 7.62mm pistols, which were carried as the badge of authority within guerrilla detachments. (The Tokarev was a prized personal capture for Rhodesian troops, especially on external raids, even though looting was officially forbidden.)

Both sides used hand and rifle grenades supplied by their respective supporters. The Rhodesian forces used Portuguese- and South African-produced M-962 fragmentation and white phosphorous hand grenades, vintage Mills bombs of British origin, NATO Z-42 rifle grenades, and a variety of Rhodesian-produced hand and rifle, phosphorous and fragmentation grenades. The guerrillas used Chinese stick grenades and Soviet and Eastern European 'egg' and standard, 'pineapple'-shaped hand grenades.

For heavier infantry weapons, both sides deployed 60mm mortars, which the guerrillas used for attacks on farms, security forces camps, PVs and other installations, as well as against security force patrols. The guerrillas also deployed 82mm mortars for attacks against static installations, and the Rhodesian artillery used 106mm mortars. These were normally deployed opposite points of border friction such as Vila Salazar and Chirundu, and used for retaliatory barrages.

The heaviest weapons normally deployed by the guerrillas were the RPG anti-tank grenade launchers, and 75mm recoilless rifles. Each section would usually carry an RPG-2 or RPG-7, but recoilless rifles were considerably less common. There were supply problems, too, and guerrillas often had a recoilless rifle and no ammunition, or vice versa.

The Rhodesians were far more lavishly equipped with heavy weapons than the guerrillas. Much of this equipment was left over from pre-UDI days, but more was amassed after the Rhodesian army began to plan for conventional warfare from 1976-7. The guerrillas were expected to attempt to go over to the 'mobile' phase of revolutionary warfare some time in the following two years, possibly with the assistance of Cuban or other Eastern bloc proxies such as Nigeria or Tanzania. In the event, the mobile phase did not materialize, and, though most of the heavy equipment saw some combat, much of it was under-utilized.

The mainstay of the Rhodesian artillery was the 25-pounder of British origin and Second World War fame. This weapon was used for retaliatory artillery strikes on Zambia and Mozambique, on some cross-border raids and on COIN operations. Artillery barrages were used to attack guerrilla base camps, in a counter-ambush role and in support of ground operations. The guerrillas feared the artillery because, unlike aircraft, it gave no warning and they were unable to gauge the origin of the fire and take effective evasive action.

The International Institute of Strategic Studies consistently reported the existence of a battery of NATO 105mm pack howitzers within the Rhodesian artillery establishment, but these were not seen in public or photographed –

because they did not exist. From time to time South African 5.5 inch medium guns, again of Second World War vintage, were deployed in Rhodesia. Designated the 140mm gun, they were used for cross-border barrages against Zambian and Mozambican military installations and guerrilla base camps in the border regions of those states. Later in the war Pretoria also loaned Rhodesia 155mm artillery pieces.

Reports of shipments of Soviet T-34/85 and T-55 tanks to Mozambique caused a scare in Rhodesia in 1976. As a result, the artillery created tank-killer teams using 106mm recoilless rifles mounted on German Unimog 2.5 ton vehicles. The weapons were worked in teams because of the huge dust clouds kicked up by the backflashes, which have universally branded recoilless rifles as suicide weapons in positional warfare. To reduce the chances of enemy retaliatory fire, the first vehicle would fire and withdraw, leaving the second to be relied on to score a lethal hit if the first missed.

Eland armoured cars, the South African-produced version of the Panhard AML-90, were imported in quantity. Armed with a 90mm gun, these vehicles were also an important element of the Rhodesian anti-tank capability. They were deployed on internal and external operations. The Eland was used successfully in Angola by the South African Defence Force in 1975-6 and in September 1979 a troop of Rhodesian Elands engaged T-34s of the Mozambique army in one battle. The T-34s were poorly handled by FRELIMO troops, but since a general rout was in process at the time of the engagement, and the tanks withdrew without pressing their attack, the results were inconclusive.

The RAF deployed another South African armoured car, a version of the Panhard AML-60, armed with a 60mm breech-loading mortar, on airfield protection and fuel convoy duties. About 20 British Ferret armoured cars, first delivered in 1960 and armed with Browning machine guns, were also used in COIN operations and for protective duties.

In 1979 the existence of eight Soviet T-55s in the Rhodesian army was disclosed. Salisbury leaked to the press that they been captured in Mozambique, but they were part of a shipment destined for Uganda when Idi Amin's regime began to topple. The French ship, the *Astor*, transporting heavy weapons from Libya to Uganda, was diverted to Angola. It stopped at Durban, where the cargo, including ten Polish-built T-55 LD (built in 1975), was seized by South Africa, which considered itself at war with Angola. Two tanks were kept by Pretoria for evaluation. The remaining eight were transported north. The tanks became part of the Rhodesian Armoured Car Regiment, in a newly formed 'E' Squadron. They were driven around on transporters for several months to give the impression that the Rhodesians possessed a large number of heavy tanks. Rhodesian crews were trained by experts from the SADF School of Armour, who kitted out the vehicles with improved communications. The squadron was put under the command of a West German captain, who was well versed in tank warfare. Despite their deployment for Operation Quartz in 1980, they remained unused.

The guerrillas excelled at land mine warfare and they employed a great variety of Soviet-designed anti-tank and anti-personnel mines. On most days at the height of the war the guerrillas could count on damaging or destroying several security force vehicles with a variety of metal, plastic and wooden-box mines. Increasingly sophisticated anti-lift and anti-detection devices were used. Small children and non-combatant supporters (*mujibas*) often laid mines, and land mine blasts became one of the most serious problems for the Rhodesian forces. They in turn sowed thousands of mines along guerrilla infiltration routes into Rhodesia and inside neighbouring countries. The standard tactical mine was a locally- and South African-produced Claymore mine. Towards the end of the war Rhodesian forces operating across the border were laying mines which, in addition to normal anti-lift devices, were equipped with sensitive photo-electric cells.

A large-scale local industry grew up during the war to produce mine-proof vehicles. Mine casualties sapped morale and hampered the security forces' mobility. Significantly, the first Rhodesian military death in the phase of the war starting in 1972 was caused by a land mine. According to Peter Stiff's history of mine warfare, *Taming the Landmine*, vehicles detonated 1,276 mines inside Rhodesia. Of those, 927 blasts involved mine-protected vehicles carrying a total of 5,830 passengers, of whom 91 were killed and 1,311 injured. There were 349 blasts involving unprotected vehicles which were carrying 1,453 passengers, of whom 331 were killed and 575 injured. These figures attest to the success of Rhodesian innovations in mine-proofing vehicles. Local manufacturers, such as the Ford plant at Willowvale in Salisbury, converted imported chassis or created new ones, and mounted engines stripped from imported commercial vehicles in a bewildering variety of types. A large number of variants were built in the difficult search for the perfect vehicle which would be simultaneously mobile, protected against ambushes, and mine-proof. There were three basic classes of vehicle: reconnaissance and utility vehicles like the Rhino and Hyena (based on a Ford V-6 engine and imported from South Africa or copied from the SADF models); and heavy troop transports such as the police Puma, and the army's Crocodile and other MAPs (mine-and-ambush-proof vehicles). Other miscellaneous mine-proof vehicles were the Pookie, an electronically equipped mine detection vehicle and the Hippo, a South African troop-carrying vehicle with a turret for a machine gun.

Rhodesian security force mobility and logistics were based on a vast fleet of troop-transport and supply trucks, all mine-proofed to some degree with sandbags and safety belts. In the early days of the war they were mainly Bedford 3- and 5-tonners and Land Rovers, but by the war's end there was also a fleet of Mercedes/Unimog vehicles. The Unimog 2.5 and 4.5 ton vehicles were highly prized for their exceptional mobility and as fighting vehicles were sometimes mounted with heavy weapons, such as recoilless rifles, 3.5 inch rocket launchers, MAGs or captured Soviet 12.7mm DShk heavy machine guns.

The use of mine-proofed vehicles and a constant propaganda campaign for safe driving at low speed reduced land mine injuries and deaths to a low level, though the damage and destruction of vehicles hit by anti-tank mines became a severe strain on repair facilities and the logistics budget.

The guerrillas used trucks and utility vehicles only in their base areas in

Mozambique, Zambia and Botswana, as their 'liberated zones' in Rhodesia were tenuously held and indefensible against security force incursions. Occasionally civilian or commercial vehicles were hijacked within the country to transport guerrillas or weapons, and buses often carried guerrillas and their skilfully camouflaged weapons. In Mozambique, ZANLA forces had the periodic support of heavy equipment of FRELIMO, including BTR-152 armoured personnel carriers mounted with 12.7mm machine guns and T-34/85s. The T-55s held by FRELIMO were deployed but not committed against Rhodesian incursions.

Nkomo's ZIPRA had by 1979 organized and equipped a conventional warfare brigade. It was supplied with Soviet equipment, including T-34s, MTU-55 bridging equipment, BTR-152 armoured personnel carriers, recoilless rifles, field guns, heavy mortars and Soviet command cars. This equipment was not deployed against the Rhodesian security forces inside the country, and was used in only a limited capacity in defence of base camps inside Zambia. The incompetence with which the equipment was used in the attempted rising by ZIPRA dissidents in February 1981 demonstrated the poor training and tactical experience of those leading this conventional force.

In the air the Rhodesian forces enjoyed supremacy, though the guerrillas' anti-aircraft defences became more sophisticated and were better handled towards the end of the war. Most observers put a great deal of emphasis on the age of the RAF's aircraft, but much of the equipment, especially propeller-driven aircraft and helicopters, was acquired after UDI. The more elderly Vampires and Provosts were relegated to a training role by the early Seventies. The Canberras were an effective light bomber force. In the attack on New Chimoio in September-October 1979, dive-bombing Hawker Hunters received a great deal of flak, but the Canberras were met with silence as the guerrillas sought cover from their loads of 1,000-pound bombs. Despite guerrilla respect for these aircraft, most of the Canberra force had been severely damaged at one stage or another, or shot down, and only one aircraft emerged from the war in reasonable flying condition.

The Canberras' most spectacular raid was that on a ZIPRA guerrilla base at Luso in Angola in 1979. The target was more than 1,000 km from the closest point to Angola on the Rhodesian border, but the seven Canberras (including three South African planes) made it there and back, unhindered by Angolan air defences, which included radar, SAMs and MiG-21s. The South African air force provided top cover and fighter back-up if the raid had gone wrong.

The Hunters were less roughly handled because of their greater speed and maneuverability. As well as having an interceptor role, they were used for strikes on guerrilla encampments and in support of Fire Forces where these encountered particularly large or determined guerrilla groups. The routine Fire Force strike aircraft was the Lynx, the Rhodesian version of the Cessna 0-2 used as a Forward Air Control (FAC) plane by the Americans in Vietnam.

The Alouette squadron was boosted by the loan of a large number of South African aircraft, including a squadron of Alouette IIs for the suppression of urban terrorism and rioting during the election of April 1979. Alouette IIIs were configured

. A Rhodesian T-55 tank: none were used in combat. Originally en route to Uganda, they were intercepted by South Africa, and were included in the Rhodesian inventory in 1979.

. A Rhodesian copy of the British anti-bomb robot developed in Northern Ireland. The vehicle was remotely controlled, mounted a TV camera and carried a shotgun to blast open packages or suspect objects.

3. A Rhodesian Air Force Hawker Hunter, a maid-of-all-work. The Rhodesians had nine.

4. A Mirage III of the South African Air Force. They did not take part in the war in Rhodesian air space, but they did provide a crucial backstop for security force raids into neighbouring states. They were a deterrent to prevent the involvement of Soviet MiGs.

. A Fire Force operation, the most important military technique developed by the Rhodesians.

. One of the Alouettes loaned by South Africa. Note the heat dispersal unit, baffle at rear. The Rhodesians modified the heat exhausts to confuse SAM-7 missiles.

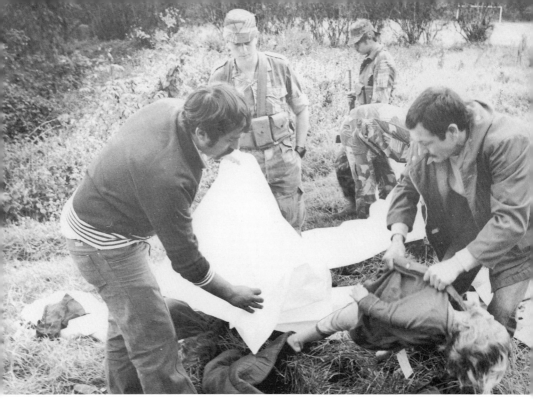

7. Slaughter of the innocents. On 23 June 1978, 12 men, women and children were variously raped, hacked and bludgeoned to death by ZANLA regulars at Elim Pentecostal Mission, near Umtali.

8. ZIPRA shot down two Air Rhodesia civilian airliners with SAM-7 missiles.

. Selous Scouts in their initial period of formation. The Scouts were ultra-secret so this rare picture was probably used for army propaganda.

0. Close-combat use of the bayonet was not uncommon in the security forces, especially in external raids, though the insurgents used bayonets regularly in punishment attacks on alleged collaborators in the black population.

11. Guerrilla attacks on urban targets forced the Rhodesians to form a Special Weapons and Tactics (SWAT) unit. Here a SWAT team drops on to a factory roof in a training exercise.

2. Rhodesian police SWAT teams wore distinctive blue denim uniforms and caps and carried Uzi submachine guns or P1 pistols.

3. On 11 December 1978, ZANLA guerrillas fired rockets and tracers at the central oil storage depot in Salisbury and destroyed 25 million gallons of fuel. The fire raged for six days. Prime Minister Ian Smith thanks the fire crew.

14. Dad's army. Towards the end of the war, whites up to the age of 60 were called up.
(Photograph courtesy of Allen Pizzey.)

5. A Security Force Auxiliary, loyal to Bishop Muzorewa.   *(Allen Pizzey.)*

16. A rare photograph of Selous Scouts preparing for Operation Miracle (September/October 1979) against a ZANLA base in the New Chimoio area of Mozambique, as part of the final total war strategy against the frontline states.

17. An early Soviet BTR-152 with a 12.7mm machine gun, used by FRELIMO. It was destroyed by elements of 2 Commando, Rhodesian Light Infantry, during Operation Snoopy, Chimoio, Mozambique, 20 September 1978.

Mike Edden, Assistant Commissioner of Police, displays a Russian-made officer's cap captured during a raid on a ZIPRA complex at Mkushi in Zambia. It was a training camp for young female administrative assistants, but Salisbury covered up the failed raid as a successful attack on combat guerrillas.

Lieutenant General Peter Walls, the Commander of Combined Operations, was popular with his troops, not least for his hands-on approach. Here he is seen helping a paratrooper before a raid.

20. Fire Force: a young troopie, exhausted by three operations in one day, Mtoko, 1977/78. *(Chris Dehon.)*

21. ZIPRA guerrillas examine a Rhodesian helicopter shot down during a raid on Victory Camp, Zambia, in 1979.

Zimbabwe African National Unio

Correct ideological education, permanent armed struggle and work... these three, fore

Comrade President Robert Mugabe has said:

'The continuance of colonialist oppression can only be effectively fought by a continuance of the oppressed masses open and armed hostility.'

'Through the war, we have submerged whatever minor contradictions have existed amongst us and we have done so out of our recognition of the need to completely destroy the common principal enemy in pursuance of our immediate common objective - the establishment of a national democratic state. This also explains why we have linked ourselves in a common front with ZAPU which we call the Patriotic Front.'

'The enemy has undergone a negativ transformation as a result of the effectiveness of our war. Once he regarded himself as invincible. Today, he is a defeatist on the verge of surrendering. Pounded heavily from cardinal points and in his major military bases and sanctuaries, he is ever retreating as we ever advance towards him in order to demolish him.'

'The enemy situation is desperate. Our situation is most favourable. There can only be one loser - the settlers and their unashamed stooges - Muzorewa, Sithole and Chirau. There can only be one Victor - the People, as led by us, for the People can never lose.'

'The Sinoia Battle was the Party's response to the Pe... call at Gwelo for effective courageous action to overthr... colonialist and settlerist system and restore the power... masses.'

'Smith thinks he can, by using stooges as shadows of th... power resting in the hands of the whites, deceive the... masses into accepting his regime as a democratic on... people of Zimbabwe have not been fighting for 12 yea... cause they detest the white looks for Ian Smith and his c... gues. Of course not! The addition of black faces doe... amount to any democratic change in the oppressive sy... Our twelve-year old war aims at the complete overthrow... entire colonialist politico-socio-economic system and i... placement by a truly democratic one vesting politica... economic power in the people. It is, therefore, not ju... change in or modification of the content, but change i... form and content of the entire system. That is the object... our struggle.'

Pamberi ne Chimurenga

22. Guerrilla propaganda was simple and highly effective. Pamberi ne Chimurenga means Forward with the Liberation Struggle.

3. Bishop Abel Muzorewa electioneering, 1979.   (*Allen Pizzey*)

24. Robert Gabriel Mugabe. He ran Zimbabwe as a revolutionary movement, not a government, still targeting all his political enemies – both black and white.

25. P K van der Byl, Rhodesia's most flamboyant and verbally aggressive politician.

26. The prime architect of the Rhodesian rebellion: Ian Douglas Smith

as gunships, mounting either 20mm cannon or twin Browning .303 machine guns, and sometimes anti-personnel rockets. At one stage there were experiments with a mounting on which the gunner operated only the gunsight, which was linked to a hydraulically aimed multiple Browning mount, but the standard equipment remained twin Brownings, manually fired.

This fleet was maintained at a high standard of efficiency by Rhodesian technicians, by private contractors, and, in the case of helicopters, by South African technicians. A helicopter pilot, Peter Petter-Bowyer, later to become a Group Captain, was a pioneer in developing the tracking potential of the Alouettes and the Fire Force concept. Although not an engineer, he also led project teams which produced the deadly Golf and Alpha bombs and the use of flechette anti-personnel projectiles. But the Bell 205 'Hueys' (Cheetahs) acquired in December 1978 created peculiar problems because they were so corroded on arrival, and one literally fell out of the sky, but these were repaired and in some cases substantially rebuilt. Spare parts were always a problem, but the RAF either made its own or acquired them through South Africa and international arms dealers.

The guerrillas enjoyed only indirect protection from the frontline states' air forces. Mozambique's and Angola's MiGs were not used to deter or intercept Rhodesian air strikes on guerrilla bases, nor to venture into Rhodesian air space. Too much has been made of South African air force assistance to the RAF, but the occasions on which it was deployed in support of Rhodesian operations served to warn the frontline states of the consequences of aerial intervention in support of the guerrillas. Zambia's British-supplied Rapier missile and Bofors gun defences were impotent to stop Rhodesian air incursions because of poor deployment and the low level of skill of the Zambian operators.

Perhaps an aviation first was the shooting down of an aircraft by a Rhodesian Air Force helicopter. In August 1979 the Rhodesian forces, including units of the Selous Scouts, raided into Botswana. Elements of the Botswana Defence Force resisted the incursion and were given air support by a Britten-Norman Defender. An Alouette III hovered in ambush behind a hill then emerged and engaged the Defender with its 20mm ground-attack cannon, forcing the aircraft down.

The guerrillas' own anti-aircraft defences were formidable by the war's end. ZIPRA pulled an ace from its sleeve with the deployment of SAM-7 Strela infra-red homing missiles. FRELIMO was reported to have used the missile to shoot down a Canberra bomber in 1973, but since ZANLA was later equipped mainly by the People's Republic of China, the SAM-7 was not in its inventory. ZIPRA scored a major victory against white morale when it shot down two civilian Viscount airliners. The Viscount was peculiarly vulnerable to the missile, for DC-3 Dakotas survived hits. Before the Viscounts were brought down there had been some 20 reports of SAM-7 firings at military aircraft, but no successful hits resulted. Rhodesian counter-measures relied on evasive flight paths and maneuvers, the painting of aircraft with grey anti-reflective paint and dispersion of exhaust gases. Deployment of the weapon was limited to border regions because of its vulnerability to poor maintenance and the short life of its specialized batteries.

The guerrillas also deployed a large number of automatic anti-aircraft weapons. United States Air Force experience over North Vietnam had shown the devastating effectiveness of small arms fire, forcing it to develop tactics which previously had taken account only of surface-to-air missile and large-calibre gun defences. The standard guerrilla weapons were 12.7mm DShk and 14.5mm machine guns. The 12.7mm guns came either on single mountings with a simple optical sight or on multiple fixtures, while the 14.5mm was most commonly found on wheeled twin or quad mountings. The accuracy of guerrilla flak was poor, but the large numbers deployed, particularly outside the country in defence of bases, and the growing determination of some gunners, posed a considerable threat to RAF operations.

In 1979 reports of larger and more sophisticated SAM defences in Mozambique sent the RAF shopping for electronic counter-measures (ECM) pods, but the threat did not materialize before the end of the war.

GUERRILLA TACTICS

Guerrilla tactics were a strange mixture of fecklessness and competence. Their combat tactics were often so bad as to border on the farcical, yet the way in which they mobilized and maintained mass support was a model of the people's war.

The guerrillas infiltrated into Rhodesia along a number of well-established corridors which were sometimes as much as 20 km wide. The crossing of the border could be dangerous as the Rhodesians created a *cordon sanitaire* (known to the Rhodesians as the 'corsan') consisting of fences and minefields, supported by periodic patrols, along much of the eastern frontier. In some areas the guerrillas were able to pass through with ease, but in others they suffered heavy casualties from 'ploughshare' mines, a large version of the Claymore.

Once across the frontier the groups, consisting of between 10 and 30 guerrillas, but up to 300 on rare occasions, followed landmarks such as hills, roads, railways, fence lines and rivers. Aggressive activity was kept to a minimum and there were few incidents along infiltration routes, to avoid attracting the Rhodesian security forces' attention. Some of the routes were extremely long, such as the 300 km route along the Lundi river valley from the south-eastern border to the Belingwe Tribal Trust Land. The guerrillas always carried heavy loads of weapons and ammunition with them as they made their way to their operational sectors. Each infiltrating group would normally carry enough for its own needs. Guerrillas or their carriers were recognizable to the security forces by the calloused marks on their shoulders where their pack straps bit into the flesh. The guerrillas put a great deal of emphasis on physical fitness in their training, for conditions on the march or in operational sectors were often gruelling.

Re-supply was a constant headache for the guerrillas. ZIPRA was more lavishly supplied by the Soviets and less active than ZANLA, which faced periodic logistics crises. Land mines were an unpopular burden because of their weight, and guerrillas would often plant them soon after they crossed the border rather than lug them into the interior.

The guerrilla groups crossed European farming areas and game parks as rapidly as possible, never staying for more than two nights in the same place, and made for the relative safety of the densely populated Tribal Trust Lands. They moved from kraal to kraal or along a network of base camps until they reached their area of deployment. In areas with less sympathetic inhabitants or in those where much of the population was in PVs, 'contact men' fed and aided guerrillas in their temporary encampments. In some areas guerrillas were able to move around with considerable safety and these were used for rest and regrouping. Some areas like Mudzi and the Melsetter District had almost the status of 'liberated zones' in that security forces could venture into them only in strength. Kandeya TTL in the north-east was a safe haven for guerrillas for much of the war.

The guerrillas normally operated in sections of 10 men, comprising the commander, political commissar, security officer, medical officer, logistics officer and three to five cadres. Standard section equipment was an RPG launcher or 60mm mortar, a light machine gun, with the rest armed with varied weapons depending on their supply state.

Once inside Rhodesia the guerrillas began operations from base camps sited near friendly villages or *povo* camps. *Povo* is a Portuguese word used by FRELIMO to denote 'the masses' and borrowed by ZANLA. Their populations consisted of Africans freed or abducted from PVs or populations moved from established kraal sites. *Povo* camps were set up in remote areas and operations were mounted from these logistics bases. These sympathetic or captive groups grew crops to feed the guerrillas, carried out base camp chores, gathered intelligence on security forces movements and generally acted as the guerrillas' 'tail'. These camps were not a major feature of ZIPRA operations as their area of operations, Matabeleland, was not as heavily covered by PVs as ZANLA areas. Occasionally guerrillas were able to use PVs as rest and recreation and feeding points, particularly when many of these were handed over to auxiliaries under Internal Affairs control in 1978 and 1979. Many auxiliaries sensed a guerrilla victory in the future and came to a *modus vivendi* with local guerrilla groups. A number of camps would be set up within any given area so that the guerrillas could move from one to another to evade the surveillance of Rhodesian forces, and in case any were discovered by enemy patrols.

One security forces' officer said towards the end of the war that if Africans lived in TTLs they could be automatically classified as supporters of the guerrillas. Certainly the guerrillas could rely heavily on local Africans' willingness to act in concert with them. Particularly effective was the guerrilla *mujiba* system, which mobilised young males from the age of five who were romantically attracted by the admiration combat guerrillas enjoyed among Africans. They carried out routine tasks such as the sabotage of roads and telephone lines, intelligence gathering, carrying messages, and even punitive beatings and killings. Sometimes this could have tragic consequences. In 1979 a Rhodesian observation post in Nyajena TTL reported a large group of armed guerrillas moving in the open. Air strikes using napalm were called in, but the group turned out to be 120 *mujibas* armed with wooden imitation AK rifles.

99

Guerrillas mounted operations from their base camps, often joining up with other sections (there were three sections to a detachment) for large operations. By 1979 guerrillas were occasionally operating in groups of 75 to 150. Movement usually took place at night, though there were some areas where guerrillas moved around openly during the day. In the Nyajena TTL, guerrillas knew that Selous Scouts posing as guerrillas were operating there because they moved through the bush and not along the open pathways.

Moving up to 50 km a night, the guerrillas would lay ambushes or attack farmsteads in the early morning. In the first years of the war, when the Rhodesian forces were not overtaxed, they would attack in the late afternoon so that they had all night to make good their escape. But later in the war attacks were typically launched just before sunrise.

The guerrillas took the maxim that they must live to fight another day more than seriously. Although some units fought determinedly, most withdrew precipitately once fire was returned. A willingness to accept a few casualties might have shortened the war considerably. Sometimes remote farmhouses defended by a single family would hold out against 20 or 30 guerrillas equipped with mortars and rockets. Although this ultimately did not matter, in that the guerrillas achieved their war aims, their irresolute tactics prolonged the conflict by years. As one Rhodesian officer commented in 1979: 'If we had been fighting the Viet Cong, we would have lost the war a long time ago.' Ambushes were often poorly sited with an emphasis on escape routes rather than on the killing zone. The guerrilla propensity for using tracer simply pinpointed their firing positions for those attacked. But their operations did not necessarily have to be totally successful, if at all. Only half a dozen ambushes on a road, no matter what the outcome, compelled the Rhodesians to mount convoys which tied down men and materials and created a siege mentality and climate of fear. The range of guerrilla activities was enormous. Farmsteads were attacked, roads dug up, cattle dips destroyed, PVs and Rhodesian security forces' bases mortared, stores were robbed, mines laid, punitive murders carried out, buses and commercial vehicles were hijacked and robbed or burnt, convoys attacked, civil airliners shot down, tobacco barns razed, bridges blown up, irrigation pumps destroyed, and railway lines sabotaged. The entire political, economic, administrative and military structure built, maintained and protected by the Rhodesian government was attacked by guerrilla groups ranging from one or two individuals to company-sized detachments.

Once the guerrillas had disengaged from their operations they moved to a number of rendezvous points. These allowed those who became detached or scattered to rejoin the group and make their way back to their base camp. Anti-tracking techniques were used if security forces' follow-up was expected. These included walking along stream beds and busy paths in populated areas, removing or changing footwear and arranging for sympathizers to sweep the tracks with underbrush or to drive livestock across them.

But most of the guerrillas' time – up to 80 per cent – was spent in 'mobilizing the masses'. The guerrillas had a number of sound starting points for politicizing the population. They were black, often from the same area in which they operated, and had the avowed intention of overturning an obviously discriminatory government and securing a better life for Africans. Politicization took place on a daily basis. Living in day-to-day contact with their supporters, emotional links were built which often transcended political beliefs. While the guerrillas lived alongside their supporters, security force contact was often limited to passing patrols, punitive actions or escorting administrative officials. Even in PVs the security forces lived separately from their charges. While the guerrillas might withdraw temporarily when Rhodesian forces were active in an area, they would usually return. Casualties were covered by claiming that guerrillas who had in fact been killed had been transferred to other sections or detachments, although the wounded were always an embarrassment.

The political commissar attached to every section had a central role to play, both within the unit and in mobilizing civilian support. Political meetings, called *pungwes*, were held in villages at night. Speeches would be made by the political commissar, and almost invariably would follow the singing of *Chimurenga* songs and often beer-drinking. Summary justice might also be meted out to those who were accused of collaboration with the Rhodesian government. Great play was made of the *Chimurenga* tradition of resistance, the need for land, the brutality of the Rhodesian forces and the general poverty of rural life. Hammering on a few simple themes was highly effective in convincing the rural population of the need for the armed struggle.

Rhodesian propaganda often spoke of an indiscriminate reign of terror inflicted on the African population by the guerrillas. There was indeed a deliberate reign of terror, but only against those who sympathized with or aided the Rhodesian cause. 'Collaborators' or 'sell-outs' were brutally murdered, or mutilated, and often whole households and kraals were destroyed. But the targets were normally carefully selected and the local population could usually see the point of the executions or mutilations. In many cases completely innocent people were suspected of collaboration and murdered, but by and large the guerrillas were careful in their policy of selective terrorism. In 1978-9 a deliberate policy of killing labourers who refused to give up their jobs on white-owned farms was adopted. The guerrillas perpetrated several large massacres of farm-workers and the tactic was highly effective in denuding farms of their labour.

There was also a strict code of ethics among the guerrillas to avoid alienating local supporters. There were even *Chimurenga* songs to spread the guerrilla code, such as this one:

There are ways of Revolutionary soldiers in behaving.

Obey all orders.

Speak politely to the people.

We must not take things from our masses.

Return everything captured from the enemy.

Pay fairly for what you buy.

Don't take liberties with women, don't ill-treat captives of war.

Don't hit people too severely.

These are the words said by the people of ZANU teaching us.

These are the words said by Chairman Mao when teaching us.

Transgressions could be dealt with by corporal punishment, as were disciplinary offences. There was no set scale of punishment: some commanders punished attempted desertion with death, while others inflicted 25 lashes; yet others gave 35 lashes and assigned offenders the section's most inferior weapon for combat. Guerrillas were theoretically forbidden to procure beer (for which there was a sentence of 20 lashes) and to 'interfere' with local women, but these strictures were generally ignored. Guerrillas often indiscriminately robbed buses and stores on their own initiative. Discipline and adherence to the code of ethics, often slack, depended on the personalities of the individual commanders and commissars. ZANLA commanders and commissars often kept detailed diaries about their operations, disciplinary procedures and success of politicization. These records often fell into the hands of the security forces after contacts. They provided a great deal of personal information, particularly on individual insurgents.

The Roman Catholic Commission for Justice and Peace, which tended to sympathize with the cause of African nationalism, remarked that:

> Although it is not possible to give a comprehensive picture, it appears that there are two distinct types of guerrilla groups operating in the country at present. One type is well-trained, well-disciplined and maintains the trust of the people. Another, however, is poorly trained and ill-disciplined and can only maintain the allegiance of the rural population through the use of terror tactics.

The ZIPRA guerrillas were usually more selective in their use of brutality and terror than ZANLA forces, whose discipline was more lax and who were less discriminating. ZANLA forces were more active than ZIPRA and covered a far larger swathe of Rhodesia, with the result that there were many more instances of ZANLA atrocities.

After spells of combat in Rhodesia, guerrillas would return to their bases in neighbouring states for re-equipment or regrouping, though some guerrillas stayed in one area for periods up to five years. Medical cases which could not be handled by the poorly trained and equipped medics attached to guerrilla units, or treated in sympathetic mission clinics and hospitals, were evacuated on foot to base camps across the borders. Messengers and political agents made frequent trips to and fro across the Rhodesian frontiers. On occasion, disciplinary sections would cross into the country to stiffen demoralized or inactive sections or to mete out justice to offending guerrillas. In 1976 Rhodesian Army Brigadier Derry McIntyre, commanding Operation Thrasher, commented:

I doubt whether the terrorists are so well organised that they can influence their cadres in the field. I would say that possibly the moon affects the terrorists more than Geneva conferences. They go mad at periods which are quite unrelated to world affairs.

But the guerrillas did in fact stay in touch with world affairs, both through their own cadres and through listening to local or foreign stations on the portable radios which they bought or stole from stores or farmhouses. The official Mozambique station, Radio Maputo, carried a great deal of information and propaganda about the guerrillas' struggle, and was an important factor in inspiring guerrillas and civilians inside Rhodesia. The speed and thoroughness with which the guerrillas honoured the ceasefire in December 1979 gave the lie to observers who saw guerrilla control over their cadres in the field as tenuous at best. It was also a comment on the guerrilla sympathizers' statements that atrocities such as the Elim Mission massacre were perpetrated by groups acting outside the control and orders of their high commands.

COIN TACTICS

While the Rhodesian forces never really developed a successful antidote to the guerrillas' mobilization of the masses, they displayed consummate skill in defeating the guerrillas in combat. Even low-calibre units such as the Police Field Reserve could easily repel guerrilla attacks, though the insurgents tended to be more aggressive against units such as Guard Force and Internal Affairs.

In the years 1966-72, guerrilla activity, no matter how small the group, would invite the full attention of regular units and the Rhodesian Air Force. Insurgents were rapidly followed up by helicopter-borne patrols, and if they failed to re-cross the frontier were almost invariably hunted down. But from 1972 both the size and geographical spread of guerrilla incursions rapidly expanded. From 1976 every area of the country became affected by guerrilla operations. There were simply not enough well-trained Rhodesian soldiers to cover all the ground, and as increasing reliance was put on reserves, the problem of pinning down guerrillas so that they could be eliminated by superior firepower and tactics became acute.

The answer devised by the Rhodesians from 1974 was Fire Force, an efficient way of stretching limited elite manpower and the RAF's helicopter fleet. A typical Fire Force comprised four Alouette IIIs. At least one was configured as a 'command car' from which the Fire Force commander directed the action. One or more of the helicopters would be a gunship. Later in the war a DC-3 Dakota carrying a stick of 15 paratroops was a standard component of Fire Forces. Strike support was given by fighter-bombers in the early days of Fire Force operations until Lynxes were acquired. After this Hunters were available for particularly large or hard-fought actions.

The Fire Force was deployed from a forward air field (FAF) at the discretion of the JOC chairman or his representative on request from observation posts or ground troops in visual or combat contact with guerrillas. Initially Fire Forces were available almost immediately, but the vast numbers of guerrillas operating inside Rhodesia from 1978 caused delays of up to four hours in meeting requests. Fire Forces could expect two to three contacts with guerrillas each day at the height of the war. In 1978 a company-sized 'Jumbo' or 'national' Fire Force was created. This roved from one operational area to another, and routinely operated into Mozambique as well.

The Fire Force was talked on to its target by ground troops, who marked their own positions with smoke or white phosphorus grenades, and then began orbiting the guerrilla position. The gunships engaged the guerrillas and air strikes were called in by the Fire Force commander. At an early stage the ground troops were landed to cut off guerrilla escape routes by means of 'stop' groups. A combined air and ground action then ensued until the guerrillas had been either killed or had fled.

So effective was the Fire Force concept that it seemed to be *the* solution to winning the war. But the sheer numbers of guerrillas operating in the country and guerrilla counter-measures upset this extremely cost-effective tactic. Fire Forces became more and more stretched to cope with incidents. The guerrillas adopted evasion tactics based on lookout positions and scatter drills, and began to move about in small groups of less than five to avoid detection, concentrating only for meetings or operations. Air strikes were evaded by running at an oblique angle to the aircraft flightpath. Initially the arrival of a Fire Force meant certain death or capture, but effective counter-measures had been devised by 1978-9. One Territorial Force major described the difficulties of locating guerrillas as like trying to pick up a handful of microscopic, coloured beads off a thick-pile, multi-hued carpet.

The tactical successes of the Fire Force system were also blunted by guerrilla measures against observation posts. Base camps were sited away from prominent features on which security forces might keep watch on the surrounding terrain. Guerrilla operations in the flat country of south-eastern and much of western Rhodesia were already facilitated by the dearth of high hills in those areas. *Mujibas* and herd boys on apparently innocent domestic chores were sent through likely OP positions to compromise their presence and booby traps were even laid in the more obvious sites. Guerrillas often wore two or three sets of civilian clothes to confuse watching security forces. By the later years of the war the Rhodesian forces were forced to move OPs well away from villages and to use telescopes with optical ranges of up to 5 km to maintain their secrecy. The Selous Scouts pioneered new, painstaking techniques for setting up OPs and keeping them secure. Teams of pseudo-guerrillas, usually Selous Scouts or Special Branch agents, including amnestied guerrillas, gathered intelligence on the locations of guerrilla bases. The guerrillas devised counter-measures, such as placing taboos on eating certain foods by their cadres. A kraal head who was suspicious of groups asking the whereabouts of their 'comrades' could test their identity by offering them prohibited foods. Another favourite identification was using certain brands of cigarettes. The stratagem needed to be spread widely, but at the same time changed frequently, to be proof against security forces' interrogations of captured guerrillas.

Ground coverage and reaction to incidents were carried out by units like the RAR, the Grey's Scouts, the territorial Rhodesia Regiment battalions, the Police Support Unit and PATU. The standard tactical sub-division was the company (except for PATU which always operated in small reconnaissance sticks), which set up a headquarters in areas assigned to it for patrolling and reaction. The company was deployed in sticks, and OPs were set up, ground patrols were sent out to sweep kraals and terrain, and to establish ambushes based on information supplied by the local Special Branch operatives or the Rhodesian Intelligence Corps.

A normal stick would comprise three or four riflemen armed with FN rifles and a machine-gunner armed with an MAG. The stick would also carry hand and rifle grenades. Every stick had a radio to maintain contact with its headquarters and other sticks in the area. The lavish provision of radios gave the Rhodesian forces the tactical flexibility they needed to cover vast areas of countryside. The guerrillas rarely operated radios (which they called 'over-overs') until the last two years of the war. Most Rhodesian equipment was locally made and maintained. The ground network of field radios was linked by a series of relay stations perched atop hills. These provided a vital service where granite outcrops and rugged terrain often severely limited the range of small, portable radio sets. Relay stations were also important for linking army and police units, which operated on incompatible sets of channels. In many cases sticks only a couple of kilometres apart were forced to communicate via relay stations on high features 20 to 30 km away.

Encounter skirmishes would be conducted by the unit itself, but OPs would usually call in Fire Force if it was available. Many of these units resented Fire Force. Since the measure of success for the Rhodesian forces was the number of guerrilla corpses produced, Fire Force was seen as snatching away the rewards of troops who had endured long marches and often painstaking work to locate guerrilla camps or positions. The fact that Fire Force rode to and from battle in helicopters merely added to the jealousy, but many of the ground troops, who considered they could handle these battles themselves, forgot that Fire Force was introduced because of the inadequacy of routine patrolling.

In 1978 it was decided to conduct 'high intensity' operations in specific areas severely affected by guerrilla operations. A whole battalion would be assigned to a district, often with the addition of the 'Jumbo' Fire Force, and would thoroughly scour it, attempting to kill the guerrillas there and break their infrastructure. These operations, a return to the old search-and-destroy pattern of the early years of the war, had great success in terms of body counts in areas where they were deployed. But the whole country could not be covered and once the high intensity force left for other districts the guerrillas began seeping back and resuscitating their network.

In areas in which PVs had been established, security forces destroyed crops found outside areas prescribed for cultivation around the PV itself. When people were moved into a PV the guerrillas tried to spirit away as many as possible to set up *povo* camps. These were treated as military targets by the Rhodesian forces. In areas where there were curfews any person moving about at night was liable to be shot by ambushes. Africans refusing to stop when challenged by security forces were shot as 'suspicious persons'.

There were also exotic variations on these ground tactics, such as the use of 'Q-cars' (military vehicles bristling with firepower and disguised as civilian or commercial vehicles) and booby-trapped radios. Other radios – nicknamed 'road-runners' – contained tracking systems. The Selous Scouts also developed a major interest in biological and chemical warfare. An organophosphate, Parathion, was used to impregnate clothing. The three most common types of clothing treated were underpants, T-shirts and denim jeans, the preferred dress code of ZANLA guerrillas. Usually sick guerrillas were left by their comrades to suffer a slow and agonizing death alone in the bush. Perhaps thousands of guerrillas were killed by this method. Such 'kills' were not mentioned in official Rhodesian communiqués, but they were frequently described in diaries recovered after contacts with guerrillas. Food was contaminated with thallium, especially canned corned beef, mealie meal (maize), tinned jam and beers. The thallium was injected into sealed tins, through bottle tops and into packets with a micro needle. Cartons of cigarettes were impregnated with toxins. Cholera and anthrax were also spread deliberately. In February 1978 the new Commissioner of Police, Peter Allum, gave a direct order to stop all covert poisoning operations, though poison manufacture and distribution by SB and the Selous Scouts continued until mid-1979.

The tactical objective was always the same: to pin down the elusive guerrillas and kill or capture them. Combat troops did not engage in any political indoctrination. Their function was purely military, and they discharged this function efficiently. Increasingly, however, the only way to find and destroy large concentrations of guerrillas was to raid across the frontiers. A network of observation posts spread into Mozambique and Zambia, and Fire Force operated into those countries as if they were extensions of Rhodesian territory. The first major cross-border raid was mounted in August 1976. An incursion of 900 guerrillas was imminent from Nyadzonya camp on a tributary of the Pungwe River about 40 km inside Mozambique. The camp was a standard guerrilla installation, a sort of 'super-*povo*' camp containing not only guerrillas but their normal 'tail' of women and children. The raid was carried out by the Selous Scouts wearing FRELIMO uniforms. They simply drove into Mozambique and entered the camp at the early morning muster of guerrillas, who were mowed down from vehicles with heavy machine guns. A number of FRELIMO troops who tried to intervene were killed, and the Rhodesian troops withdrew without severe casualties. The raid caused jubilation among whites in Rhodesia and outrage abroad. The United Nations claimed that the camp was a refugee centre and that more than 600 civilians were killed and more wounded. The Rhodesians countered with claims of only 10 civilians killed. The incident was ruthlessly exploited for propaganda purposes by both sides. The Rhodesians questioned the morality of stationing combat troops alongside civilians in base camps, while the guerrillas countered that, if there were any soldiers at all, they were there to protect innocent refugees against Rhodesian savagery.

The pattern of raids remained much the same over the next three years. Camps in Zambia, Botswana and Mozambique were attacked by different methods to keep the initiative in Rhodesian hands. Ground operations were preferred because of their more successful results. In 1979 an SAS intelligence officer complained that air strikes were not effective – although many direct hits were scored on the guerrilla camps, the high explosive and napalm bombs did not kill as many guerrillas as expected. Large-scale raids were designed to do two things: to kill guerrillas where they were concentrated outside Rhodesia and to destroy or disrupt their infrastructure, weapons and supply. A number of different tactics were used: troop-carrying, heavily armed vehicles drove across the borders, paratroops made low-altitude combat jumps, ground forces were landed by helicopter or walked in and were evacuated by helicopter. The SAS infiltrated raiding parties across Lake Kariba with the assistance of the army's boat section. Small-scale raids became more frequent once the principle of striking across the border had been adopted. During one typical small operation in August 1979 a platoon of the Selous Scouts' Support Troop attacked a base camp deep inside Zambia. The ZIPRA occupants fled without resisting, but a combined guerrilla and Zambian army mobile relief column attempted to eliminate the withdrawing unit. A section-sized stop group ambushed and drove off the numerically superior column and then withdrew, laying land mines on the way back to Rhodesia. The guerrillas then set fire to the whole area in an attempt to burn down the retreating unit's cover.

This sort of operation went on week after week in the closing two years of the war. The guerrillas often felt safer inside Rhodesia than they did in the border regions of their host states, for the marauding troops were the highly trained and motivated elite of the Rhodesian Army. Guerrilla offensives were often disrupted by timely Rhodesian spoiling attacks, and camps had to be moved back from the borders, dispersed and more heavily defended. The series of raids culminated in an attack on the massive guerrilla base at New Chimoio in September 1979. The Rhodesian blitzkrieg put significant pressure on the leaders of the Patriotic Front to remain at the Lancaster House conference which ended the war.

In a letter to *The Times* in January 1978 retired British General Sir Walter Walker wrote of the Rhodesian forces:

> Their army cannot be defeated in the field either by terrorists or even a much more sophisticated enemy. In my professional judgement based on more than twenty years' experience from Lieutenant to General, of counter-insurgency and guerrilla type operations, there is no doubt that Rhodesia now has the most professional and battleworthy army in the world today for this particular type of warfare.

The general was probably right. A further, backhanded compliment to the Rhodesian forces was paid by an official of the Mozambique government when he claimed that they had destroyed a vital bridge deep inside his country. 'It must have been the Rhodesians,' he said, 'because it was done so well.' But the 'field' in revolutionary warfare is not the same as that in conventional warfare. In a guerrilla war the battlefield is the political loyalty of the mass of the population. The Rhodesians did not develop tactics to win enough battles in that more subtle war.

107

GUERRILLA AMBUSH

(The skirmish described here lacked the spectacular violence of the Rhodesians' cross-border raids, but was more characteristic of the low-intensity bush war.)

From early 1979 much of Rhodesia's petrol was shipped via Durban and then transported to the South African railhead at Beit Bridge. Then it was trucked north. Daily convoys of 10-15 tankers, each carrying 30,000 litres of fuel, rumbled towards depots in Salisbury. Before then the guerrillas had mounted only periodic ambushes along the 300 km stretch from Fort Victoria to Beit Bridge, or had organized *mujibas* to dig ditches across the road at night. But from mid-1979 their aim was to make the route impassable for protracted periods and turn the Rhodesian lifeline into a costly chokepoint. By October 1979 several tankers had been burnt out and the Rhodesians were forced to deploy armoured cars to keep the fuel flowing.

One small guerrilla section operated for months against the road from the 70 km peg south of Fort Victoria to the Lundi River, 40 km further south. The guerrillas switched their attacks back and forth along the road, sometimes marching 40 km in a night from their base camp in the hills west of the 75 km peg. They bore a charmed life and successfully eluded many security forces' sweeps and counter-measures, while killing and wounding several members of the BSAP Reserve assigned to clear and protect the vital economic artery. The gadfly section was so effective that the Rhodesians had to commit more and more men and material to convoy duties.

The section, numbering a dozen cadres, mounted a classic guerrilla ambush in early September 1979. The firing positions and killing zones were carefully laid in the pre-dawn hours, after a night march in pitch darkness. Two guerrillas were detailed to act as a decoy group to the east of the road. Six formed the main ambush line behind an embankment running along the west side of the road, and the rest formed a stopline on a hillock to the south of this line. The guerrillas lay wrapped in chill silence until they heard the approaching engines of Rhodesian military vehicles soon after sunrise.

The Rhodesian task force, operating from a base on the Lundi River to the south, was charged with checking the road for land mines, ditches and ambushes every morning, before linking up with the south-bound, civilian 'Blue Convoy' from Fort Victoria. The force comprised a road-clearing party of a heavy truck mounted with a machine-gun turret, an armoured troop carrier, and two roving Police Anti-Terrorist Unit (PATU) vehicles carrying squads to chase ambushing guerrillas. The Rhodesian timetable was so regular (to fit in with scheduled civilian convoy times) that the guerrillas could almost set their watches by it. On that day an armed Police Reserve Air Wing (PRAW) aircraft provided an air observation post and fire support for the task force. The scale of the security forces' equipment was testimony to the success of the guerrilla high command's strategy of burdening the Rhodesians with protection duties to stretch their manpower and resources to breaking point.

The guerrilla ambush was triggered with an RPG-2 anti-tank grenade launcher, fired point-blank at the second Rhodesian vehicle from the rise at the south end of the embankment. The guerrillas tried whenever possible to use either an RPG or a

GUERRILLA AMBUSH

1 Guerrilla initiates ambush with RPG-2.
2 Main guerrilla killing group.
3 Guerrilla decoys.
4 Rhodesian police 'Puma' heavy mine-proofed vehicle mounting Browning machine-gun turret.
5 Rhodesian police 'Hyena' mine-proofed vehicle.
6 Police Reserve Air Wing aircraft orbits skirmish after contact erupts.
7 Secondary guerrilla ambush group.
8 Rhodesian police 'Kudu' with PATU stick.
9 Rhodesian police 'Leopard' with PATU stick.
10 Kraal through which guerrillas flee and where cattle slaughtered by pursuing PATU squad.
11 Guerrilla base camp attacked by Rhodesian artillery in afternoon after skirmish.

rifle grenade to initiate an ambush in the hope of frightening and disorienting Rhodesian patrols. In this case the anti-tank rocket missed the Rhodesian vehicle, but the guerrillas engaged the patrol with small arms fire. The decoy party opened fire to confuse the Rhodesians' fix on the direction of the fire. The PATU vehicles were half a kilometre behind the clearing party and as they entered the guerrilla killing zones were engaged by the well-sited flank group.

While the clearing force sped on north without stopping to rendezvous with 'Blue Convoy', the PATU sticks debussed and attacked the guerrillas. An intense firefight erupted around the hillock on which the guerrillas had now regrouped. The Rhodesians used a 60mm mortar to pound the guerrilla positions, but the PRAW pilot simply circled over the Rhodesians instead of trying to pin the guerrillas with his Browning machine guns. The troops were so close that they were able to shout obscenities at each other. The guerrillas' machine-gunner used his rock-steady RPD to break up the Rhodesian rushes. The decoy group drew off part of one PATU squad by firing on the Rhodesian vehicles left unguarded on the road.

After a 10-minute battle the guerrillas skilfully disengaged under fire and withdrew towards their base 5 to 6 km away. The Rhodesians regrouped and pursued them. The guerrillas' tracks passed through a tiny kraal. The PATU sticks, their blood up, wantonly slaughtered the old kraalhead's small herd of cows before pressing on after the guerrillas. A senior police officer who went to the skirmish area to direct the follow-up found the old man weeping near the carcasses. In sheer anger, frustration and weariness with the war he pointed out the hill where the guerrillas had had their base camp for months. That afternoon, following up this intelligence windfall, a Rhodesian battery of 25-pounder field guns blasted the suspected site. A young, unarmed African man fleeing from the barrage was gunned down by the PATU observation post which was directing the fire. It was claimed that he must have been a guerrilla since there were no identification papers on his corpse. The bush war in Rhodesia rolled on and on.

FIRE FORCE! FIRE FORCE!

(The action described here was the last major battle between ZANLA guerrillas and the Rhodesian security forces before the ceasefire on 28 December 1979. It was a classic firefight between the two armies and typified the disparity in tactical ability, and capability, between them.)

For years guerrillas operating in the Chiduku TTL 150 km east of Salisbury used a large mountain, called Rombwe after a former tribal ruler, as a base. Because of its prominence, it was an ideal rendezvous point for groups infiltrating from Mozambique. The mountain lay 8 km from the main Salisbury-Umtali road. From Rombwe the guerrillas crossed the narrow strip of European farming land around the tiny hamlet of Inyazura to and from operations in the Makoni TTL. By 1978, about 500 guerrillas fighting in the region were using it from time to time.

In late December 1979 an African herder on a European farm bordering on the

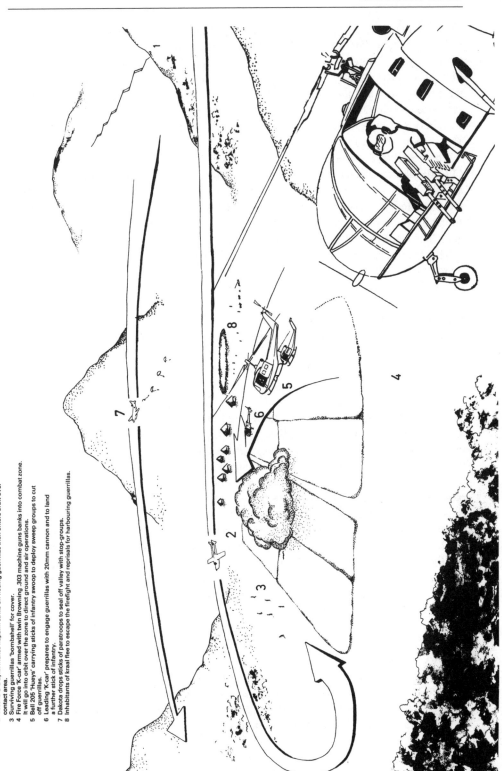

FIRE FORCE

1 Rhodesian Observation Post (OP) detects guerrillas in kraal and radios for Fire Force.
2 Cessna O-2 Lynx makes napalm strike on fleeing guerrillas then enters orbit over contact area.
3 Surviving guerrillas 'bombshell' for cover.
4 Fire Force 'K-car' armed with twin Browning .303 machine guns banks into combat zone. It will go into orbit over the zone to direct ground and air operations.
5 Bell 205 'Hueys' carrying sticks of infantry swoop to deploy sweep groups to cut off guerrillas.
6 Leading 'K-car' prepares to engage guerrillas with 20mm cannon and to land a further stick of infantry.
7 Dakota drops sticks of paratroops to seal off valley with stop-groups.
8 Inhabitants of kraal flee to escape the firefight and reprisals for harbouring guerrillas.

Chiduku TTL spotted a group of guerrillas moving across the farm and reported this to his employer. For the next four days guerrilla tracks were found on the farm, trailing west. There was obviously a large-scale movement of guerrillas from Makoni TTL to Chiduku. The farmer and a handful of his African militiamen sprang an ambush on a guerrilla group filtering across the farm the night before the ceasefire was due to come into effect. The next morning two Alouette III helicopters searched Rombwe mountain as it was suspected the guerrillas had hidden there. They reported nothing.

The BSAP at Rusape deployed two sticks of their COIN 'strike force' comprising 11 European regulars, reservists and African auxiliary constables to search the kraals and the valley at the base of the mountain. The sticks were dropped to the north of the mountain by Alouette IIIs at noon, and began to sweep along its western face. Towards the south-western spur they picked up the tracks of a large number of guerrillas leading up the steep mountainside.

The guerrillas were, in fact, assembling their forces on Rombwe before moving on to St Anne's mission to the east, and then to a Commonwealth Monitoring Force assembly point for the ceasefire. The increase in the level of guerrilla movements observed in the area by Rhodesian security forces had come from outlying sections and detachments making their way towards Rombwe. The Rhodesians' initial estimate of guerrilla strength on Rombwe was 200, but after the end of the war guerrillas testified that their strength was more than 400 on that day. Yet they had skilfully hidden themselves from the prying eyes of the Alouettes which overflew the rugged mountain. The guerrillas had gathered there over preceding days, and their logistics squads had cached water and *sadza* (maize meal porridge) among the rocky outcrops high above the surrounding plain.

A well-worn path alerted the Rhodesian patrol to the presence of what was one of the largest-ever concentrations of guerrillas inside Rhodesia. The patrol wound up the path in single file, and among the thick vegetation came across clearings, fire places and other signs of the guerrillas' presence. At two o'clock in the afternoon the patrol stumbled on a group of guerrillas resting among trees near the crest. The ceasefire was still 10 hours away. Both sides opened fire simultaneously and the mountain-top erupted in volleys of small arms fire.

The guerrillas were spread in their sections in a long, half-kilometre crescent on ground overlooking the Rhodesian patrol, and soon had it pinned down with small arms and mortar fire. Within minutes they had the range and one Rhodesian policeman was wounded by a mortar burst. Every time one of the patrol moved he attracted heavy, accurate fire.

The guerrillas roared obscenities at the pinned patrol and dared them to call Fire Force. The patrol had already done so. The controller at Grand Reef Forward Airfield, the nearest Fire Force base, replied to the request that it would be available only after two or three hours. But, in a move typical of the informal arrangements at JOCs, an Air Force Wing Commander at Rusape JOC, who was listening in on the contact, intervened and scrambled Fire Force immediately. Flight time from Grand Reef was 45 minutes. The Fire Force, comprising two Alouette III K-cars (one armed with a 20mm cannon, the other with a multiple Browning .303 mount), two Bell 205 troop-carrying helicopters, a ground-strike Lynx and a Trojan utility craft mounted with 'Skyshout' loudspeakers, arrived at 2.45 pm.

The police patrol threw two white phosphorus grenades to mark its position. The Lynx made two strikes on the guerrilla positions with napalm. Great orange tongues of flame splashed across the mountain, but the napalm's effectiveness was lessened by the rocky, broken terrain. The K-cars closely followed the Lynx strike and passed across the front of the widely spread guerrilla positions, pouring in fire. They were engaged by 12.7mm DShk anti-aircraft machine guns the guerrillas had on the mountain.

While the duel between the Alouettes and the guerrillas raged, the Bells deployed six sticks (30 men) of the RLI at the extreme northern tip of the guerrilla positions. These troops began to sweep the flank of the guerrilla line. One guerrilla nestled in a tree and pinned down one of the RLI sweep sticks with his machine gun.

As a fierce firefight developed between the guerrillas and the outnumbered RLI squads the police patrol was able to extricate itself, and withdrew to the base of the mountain and the kraals straggling along the shallow valley below it. Long before the engagement broke out the inhabitants had smelt trouble and had fled with their cattle. The patrol burnt their huts in retaliation for their failure to inform the security forces of the guerrillas' presence on the mountain. The police patrol was then evacuated by a Bell, which had returned from Grand Reef FAF with ammunition for the 20mm cannon of one of the Alouettes.

The ground support Lynx returned from Grand Reef towards sunset and once more seared the guerrilla positions with napalm. By this stage the guerrillas were withdrawing southwards on the mountain top and working their way up into the rocky outcrops on the crest. A guerrilla mortar squad tried to knock down one of the Alouettes with its 60mm mortar. Two Hawker Hunters orbited high overhead in the late afternoon sun, but were unable to make their attack runs because the RLI sweep groups were so close to the guerrillas. They made a dummy run, but they needed a 150-metre safety margin and called off the strike.

At sunset the RLI sticks were evacuated to Grand Reef, and an eerie quiet settled over the napalm-scorched mountain-top. At two o'clock the following morning, two hours after the ceasefire came into effect, a company of 8 Battalion Rhodesia Regiment deployed into the combat zone from Rusape to cordon off the guerrillas. Early next morning the Fire Force dropped on to the mountain again and swept it. One wounded guerrilla who had been left behind put up resistance and was killed, but the rest of the force had escaped under cover of darkness and fled towards St. Anne's mission.

Despite the intensity of the action, only 15 guerrillas had been killed. The rocky outcrops which dominated the crest had reduced the effectiveness of the napalm strikes and the fire from the helicopter gunships. The withdrawal of the Fire Force at dusk had enabled the guerrillas to retreat in good order and escape – to the nearby ceasefire assembly point and the end of the war.

THE DESTRUCTION OF NEW CHIMOIO

By late 1979 Rhodesia teetered on the brink of a conventional war. The guerrilla build-up in the previous year had been enormous, and a flood of weapons, accompanied by Eastern bloc advisers and technicians, had been flowing to ZIPRA and ZANLA. Rhodesian cross-border raids had thrown the guerrilla infrastructure back from the border areas and inflicted thousands of casualties on the guerrilla armies. Yet those bloodied armies continued to swell in size and power.

Inside Mozambique, ZANLA resolved to abandon dispersion tactics and to stand and resist further Rhodesian incursions. The base camp areas at Chimoio had been repeatedly attacked and overrun. A vast new base was built near this devastated site and called New Chimoio. The camp was dominated by a high hill. East German advisers supervised the blasting of bunkers into its granite summit. They were roofed with thick logs and layers of earth. The largest concentration of flak weapons ever assembled by ZANLA, including 23mm mountings, was deployed on the hill and in the trench complexes on the plain below. A system of concentric trenches, each with a flak site at its centre, was spread throughout the 64-square-kilometre encampment.

Rhodesian Combined Operations Headquarters was determined to smash the complex at the time when international efforts to solve the Rhodesian conflict were reaching a climax – a massive military defeat for ZANLA would weaken its leaders' bargaining position at the Lancaster House constitutional conference.

But the Rhodesian security forces were at that stage of the war fully stretched on internal and external operations. Only 200 men were available to assault the camp. The elite Selous Scouts' Support Company was allocated the assault, with the RLI providing stop groups beyond the camp to hem in the guerrillas.

For the Rhodesians, information on the camp was sketchy. Rather blurred aerial reconnaissance photographs showed most of the flak positions, but little else. Two small teams, first from the SAS (with four RENAMO men in tow) and then Selous Scouts, made brief reconnaissances, but had to exit rapidly. Guerrilla strength was estimated at not more than 2,000. This, however, was a miscalculation. The camp probably contained 12,000 inmates, comprising troops and various hangers-on. The guerrillas were completing a large training intake at the time of the raid. Such massive quantities of arms had been shipped into New Chimoio to equip these fresh cadres that crates of mint AKs and heavy weapons lay under tarpaulins among the trees – the existing armouries and caches had simply overflowed. Rex Nhongo, the deputy commander of ZANLA, and other senior officers were in the camp at the time. They had 6,000 guerrillas with them when the Rhodesians opened their attack.

The Selous Scouts rehearsed mock assaults for a week before the raid. The task force was mounted on Unimog 2.5 ton vehicles armed with machine guns. The shock force of 100 men had 10 of these highly mobile trucks, one for each stick. Breakdown vehicles formed part of the convoy, which was escorted by a troop of Eland armoured cars. The convoy left the Selous Scouts' camp at Inkomo Barracks

THE DESTRUCTION OF NEW CHIMOIO

AA Main guerrilla anti-aircraft emplacements protected by concentric trench systems.
RLI Rhodesian Light Infantry 'stop-groups' and ambushes.
1 Store used as Rhodesian forward staging position, code-name 'Madison Square'.
  Position of 25-pounder artillery battery giving supporting fire on to guerrilla positions.
2 Guerrilla trenches cleared by Selous Scout task forces in first assault.
3 Guerrilla huts.
4 Selous Scouts' observation post on Day 2 of battle.
5 Selous Scouts' battle HQ and 81mm mortar battery.
6 Night base of Selous Scout task force assigned to storm Monte Cassino on Days 1 and 2.
7 Guerrilla HQ and logistics camp.
8 Main guerrilla training camp.
9 Flightpath of Rhodesian Air Force Canberra bombers.

Main assault force on Day 1
Main assault force on Day 2
Main assault force on Day 3
Secondary assault force Days 1 – 3

near Salisbury under cover of darkness on 26 September 1979. That night the force reached Ruda base camp, a kilometre from the Mozambique border, and then pressed into guerrilla country.

While the ground raiders drove towards New Chimoio, the RLI stop force, fewer than 100 strong, parachuted on to a landing zone 10 km from the guerrilla base and infiltrated into ambush positions around it.

The assault force divided into two columns of 10 vehicles each, and these were further divided into task teams of two vehicles. Their staging base was a tiny hamlet, code-named Madison Square Garden, a few kilometres from New Chimoio. The first column drove unmolested through the main gate of the camp as the RAF made its bombing strikes on the camp. These Unimogs struck on into the main camp, but the second column was attacked by the now alerted guerrillas. The assault teams believed that the guerrillas had been alerted by the noise of the aircraft dropping the RLI, but one guerrilla, who was interrogating a captured black Selous Scout when the assault began, later testified that the first he knew of the raid was the scream of jet engines from the west. He sprinted towards Nhongo's headquarters to protect the guerrilla leader.

The guerrillas, once they realized that a ground attack was taking place, responded with a devastating hail of fire. The multiple flak mounts, recoilless rifles and mortars poured heavy barrages on to the attacking Selous Scouts. Trees crashed to the ground as the assault force drove into the guerrilla defences.

The defenders in the trenches were systematically winkled out by classic flanking attacks, which almost invariably worked in an encounter with guerrilla forces. When a Rhodesian task team ran into guerrilla fire the stick on the lead vehicle debussed and aimed suppressive fire at the guerrilla trench, leaving one man to fire the machine gun, either an MAG or a DShk 12.7mm, from the exposed back of the truck. The men on the second vehicle all debussed and worked to the flank of the guerrilla position, then skirmished on to it, killing the defenders with phosphorus and fragmentation grenades and small arms fire. In this way the teams leapfrogged through the trench system. In one trench a number of women guerrillas tried to fight off the Rhodesians but were all killed in the fire-fight.

So heavy was guerrilla resistance that the Rhodesians' plans were thrown out of gear. One day had been allocated for the capture of the dominating heights, dubbed Monte Cassino after the famous battle site in Italy in 1944, but the assault force took three to achieve its objective. After that the training camp in a shallow valley to the east of the main entrenchments was to be overrun. Repeated air-strikes by the RAF pulverized the guerrilla positions. The guerrillas manning the anti-aircraft weapons had little fear of the Hawker Hunters making steep dives to deliver their rockets, bombs and cannon fire. Their strike runs were met with curtains of flak from the anti-aircraft positions on the hilltop and in the trenches. No helicopters could get near the enemy for three days. But the Canberras were met with eerie silence as they dropped their loads of 1,000-pound high-explosive bombs. The use of napalm was ruled out in this raid for fear of incinerating the Rhodesian assault troops in the close-quarters combat.

After three days guerrilla resistance began to crumble under the relentless pressure of the assault force and the air strikes. The guerrillas began to run out of ammunition – their extravagant mortar barrages and vast expenditure of small arms rounds told in the fizzling out of fire directed at the attacking Rhodesians. A troop of FPLM Soviet-supplied T-34 tanks tried to intervene in the battle, but they were engaged by the Rhodesians' Elands. East German advisers and ZANLA commanders were unable to keep the defence from disintegrating. One white adviser was spotted through a Rhodesian sniper's telescopic sight directing operations on the hill.

Unable to sustain their resistance, the guerrillas finally broke. The survivors streamed from the camp as the Selous Scouts set fire to the tall grass in the complex. The crowds of fleeing guerrillas ran into the waiting RLI stop-groups. One of four machine-gunners in a single ambush position fired a thousand-round belt without taking his finger off the trigger – he later found 60 guerrilla corpses in his arc of fire.

On the afternoon of the third day of the assault the small group of Selous Scouts stood on the charred summit of Monte Cassino. They had suffered two dead and one severely wounded. Around them on the summit lay only 11 bodies. Hundreds of others had been killed or wounded elsewhere in the camp. Nevertheless, it was a costly victory. A Canberra, a Hunter and an Alouette had been brought down, the largest loss of any air force operation during the war. The guerrillas had put up very stiff resistance. While some had broken, other parts of the evacuation had been an orderly fighting retreat with many strong points being held until the right moment to withdraw.

Chapter Seven

INTERNATIONAL INTRIGUES

The Rhodesian war had a kaleidoscope of international ramifications. Nearly all the major powers and world organizations got in on the act at some time or another. The most significant issues revolved around oil and guns for Salisbury, and cash and weapons for the guerrillas.

Two of the most active organizations were the UN and the OAU. Unlike the wrangling over the wars in Angola and Biafra, the OAU managed usually to present a united front on Rhodesia. During the detente period (1974-5) OAU funds were channelled to the ANC umbrella grouping; by 1976 the Patriotic Front was recognized as the authentic liberation movement. The warnings from the OAU Liberation Committee that it would cut off funds from the PF unless it maintained a unified ZANU-ZAPU front did much to enforce a semblance of co-operation in an inherently unstable alliance.

The UN also favoured the PF. Even after the March Agreement in 1978, the internal black leaders were refused the opportunity to take part along with PF spokesmen in the various UN debates on Rhodesia. Besides diplomatic support, a number of UN agencies were involved in assisting Rhodesian refugees and guerrillas in the frontline states. The most obvious symbol of UN support for the nationalist movement was of course the imposition of sanctions. Although Harold Wilson promised that sanctions would end the rebellion within weeks and not months, from 1969 to 1974 Rhodesia's economic growth was far more impressive than Britain's. In fact, until 1974 the periodic inclemency of the weather in southern Africa did much more harm than all the strictures of the UN.

The Rhodesian economy had rested traditionally upon three legs. The first, minerals and metals, was well developed before 1965. The other two, farming and manufacturing, were strengthened by sanctions. As late as 1978, agricultural and mineral outputs (gold, chrome, asbestos, etc.) were expanding. The world boycott had forced Rhodesia to adopt the popular development strategy of the 1950s – import substitution – and then the later fashion of agricultural diversification. Unlike most other African countries, Rhodesia became remarkably self-sufficient, especially in food production. The fact that Rhodesia's well-balanced economic structure was the most industrialized (after South Africa) in sub-Saharan Africa provided a resilient base for a vigorous anti-sanctions campaign.

More important than indigenous resources and skills, however, was the assistance from Portugal and South Africa. Neither state had any interest in seeing sanctions work. Neither would accept the principle, as it might have been applied to it. And in the case of Pretoria, a tidy profit was to be made in trading with the captive market in Rhodesia (although profit turned into loss when South Africa was compelled to bankroll her neighbour's escalating war effort). In addition, Mozambique and Zambia continued to trade with Salisbury, sometimes secretly, and in the case of Zambia in 1978, openly. Ironically, while PF leaders in Maputo and Lusaka were urging the guerrillas to drive white Rhodesian farmers off the land, both countries were receiving food supplies from these same farmers. Moreover, the railways system inherited from the colonial era compelled a reluctant interdependence upon the southern African states. Goods in transit into and from South Africa continued to pass through Botswana (where Rhodesia Railways owned and ran the rail link) into Rhodesia and then on through Zambia to Zaire via the Victoria Falls bridge.

Sanctions then were hardly more than a nuisance to Rhodesians, although luxury goods, particularly electrical gadgets, whisky and razor blades, were in short supply. And cars were expensive. Imported wines were rare, and the local variant almost undrinkable. But in the boom period of the early 1970s such minor privations were shrugged off. British goods were scarce but the West German, Japanese and French substitutes proved superior to their British counterparts in price, quality and promptness of delivery. London could retaliate by blaming Russia, East Germany, Romania and Czechoslovakia for 'regular trade' with Rhodesia. These socialist states had bought tobacco and agricultural commodities through a Swiss intermediary in Geneva, the British claimed. Rhodesia had indeed set up a string of holding companies in Switzerland, Liechtenstein and Luxembourg.

Many African states treated sanctions with disdain. As President Omar Bongo of Gabon said in 1975: 'The majority of member states of the OAU, of which Gabon is a member, trade with Rhodesia. If I do not give you the list, it is out of courtesy.' Gabon became the main base for a number of Rhodesian companies which rapidly changed their names but not their illegal cargoes: plane-loads of Rhodesian beef went to all the top tables in African presidential palaces. The most active Rhodesian air-pirate was Captain Jack Malloch (who regularly took part in military raids as well). His company (called Affretair, Air-Trans Africa and Cargoman to name a few of the disguises) smuggled large quantities of Rhodesian goods to Europe via Holland and then brought back illegal imports, including, occasionally, arms. Many Rhodesian VIPs (most regularly P K van der Byl) as well as sanctions-busting businessmen and intelligence agents used Malloch's planes to enter Europe quietly. Malloch's planes and operational costs were funded by the CIO. Much of Malloch's business, however, did not involve direct Rhodesian sanctions-busting. For example, the use of the Comoros for weapons shipments by Malloch's planes led to Rhodesian involvement in the pro-Western coup in the islands in 1978. The Rhodesians provided logistic support for the coup on the island which they needed for end-user certificates for illegal arms shipments. The coup forces, led by the mercenary Colonel Bob Denard, were in daily radio contact with Salisbury. (Despite Malloch's swashbuckling career fighting against sanctions, after the war his company became the official Zimbabwean freight carrier.)

Rhodesian bravado could not prevail against world economic trends, however. In 1974 everything started to go wrong for the Rhodesian economic war effort. The fall of white rule in Mozambique coincided with a world-wide recession. The OPEC-induced crash hit Rhodesia hard. Arab petro-politics created the swiftest transfer of money in history and, by accident, helped to sweep away minority rule in Rhodesia. Western Europe went into a slump. The West had to pay quadrupled prices for oil; and so did Rhodesia, which was already buying oil at a premium. In 1976 Mozambique closed its border with the rebel state in retaliation for Rhodesian raids. As South African subvention for Rhodesia's war burgeoned, Pretoria grew increasingly restive, especially when the collapse of the Shah of Iran's regime caused the rupture of Pretoria's oil supplies.

Until 1974 there had been a steady growth in the Rhodesian Gross Domestic Product. Then the growth rate slumped. In 1975 the GDP growth rate was just 1 per cent. The decline quickened in 1978 and 1979, despite the increase in South African support. By 1979, 35 per cent of the national budget went on the war effort. Black and white employment levels fell from the high point of 1975. Between 1969 and 1975 the economy had absorbed almost all the 40,000 black school-leavers entering the labour market annually. It could not absorb the growing number of school-leavers (70,000) after 1975. These disgruntled and educated young men and women, unable to find jobs, swelled the ranks of guerrilla recruits. Tourism, an important source of foreign exchange, suffered heavily from the war. The number of visitors to Rhodesia dropped by 74 per cent from a high point of 339,210 in 1972 to 87,943 in 1978. So, compared with the disruptions of the war, sanctions were a minor aggravation.

Many members of the UN argued that sanctions could be made more effective. Total sanctions were never imposed. Mail, for example, was excluded. Most white Rhodesians had relatives in Britain. The stoppage of mail would have dealt a telling blow to white morale. But the most explosive issue was the supply of oil to Rhodesia. British companies continued to supply oil to the besieged state in a hypocritical exercise. According to Martin Bailey's exposé, *Oilgate*, official sanctions-busting which emanated from the highest level of government created a more disturbing malaise in Britain than even the Watergate affair. Although some Labour politicians used to point sanctimoniously at the Royal Navy's blockade of Beira, which cost British taxpayers more than £100 million, it was a complete waste of money. The oil came from Lourenço Marques and South Africa – with the arrangement of British oil companies. As one letter writer to the *Guardian* suggested: 'Presumably the British Government calculated that the profit from the sale of oil to Rhodesia would offset the cost of the naval blockade that was supposed to stop it getting there.' UN sanctions were riddled with hypocrisy and deliberate contraventions. No wonder Rhodesia survived the economic war.

Another kind of war, if perhaps less hypocritical, was being fought in Rhodesia: a religious struggle. A number of international church bodies provided moral, material and financial aid to the guerrillas. The best known was the World Council of Churches. In May 1978, for example, the WCC gave ZANU and ZAPU £45,000. Although the amounts were small, international support stiffened the Rhodesian churches' opposition to the RF government. This was especially true of the Catholic Church, which had 600,000 African adherents and 40,000 white members in Rhodesia. Not all Catholics supported the guerrilla cause, however. Many white Catholics, particularly in the urban areas, opposed the radicals within their church. Nearly all the nationalists had religious backgrounds: for example, Mugabe (Catholic), Muzorewa (United Methodist), Sithole (Congregationalist). Many of them had been preachers before going into politics. This pattern had developed elsewhere in Africa: Kaunda, Banda and Nyerere were all mission-educated. Although other denominations had elements which were hostile to the government, it was the Catholic Church with its large numbers of African members and deep roots in the countryside which had the biggest impact on church-state relations. Criticism from clerics was acutely irritating to the RF government, which had declared UDI partly in order to preserve 'civilization and Christianity'.

Donal Lamont, the Catholic Bishop of Umtali, refuted these claims in August 1976 when he wrote an open letter to the government which said in part: 'Far from your policies defending Christianity and Western civilization, as you claim, they mock the law of Christ and make communism attractive to African people.' Although many white Catholics opposed Lamont, his criticism (until he was deported in March 1977, after a failed Special Branch assassination) rattled the government. The Catholic newspaper *Moto* (before its banning) and the Catholic Justice and Peace Commission did much to expose the security forces' excesses. In the countryside many missionaries ignored the law and continued to assist the guerrillas, particularly if they were injured. Cecil John Rhodes's dictum that missionaries were better and cheaper than policemen proved to be false.

Rhodesia was battered by the UN, OAU, WCC, guerrillas and their superpower allies. Salisbury also had a few friends. A conservative group within the American Senate, in alliance with business interests, had secured the passage of the Byrd Amendment (1971) which allowed America to buy Rhodesian chrome, until President Carter repealed the amendment. In Britain, vociferous pro-Rhodesia lobbies within the Conservative Party and muted ones within the armed forces proliferated. (Immediately after UDI, for example, the Royal Air Force Javelin squadron, based in Zambia and commanded by a South African, conducted unofficial joint flying exercises with the Rhodesians and holidayed in Salisbury. The British pilots, disdainful of the Labour government in London, made it clear that they would refuse orders to attack the rebel colony.) Belgium allowed an unofficial Rhodesian trade delegation to operate. Arms shipments came from Israel, India and Jordan as well as the usual arms bazaars in Europe and America. The Rhodesian CIO co-operated with the CIA (whose liaison officers were still stationed in Rhodesia even though they were supposed to have been withdrawn on the orders of Washington) and the old links between the CIO and British intelligence were never broken. Senior CIO men regularly commuted to Britain throughout the UDI years. On occasions British intelligence even helped Salisbury to vet the records of ex-British army personnel who had volunteered to fight in Rhodesia. It was the old boy network with a vengeance. Rhodesian intelligence agencies in the army and police as well as the CIO had very close ties with their South African counterparts, though that did not stop them also spying on their white neighbours. But Rhodesian electronic eavesdropping on South Africa was thwarted by superior technology in the apartheid state.

Rhodesia's closest ally remained South Africa, even though Pretoria had cautioned Smith against the rebellion. Nevertheless, two months before UDI, South Africa joined Rhodesia and Portugal in a secret tripartite military alliance. But although relations were good among senior officials, some elements of the Portuguese intelligence service, the PIDE, and its successor, the DGS, grew to be suspicious of Rhodesia's CIO. Until the Portuguese collapse in 1974, Rhodesian secrets trickled through to Whitehall, and then via an alleged Russian mole in British military intelligence (and occasionally through British agents) to the guerrillas in Mozambique. (Rhodesian counter-intelligence knew that the army, police and air force had been thoroughly penetrated by British agents.) The leaks became more regular after Combined Operations was set up in 1977. Intelligence officers grew alarmed at General Walls's propensity for including large numbers of lower-ranking officers in the top secret planning of the war. Eventually Walls excluded all except senior ComOps staff and the special force commanders for discussion of important raids. Crucially, the timing of the raids was kept a tight secret from the CIO, and even then the timings were sometimes brought forward. These later raids were successful. Walls had his faith in ComOps restored, but the CIO was even more distrusted. South African military intelligence is alleged to have eventually traced the source to a very senior white member of the Rhodesian security elite, but then the election of Mugabe resulted in hushing up of the affair. Pretoria, however, became agitated when the formerly Rhodesian-backed RNM (RENAMO) group began to suffer reversals in Mozambique. Their bases were accurately located and destroyed. South African military intelligence accused senior members of the Rhodesian CIO of betraying their former confidences in order to gain favour with the new Mugabe administration. Ken Flower, the CIO chief, was lambasted by South African intelligence officials for his alleged betrayal of the operations in Mozambique. They also blamed him for their intelligence failure in the 1980 election. Flower was innocent of all the charges, but a very senior CIO official was not. In fact Flower made it clear to Robert Mugabe, when he became premier, that if he remained head of the CIO he would cut all ties with the resistance movement. The post-war RNM setbacks in Mozambique were a result of initially heavy-handed management by the SADF, not a betrayal by Flower, who resigned from running the CIO in June 1981 (although he remained as a part-time consultant to Mugabe). By the end of 1981, however, the Mozambican resistance movement had recovered from the loss of Rhodesia as its main base. It had become such a growing threat to FRELIMO authority in large swathes in Mozambican territory that Machel was forced to ask for the assistance of Tanzanian soldiers and later nearly 20,000 Zimbabwean troops.

Rhodesian intelligence officials had a low opinion of South African military intelligence which, they maintained, passed on a great deal of faulty information to Salisbury. One of the problems was the poor co-ordination between South Africa's intelligence services. The police Security Branch had the best intelligence on the Zimbabwean nationalist movements, whereas the Bureau for State Security (BOSS) produced the best politico-economic analyses. The SADF was responsible for gathering purely military data. The difficult relations between the Rhodesian and South African intelligence services were exacerbated by Pretoria's breaking of a gentlemen's agreement not to poach each other's agents nor to operate clandestinely in each other's territories. (The military-military relationship remained very cordial, not least in the supply of equipment. Often without the knowledge of South African senior politicians, Pretoria's special forces played an active role, especially in operations in Mozambique.)

The bitter-sweet nature of the intelligence nexus was paralleled in other spheres, particularly in economic relations. Once UDI was declared, Pretoria had a vested interest in proving that sanctions did not work. Still, South African businessmen manipulated Rhodesia's captive market (between 80 and 90 percent of Rhodesian imports after 1976 came from the south) and made huge profits. But generous voluntary support was provided by such bodies as the Friends of Rhodesia, the South Africa-Rhodesia Association and, immediately after UDI, the Petrol for Rhodesia Fund. Although some South Africans had historically regarded Rhodesia with suspicion because of the Jameson Raid, and the Rhodesian rejection of union with South Africa in 1923, Afrikaners made up roughly 20 percent of the white population in Rhodesia. This kith and kin factor, plus the South African origins of many English-speaking whites, forged a strong emotional bond, which was enhanced by the large influx of South African tourists into the rebel state. Although white rule in Rhodesia later became a serious obstacle to the development of Pretoria's outward policy in Africa, right-wing opinion in South Africa could not be ignored. The ultra-right Herstigte Nasionale Party, although small, commanded a disproportionate influence over the ruling National Party. The HNP had always regarded the Zambezi and not the Limpopo as South Africa's military border.

In 1967 Pretoria sent units of the South African police to the Zambezi valley, and they stayed until 1975. On average, their strength was about 2,000, but some sources suggest that the figure was higher. The *Guardian*, for example, stated in 1970 that South African troops and police numbered 3,000 to 4,000. Rhodesian troops regarded their South African allies with near contempt because of their poor bushcraft. But the South Africans gradually improved, for they were in Rhodesia to gain experience as much as to help their white brethren. Although most of the South African forces were withdrawn in 1975, South Africans continued to train with the SAS and take part in the cross-border raids from 1976 to 1979 as observers, in combat on the ground and as chopper pilots. Meanwhile, Rhodesians trained in the south. (The Selous Scouts, for example, were given para training near Durban.) Even after Mugabe's victory, Rhodesian air force personnel continued to train (and instruct) on SAAF Impala jets in the Republic. Rhodesian air force personnel needed to practise on modern aircraft (one of Rhodesia's Dakotas had flown at Arnhem); it stopped them going stale and boosted morale.

In 1976 South Africa choked off military supplies and oil to Rhodesia to force Ian Smith to accept the Kissinger initiative. This caused a great deal of resentment, particularly in the armed forces which were desperately short of small arms ammunition during late 1976. But elements within the South African government and armed forces resented Vorster's arm-twisting. Vorster's hawkish minister of defence, P W Botha, was anxious to continue the military subvention of Rhodesia. During the detente exercises of the mid-1970s, Vorster had to countermand a P W Botha plan to send extra equipment to Rhodesia and to anti-FRELIMO forces in Mozambique. When Botha became prime minister in 1978, he stepped up the flow of strategic supplies to the transitional government in Salisbury. During the 1979 election, South African Puma helicopters and pilots, as well as military vehicles, were lent to Rhodesia to assist with the logistics of the first universal franchise poll. Also, funds poured into the coffers of the internal black politicians. According to Eschel Rhoodie, the former Department of Information official at the centre of the Muldergate scandal, South Africa was involved in a R400,000 plot to 'buy' James Chikerema, the leader of the Zimbabwe Democratic Party. The plan involved the option of blackmailing Chikerema with secret photographs and tapes if he should dare to doublecross Pretoria. And in both the 1979 and 1980 elections Bishop Muzorewa received millions of rands for his political campaign from the South African government and businessmen. The OAU made the exaggerated claim that Pretoria had given Muzorewa US$55 million for his 1980 election campaign. Whatever the amount, and wherever it came from – there were European and American sources as well – certainly the Bishop's UANC was awash with cash. The CIO was concerned at the political backlash of South African financial support of Muzorewa; it also conducted a secret inquiry into the allegations that top UANC men were salting away large sums in Swiss bank accounts.

In the latter stages of the war in 1979, South Africa became heavily involved in shoring up the sorely tried Rhodesian forces. Officially, SADF troops were only guarding both sides of the crucial rail and road link at Beit Bridge. In fact SADF troops and air force pilots were stationed throughout Rhodesia. Some estimates suggest that just prior to the February election, about 6,000 SADF personnel were engaged in the country. These troops could have been used for an all-out war against the guerrillas if the Lancaster House talks had broken down, or later in March 1980 to support a pro-Muzorewa coup. But this could not happen once Mugabe had secured a stunning victory.

The Pretoria government had ignored its military intelligence again (as it had over the Angola incursion, although Pretoria had listened when BOSS accurately predicted the coup in Portugal). Following the Muldergate scandal, the Bureau for State Security had gone into eclipse and was renamed the Department of National Security, DONS, which was appropriately headed by a 31-year-old academic who replaced the sinister, but capable, General Hendrik van den Bergh. (DONS later became NIS, the National Intelligence Service.) The SADF's Department of Military

Intelligence took over all the major responsibilities of BOSS and proceeded to work closely with P W Botha. As in Rhodesia, intelligence sources on the ground made it clear that Muzorewa could not win; but the top-level political intelligence experts in Salisbury and Pretoria refused to listen to their men in the field. Like the Israelis before the Yom Kippur war, Pretoria and Salisbury had the hard intelligence to hand, but they failed to make a clear political appreciation of that data.

(One of the main reasons for the failure in South Africa was the aftermath of the Muldergate scandal, relating to financial scandals, where money was misused in propaganda campaigns in South Africa and in the West. When Vorster, Van den Bergh and Connie Mulder were forced to retire from public life, BOSS was reformed as DONS. Many of the skilled BOSS professionals resigned in disgust. The inexperienced civilian leadership of DONS and the inefficient SADF military intelligence mismanaged their joint operations in Rhodesia during the period of direct British rule. Despite the increasing power of military intelligence in South Africa, the rivalry with DONS, later NIS, as well as the Security Police, continued. It was this rivalry which was a contributory factor in the abortive Seychelles coup of November 1981. [A large component of the 45-member strike force were seasoned ex-Rhodesian soldiers; some members of the expatriate Rhodesian community in South Africa felt that this force should have been aimed at Salisbury, not the Seychelles.] Though South African intelligence agencies were up to their necks in the Seychelles coup, the SADF military intelligence publicly criticized the attempted coup, and quietly the focus of blame shifted on to the NIS, which suffered a further downgrading of its responsibilities. By the beginning of 1982 the intelligence community had been reorganized: the police Security Branch continued its highly effective role in gathering political information, particularly on the ANC, while a revamped military intelligence improved its intelligence gathering both at home and abroad. The NIS became largely a think tank.)

In March 1980 a vast array of South African equipment was spirited out of the country, along with such Rhodesian military mementoes as mess silverware, for safekeeping. One of the reasons General Walls stayed on as head of the integrated forces was a moral obligation to return the arsenal that Pretoria had merely loaned, though this could have been, and was, regarded as treasonous by the new order in Salisbury. South Africa had provided most of Rhodesia's small arms, plus vehicles such as the Unimog, Eland, Alouette IIIs and, in 1979, eight T-55 Russian tanks. Usually Pretoria provided the assistance of its extensive arms network in Europe, America and Israel, but sometimes Rhodesian arms smugglers acted independently via Jack Malloch's airline. Often such sanctions-busting was highly successful. In 1978, however, some of the Rhodesians involved in arms supplies doublecrossed the Salisbury government by using their arms connections to build nest-eggs outside the country. On one occasion Rhodesian swashbuckling led to a near disaster. The eight Bell helicopters that were smuggled into Rhodesia in 1978 were found to be in poor condition; most could hardly be flown. South Africa was not to blame; Pretoria had helped only with the transit from Israel.

Towards the end of the war everyone had a finger in the pie. In 1978 and 1979 senior American officers were on fact-finding missions in Rhodesia. Even some of the Israelis on loan to the SADF were occasional visitors. The Nigerians and Tanzanians were preparing combat brigades for entry into the war; by late 1979 more than 500 Mozambican troops were in Rhodesia. A plan to introduce Cuban regulars was also mooted. If South African troops had officially entered the fray, all hell might have broken loose in southern Africa. Instead Mugabe won a convincing victory at the polls. Russia and Zambia had backed the wrong horse; China, Tanzania and Mozambique celebrated. In South Africa, Mugabe's triumph led to a wide-ranging reassessment of the SADF's strategy regarding the use of Zimbabwe as a possible staging post for South Africa-bound guerrillas and Pretoria's attempted internal settlement of the war in Namibia.

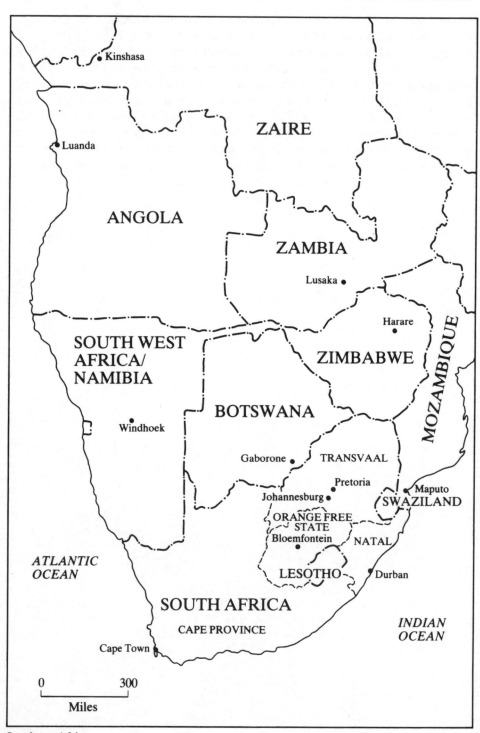

Southern Africa

Chapter Eight

THE SOCIAL IMPACT OF THE WAR

THE WHITES

Between December 1972 and January 1980, 1,047 members of the security forces were killed in action; about one-third of this figure was European. The guerrillas also killed 374 white, Asian and Coloured civilians on the ground and another 107 died in the Viscount air disasters. In a small community of 250,000 whites, these fatalities had a big impact, although the death rate was not as significant as the first *Chimurenga* which decimated the settler community. The whites also made proportionately a greater sacrifice in the two world wars: 732 were killed in 1914-18 and 742 in the 1939-45 war.

As the war spiralled, so did taxes in a conflict that was costing Rhodesia Rh$1 million a day. Business suffered as the call-ups cut into every sector of economic life. Men under 38 could spend as much as six to seven months 'in the bush' each year.

How then did the rebellion last so long? Perhaps the main reason was high morale, despite all the adversities. In fact, world pressures actually helped. Just as sanctions boosted the local economy until 1974, so UN harangues galvanized the spirit of white nationalism within the besieged laager.

Another important factor was the psychological war. Rhodesian propaganda had little effect on the blacks, but it did work on the whites. The army's Psychological Action Unit (PsyAc) did little to stem the tide of guerrilla advances, nor did the government Psychological Warfare department (set up in February 1977 under the command of Major General Andrew Rawlings) have much success abroad (though many of the international pressmen, particularly those belonging to the conservative British Press, 'went native' and wrote 'on-sides' [pro-government] articles). But many Rhodesians fell hook, line and sinker for the Rhodesia Broadcasting Corporation's view of the world. The TV and radio hypnotically harped on a few basic themes: the chaos in black states, the disorders elsewhere in the world (especially in those countries such as Britain which attracted southern African emigrés), and the monolithic communist threat. Patriotism was always put above perception. The censorship of news and the pitifully small holiday and emigration allowances made many whites captives rather than supporters of the RF government, although Smith continued to receive an average of 75 per cent support from the white electorate during UDI and in elections after 1980. The negative portrayal of the outside world intensified the cancer of isolation in what was already a parochial society. Rhodesians seemed to understand little of the modern world and heartily disliked the little they did understand.

Many whites believed they were sincerely battling against communism to preserve a civilized Christian order; it was not merely to protect a three-servants-two-cars-one-swimming-pool way of life. But although the whites did fight long and hard, Rhodesia was not a militaristic society, despite the ubiquitous weaponry and uniforms. By 1979, as black rule became imminent, the whites looked back on the tragedies of the war. The mood was one of sorrow and resignation rather than anger; and they displayed a bruised pride in having survived for so long against such steep odds.

Morale was plummeting; the call-ups were making the bulk of the security forces, the reservists, incessant and reluctant commuters to an escalating war. One-man businesses were going under. The government system of 'make-up' pay for employees could not avert the loss of bonuses, profits or promotion prospects. And blacks were taking the places of whites who were constantly in the bush – some employers were looking to the future. Others were just sick and tired of having their white employees away in uniform. So the white soldier or policeman on call-up worried about his job; and also about his wife – as early as 1976 a wave of poison-pen letters reached the troops, suggesting that their wives back home were indulging in orgies. There was sometimes a grain of truth in the accusations. The strain of long call-ups led to a drop in fidelity and one of the highest divorce rates in the world.

The various compensation bodies, such as the Terrorist Victims' Relief Fund, could not bring back the dead nor the gutted farms. What is it all for? many whites asked, especially after Muzorewa came to power. Why fight on – let the black man do his own fighting, was a pervasive feeling. As one white put it: 'The First and Second World Wars were wars of honour. But what are we fighting for in the Rhodesian war: just to keep squabbling kaffirs in parliament.'

In war, morale is often lowest at the furthest point from the front. Rhodesia was no exception. By 1979 the remaining 5,000 white farmers were bearing the brunt of the war. In the face of almost daily alarms, agricultural output was high, despite mounting stock thefts and crop burnings. Women in the rural areas were thrust into the front line, defending their farms while their husbands were on call-up – the Agric-Alert crackling all night – and then helping out with WVS (Women's Volunteer Service) canteens at weekends. Although the pressures caused some farmers to quit, especially in the Cashel Valley, Melsetter, Headlands and Mtoko areas, most stuck it out with stubborn courage.

Not all white farmers resisted the guerrillas, however. In certain areas, near Umtali and Fort Victoria, for example, some farmers had reached an accommodation with the guerrillas during the last stages of the war. They turned a blind eye to guerrillas crossing their land or being fed in their labourers' compounds. (After the war, Garfield Todd, a former prime minister of Southern Rhodesia, admitted that he had helped guerrillas who came to his farm in Matabeleland.) And guerrillas often concentrated on those farms which had particularly bad labour relations. In contrast, one farmer who was captured near Rusape, Johannes Maartens, was well treated by ZANLA when he was taken to Mozambique along with three other white prisoners, John Kennerly, Tom Wigglesworth and Jim Black. Maartens had a heart condition and the guerrillas were careful not to overstrain the Afrikaner farmer during the long marches. Although taking white prisoners was not a regular policy of the guerrillas, ZANLA did offer to release these four men in exchange for better treatment, or the release, of ZANLA men in Rhodesian prisons. Salisbury refused point blank. Nevertheless, the four men were released unharmed by ZANLA in February 1979.

By late 1979 the white core had been seriously eroded. The strains of constant call-ups were evident in the increasing breakdown in European family life: the rise in divorce, alcoholism, suicides and illegitimate births. Soldiers on leave rarely admitted to the strains of conflict or what later became known as Post-Traumatic Stress Disorder. For many it was just too much. They 'took the gap' and emigrated with their meagre allowance of Rh$1,000 a family plus a few household effects (the allowance had been reduced from $5,000 as a deliberate disincentive to leave). It was not a lot with which to start a new life in Britain or South Africa. At the end of the war the official emigration rate was nearing 2,000 whites a month and many of these were artisans, doctors and engineers. Others left unofficially 'on holiday'. This exodus undermined the war on the economic front and depleted the crucial white conscript element of the armed forces. One white businessman commented: 'You're down to the die-hards now. You could call us the intrepid, the loyal or the financial prisoners.' But there were also fanatics: some sections of the army had planned to fight to the last with a scorched-earth retreat to the South African border. Although these same groups had wanted a coup in March 1980, it was not to be. Rhodesian whites did not fight to the last man and cartridge as P K van der Byl had threatened.

THE BLACKS

The battle for control of the African civilian population in the Rhodesian war was waged incessantly from 1972. Before then guerrilla strategy and tactics minimized the contact of either army with the vast majority of Africans. But the Maoist revolutionary war fought after 1972 brought more and more African civilians into the firing line. Unarmed men, women and children became the archetype of 'the man in the middle' and were cajoled, wooed, battered and abused by both sides. The Rhodesians wanted their 'hearts and minds' and the guerrillas needed them as their 'sea', but all too often it was their lives, not their loyalties, that were given.

The confinement of the war to Operation Hurricane until 1976 saw a commensurably small civilian African involvement in the war. The Budja and Korekore peoples of the Shona tribe were those in the fighting zones at that time. The first indication that the civilian population would become heavily involved was the imposition from early 1973 of communal fines and other collective punishments on villages suspected of aiding the guerrillas. One kraal was forcibly moved hundreds of kilometres to the south, to the Beit Bridge area, for assisting guerrillas.

In due course it was made a punishable offence not to report the presence of guerrillas in an area, and rewards of Rh$5,000 or more were offered for information leading to the death or capture of guerrillas and the seizure of arms caches. In early 1973 Africans living in the Chiweshe and Madziwa TTLs were sealed into the first PVs to deny their food to and co-operation with the guerrillas.

The guerrilla response was to stiffen the resolution of their collaborators by a policy of terror. Mutilations and executions of 'sell-outs' and 'suspects' became commonplace, especially after incidents in which guerrillas were killed or ambushed. Often the merest suspicion was enough, and many family feuds were dragged into the struggle. Rhodesian Special Branch operatives often 'blackened' suspected guerrilla sympathizers or contact men by planting false information. The guerrillas would then oblige the Special Branch by killing the suspect for treachery.

Eventually about 500,000 people were living in PVs which official propaganda portrayed as model settlements in which civilians could pursue their lives unhindered by the exactions and atrocities of the guerrillas. They were also touted as future growth points for a policy of industrial and commercial decentralization to the TTLs. By the end of 1976, 41 PVs had been established, with another 138 in various stages of construction. Guerrilla propaganda portrayed them as concentration camps or torture installations. That they were concentration camps was true up to a point. Like British camps for Boer civilians during the South African war (1899-1902), they were designed to concentrate the African population so that they could be better controlled. But the horrendous pictures painted by the guerrillas of life behind PV wire were largely inaccurate, despite grains of truth. The movement of such a big proportion of the peasant population obviously inflicted hardships. Some PVs were model villages with well-constructed huts, clean, running water and medical and educational facilities. But these were rare, particularly among those formed in the later stages of the war. The general picture was one of rural poverty transplanted behind wire. African peasants generally loathed life in the PVs. Not only was there no significant improvement in their living conditions (and often a deterioration), but they were subject to tedious controls and restrictions. Peasants resented being uprooted from their ancestral lands. The loyalty of peasants to the soil they had tilled for generations was a potent factor in making PVs a widely hated feature of rural life. Fields were tilled around the PVs, but farmers were not permitted to take food with them when they went out for their day's work lest they fed it to the guerrillas. There were constant security checks and often abuse by the security force personnel guarding the PVs. Stores within the PVs often charged extortionate prices for their limited ranges of goods. So unpopular were the PVs that some in the Mtoko-Mrewa area were dismantled at the insistence of black politicians taking part in the internal political settlement. There was an immediate upsurge of guerrilla activity in the areas to which the freed civilians returned.

The PVs may have been unpopular and irksome, but they did at least spare their inhabitants from the deadly ebb and flow of guerrilla and security force activity. Those living freely in the TTLs suffered mounting casualties in the years 1977-9.

Curfews covered most of the areas affected by guerrilla activity and hundreds of curfew breakers were shot over the years, particularly after the introduction of martial law. Guerrilla mines, being indiscriminate weapons, inflicted enormous casualties on African bus passengers and those travelling in passenger cars, on scotch carts and on foot.

Travel for Africans became laborious as they were subjected to searches at roadblocks which often doubled their travel time. Often soldiers, policemen and other government personnel on leave at their rural homes were murdered by guerrillas or even *mujibas*. Their families also went in constant fear of guerrilla reprisals. In 1978-9 many service personnel could never go on leave to their home villages, unless these were PVs.

From time to time massacres of entire villages were inflicted. The guerrillas destroyed many kraals of unco-operative headmen or household heads. Security forces units acting as pseudo-guerrillas attacked and destroyed villages which persistently supported the guerrillas. The spectre of My Lai reared its head more than once when both sides massacred *pour encourager les autres*. In one not untypical incident in August 1979, a section of Selous Scouts attacked a village in the north of Rhodesia which supported the guerrillas. White phosphorus grenades were thrown into the grass-roofed huts and their mud walls were blasted with small arms fire. A number of men were then marched away from the village and were executed. An Alouette III helicopter then landed with a cargo net and carried the corpses to a remote escarpment where they were dumped over the edge. There were many similar instances in which guerrillas punished recalcitrant kraals. Often whole families would be driven into their huts and then incinerated when the guerrillas set fire to the roofs. In 1979, as part of their strategy of breaking the white economic infrastructure, ZANLA guerrillas began a series of calculated massacres of labour on European farms, especially on estates along the border.

The whole question of atrocities became embroiled in the propaganda war. Each side accused the other of having a monopoly of massacre. The Selous Scouts were vilified by guerrilla propagandists as perpetrators of virtually every atrocity committed in the war. Their clandestine activities made them a convenient scapegoat. The Rhodesian Ministry of Information frequently published gory booklets cataloguing guerrilla atrocities, with photographs of mangled corpses and tribesmen with mutilated lips and ears. The classic moderate position was to condemn both sides for atrocities. But the atrocity issue became a sterile debate because of the difficulty of separating fact from propaganda fiction. The important point, missed by many observers of the war, was that atrocities were not indiscriminate. The targets were usually carefully and deliberately chosen for the exemplary effect they might have on the civilian population.

A whole generation of African children was exposed to violence. Their attitudes towards law and order were strongly negative, since every part of the white-built administrative system was fair game. Vandalism became a way of life for youngsters, and virtually every administrative or commercial structure in the TTLs outside PVs was destroyed. Youths as young as 13 enjoyed immense authority through their association with the guerrillas in the *mujiba* system and often held the power of life and death over adults. Unarmed boys in their early teens could rob buses packed with adult males merely by invoking the authority of the guerrillas.

The guerrilla campaign to break the back of the Rhodesian civil administration in rural areas was highly successful, but had serious consequences for the peasant population. Guerrillas or *mujibas* destroyed cattle dips, with a resultant proliferation of tick-borne diseases. Anthrax and foot-and-mouth carried off large parts of the African national herd. Veterinary staff of the Rhodesian government could not control the epidemics because of the security position. The rudimentary but widespread rural health service was effectively shut down and the buildings destroyed. More than 1,000 schools were closed down by the guerrillas, throwing several hundred thousand children, and their teachers, out of the educational process. The offices of African local administrative councils were pillaged or razed. Buses were robbed or hijacked. Mosquito, rabies and tsetse fly control became impossible over large swathes of the country and malaria became endemic in most TTLs. For the African civilian the problem was that the guerrillas provided no alternative administration or services. Guerrillas made few attempts to claim the existence of true 'liberated zones', in which an alternative system of government had been established, mainly because there were none. Strangely, many guerrillas spoke of their base areas in Mozambique or Zambia as their 'liberated zones', which was a significant comment on the absence of such areas inside Rhodesia.

The tempo of the disintegration of civilian life in the TTLs accelerated in the last two years of the war. The numbers of civilians killed in 'crossfire' rose alarmingly from late 1977. As the guerrillas became more and more ensconced within the framework of peasant life so the number of casualties increased. The Rhodesian forces attempted to punish and deter peasants from aiding the guerrillas by inflicting a blood price for having anything to do with armed guerrillas. 'Crossfire' became a codeword for indiscriminate shooting. The guerrillas also showed little concern for civilian casualties in their attempts to escape security force ambushes. This sort of violence reached a crescendo in the 'Gutu Massacre' of 1978. More than 50 civilians were killed when security forces interrupted a guerrilla *pungwe* at a village in the Gutu district. Although officials blamed the guerrillas for opening fire, which appears to have been true, one member of the security forces involved later admitted that no attempt was made to discriminate between guerrillas and civilians in the night-time encounter. This incident forced black politicians taking part in the internal settlement to press for curbs on the security forces' freedom of action; they wanted to limit the high civilian death toll, which was politically damaging to their claims to represent African voters. During the 1979 election security force pressure reached a peak. A senior Rhodesian officer was heard to comment: 'If we carry on the way we're going we'll have a white majority.'

Hut-burning and the slaughter of cattle became more common security force methods of punishing civilian co-operation with the guerrillas. First dwelling huts would be razed, then grain storage bins would be destroyed and livestock killed if co-operation persisted. It also became a routine procedure after actions against the guerrillas to raze kraals in the immediate vicinity. African livestock was slaughtered by security forces if civilians took part in, or concealed knowledge of, stock thefts. The policy became applied so indiscriminately by security forces, often frustrated by civilian recalcitrance, and stock theft so prevalent, that the national herd was depleted by nearly a million beasts in the last two years of the war. The security forces then introduced restrictions on the punitive killing of cattle and there were cases of disciplinary action against those who needlessly killed livestock. The guerrillas contributed to the carnage with their own destruction of the livestock of unco-operative civilians.

The Rhodesian 'get-tough' policy tended to be counter-productive. Guerrilla methods of enforcement were far more brutal and effective than those of the Rhodesian forces, and where they had the emotional and political loyalty of civilians, the Rhodesian forces could do little to counter this. The guerrillas also turned this use of punitive measures to their own advantage. Knowing that Rhodesian forces usually reacted to land mine incidents by firing to their flanks in case there were ambushes as well, and often simply at the nearest kraal, they planted land mines near villages which wavered in their support. The Rhodesian forces' reaction often pushed these villages finally into the guerrilla camp.

The end-product of the long conflict was a massive refugee problem. Many thousands flowed into the major cities of Rhodesia to live with relatives or in squalid squatter camps on urban outskirts. Many fled across the borders into Mozambique and Botswana (from where many were airlifted to Zambia) to live in overcrowded refugee camps run by the UN or other international relief agencies. The guerrilla system of conscription scooped up many thousands of young people from schools and kraals. Rhodesian plans to conscript Africans for the first time from 1978 netted some recruits, but many hundreds of others fled into the bush or across the heavily guarded borders to join the guerrillas rather than serve with the Rhodesian forces. In 1978-9, after the transitional government took power, hundreds of youths were press-ganged into the Security Force Auxiliaries. Rhodesian authorities took the attitude that if they did not grab them the guerrillas would. One SFA more was one guerrilla or *mujiba* less. Probably about 500,000 people were displaced by the war, the addition of the PV populations bringing the total to nearly 1,000,000. Refugees across the border often had little respite from fear, as the policy of mixing guerrillas and civilian refugees in camps exposed them to Rhodesian raids. The total civilian death toll for the war years was about 20,000. This was not an enormous figure compared with the casualties in other guerrilla wars, but Rhodesia was a small country in which individual deaths had a greater impact than in a larger nation. It was also a country with a strong legacy of racial antagonism and the death tolls made it an even more embittered land.

THE GREEN LEADER RAID

(On 18 October 1978, Rhodesian Air Force units attacked a ZIPRA guerrilla camp near the Zambian capital, Lusaka. For a brief period the Rhodesians assumed complete control of Zambia's air space. A tape recording of the exchanges between the leader of the flight of four Canberra bombers on the raid [accompanied by six Hunters] and the Lusaka control tower was broadcast to the world. But it was an edited version of the recording of the entire raid on a tape recorder in the cockpit of 'Green Leader'. The following is a transcript of the full version. Most of the conversation takes place between Green Leader and his navigator/bomb aimer, but other actors also appear. Squadron Leader Chris Dixon was Green Leader and his navigator was Mike Ronnie.)

Canberra pilot: I can see smoke.

Green Leader: Affirmative. Colour's unreal... Left five ... Get your speed up. Take it up... We're at sixteen hundred feet... We're coming up to the stream now ... We're crossing the stream now. [*The 'stream' referred to is the Zambezi river, the Rhodesian-Zambian boundary.*]

Navigator: Check.

Green Leader: Well done, J.R.... three zero four, rolling out now. How's your speed? We're at two nine zero. Roger, uhhh, go left two degrees.

Navigator: Roger, three zero two. [*The aircraft are heading on a course north-north-west inside Zambia.*]

Green Leader: Pull your speed back.

Navigator: Roger.

Green Leader: Five knots... Dead right... Those Hunters are with us. Their golf bombs are painted red; something fucking brilliant... Check your speed, two seven five. Which is the fifteen knots I wanted. Stick on three zero three. [*Golf bombs were anti-personnel weapons which first bounced and then detonated in an airburst. They were packed with hundreds of 'flechettes', darts made from steel six-inch nails with tiny plastic fins. These darts could rip through a moderately thick tree-trunk.*]

Navigator: Roger, three zero three.

Green Leader: Ah, shit, I hope these wings don't fall off... Roger, go down a bit. Dead right... Two starboard. [*By this stage of the war metal fatigue was a serious problem for the Canberras, and this fear was a real one.*]

Navigator: Three zero four.

Green Leader: No, make it three zero five.

Navigator: Okay.

Green Leader: No, three zero six.

Navigator: Okay, I've got it.

Green Leader: There's not a peep out of tower. That's superb, we won't have to talk to them. [*The Rhodesians were listening out on Lusaka Control Tower's frequency to see if they had been picked up on Zambian radar screens.*]

Green Leader: About a minute and a half before the Hunters leave us ... The Hunters are going to be going in about fifty seconds. [*Lusaka Tower is heard in the background speaking to a Kenya Airways flight.*]

Green Leader: Ah, that's bloody tower... Just stand by so we can hold back.

Navigator: Roger ...I think we've passed it, sir. I think that ridge on the right is the one. It should have been our turning point.

Green Leader: Ah, shit! Ah, shut up man ... Coming up for the Hunters to go ... Blue Section go! Blue Section go! [*Blue Section, the accompanying flight of Hawker Hunters, peels off to carry out its mission.*]

Green Leader: Two seventy knots. You got it now? ... Shit, they only accelerate bloody quickly ... We must hold on the other frequency.

Navigator: Confirm tower frequency?

Green Leader: I'm sure there's someone on that... Well, I'll switch off, I think, at this time anyway.

Navigator: Oh... Okay, we're coming up to thirty seconds to turn, sir.

Green Leader: Roger.

Navigator: It's supposed to be on our right here... We should see the bridge fairly shortly.

Green Leader: Turn now... There's a road... We've just missed it ... We passed two eight one, so I'll turn back on it now ... Steady, two eight one. Two thirty knots. [*The Canberras of Green Section are now heading on a more easterly course, which will take them over the guerrilla camp.*]

Navigator: Bring your speed up, cap. Two thirty.

Green Leader: Roger, have you got us... Roger, now I have three ten knots. About two eight zero and four thousand five hundred. Two eight one, zero eight seven.

Navigator: Steer on two eight one.

Green Leader: Roger, two eight one... There's a school coming up... There's nothing from tower. I'm not going to call them, okay?
[*At this stage Green Leader does not have to warn Lusaka Tower to keep Zambian Air Force aircraft on the ground because they have slipped in under the radar scan.*]

Navigator: Okee-dot.

Green Leader: It's going to be perfect.

Navigator: We're coming up to about two minutes to target. Two eight two ... Two minutes to run. Go left a bit. Okay, that's better. That's two seven eight. Two eight two.

Green Leader: There's a dam coming up.

Navigator: Roger, two eight two. No, two eight five.

Green Leader: Roger, a power line's coming up ... That's good. Coming up to our acceleration point.

Navigator: Okay. We should start acceleration now.

Green Leader: Roger, should I go?

Navigator: Just leave it in case they're going to be a bit late.

Green Leader: Okay ...

Navigator: Accelerate! Other aircraft in formation: Greens accelerating!

Navigator: You want to get your doors open?

Green Leader: Yah, as soon as I get my speed.

Navigator: Go left a bit ...go left.

Green Leader: Little more?

Navigator: No. Okay, go on to two eight two, quickly!

Green Leader: How's your ...

Navigator: Roger, got the target. Target!

Green Leader: Ah, beautiful, yes! [*The Canberras have navigated to the camp perfectly. As they begin their bomb run the aircrew's voices grow more excited and tense.*]

Green Leader: Speed up, or is it okay?

Navigator: It's fine ...go left... steady!... steady! Two seven eight! Roger D ... Steady!... steady ... Left a touch!

Green Leader: Beautiful, Fanie...

Navigator: Steady!... steady ... left a touch... steady!... steady!... steady! Can I switch the doors open?

Green Leader: Yes, switch on doors!

Navigator: Right! I'm going to put them [the bombs] into the field! Steady! I'm gonna get them!

Green Leader: Yes!

Navigator: Steady!

Green Leader: Fucking beautiful!

Navigator: Steady! Steady! NOW! BOMBS GONE! THEY'RE ON!

Green Leader: Beautiful! Jesus Christ, you want to see all those fuckers! The fucking bombs were beautiful!

Navigator: Roger, it went straight through.

Navigator: They're running into the other fran [*Short for 'frantan', the Rhodesian name for napalm.*]

Green Leader: Yah, I know.

Navigator: Beautiful.

Green Leader: Fucking beautiful! Roger, just let me get on to fucking tower to give them our bloody message. Where's this fucking piece of shit? [*Rummages for paper on which message is printed.*]

Navigator: I think we'd better wait till we've climbed, sir.

Green Leader: Yah, just trying to get the thing ready ... Fuck, that was beautiful. Fuck, that was mush. [*Rhodesian slang for 'good'.*] Fucking hundreds of the cunts. Fucking magnificent!

Navigator: Go left here.

Green Leader: Jesus, those fucking kaffirs ... There's the bloody city. [*Green Section is now nearing the Zambian capital, Lusaka. From now on the soundtrack is interspersed with conversations between the helicopter gunships, dubbed 'K-cars', attacking the remains of the guerrilla camp.*]

K-car: There's people running on the left.

Another K-car: Got them visual. There in the hut.

Navigator: Are we putting in K-cars here?

Green Leader: Huh?

Navigator: K-cars.

Green Leader: Yah, they've got K-cars in there. They'll have a beautiful time. They're like fucking ants running around there.

Navigator: Steady for one more minute.

Green Leader: Okay.

Navigator: Remember the tape recorder, sir.

Green Leader: Ah, fuck it!

Navigator: Keep an eye out, sir.

Green Leader: Yah, I was going to say, for a big pylon.

K-car 3: K-3 has a stoppage. [*The K-cars report to the lead gunship whenever their guns jam so that they were not called on to perform any tasks while the gunner tries to clear the stoppage.*]

Dolphin 3: Green Leader, this is Dolphin 3. [*Dolphin was the call-sign of Rhodesian Air Force headquarters, a relic of the days when it was situated in Dolphin House in Salisbury. Dolphin-3 was an airborne command post in a Dakota. The air commander was Norman Walsh.*]

Green Leader: Roger, I'm on tower now. I'll give them a shout.

Navigator: Right, we crossed a road.

Green Leader: Just check the tape recorder if you've got time. If not, just leave it.

Navigator: Still turning.

Green Leader: Okay, let me try and get this spiel off.

K-car 1: K-1 stoppage.

Green Leader: Lusaka Tower, this is Green Leader. [*Interruption from another radio.*]

Green Leader: Just turn it off ... Lusaka Tower, this is Green Leader.

Lusaka Tower: Aaaahhh, station calling tower.

Green Leader: Lusaka Tower, this is Green Leader. This is a message for the station commander at Mumba. From the Rhodesian Air Force. We are attacking the terrorist base at Westlands farm at this time. This attack is against Rhodesian dissidents and not against Zambia. Rhodesia has no quarrel, repeat, no quarrel, with Zambia or her security forces. We therefore ask you not to intervene or oppose our attack. However, we are orbiting your airfield at this time and are under orders to shoot down any Zambian Air Force aircraft which does not comply with this request and attempts to take off. Did you copy all that?

Lusaka Tower: Copied that.

Green Leader: Roger, thanks, cheers.

K-car 4: K-4 stoppage.

K-car Leader: Roger, call us back.

Green Leader: Jesus, you should have seen the bombs rolling down from the other aircraft here. Fucking unreal.

Unidentified K-car: Confirm you're still going for the buildings?

K-car 3: Okay, we've got a stoppage now, sir. We're moving out.

Unidentified K-car: Roger, we're coming over.

Another K-car: Can you see those people running on the path down there?

Navigator: I hope those K-cars get those buggers. I was so tempted to drop short, you know.

Green Leader: But the other ones [napalm bombs] were going on to them... Yah, they were running okay.

Lusaka Tower: Rhodesian Air Force, one one eight one.

Green Leader: Should I answer them?

Navigator: Yah.

Green Leader: Go ahead.

K-car 3: K-3 stoppage.

Lusaka Tower: Can you confirm we can let our civil aircraft take off from here and you have no objections?

Green Leader: We have no objection, but I advise you for the moment to stand by on that. I'd request that you hang on for about... a short while, half an hour or so.

Lusaka Tower: I copy. Can you please keep a listening watch on this frequency so we can ask you what we want to ask?

A K-car: Ammo's finished.

Green Leader: Roger.

Lusaka Tower: What do I call you?

Green Leader: Green Leader.

Lusaka Tower: Green Leader, will do.

Green Leader: Thanks.

K-car 3: K-1, K-3. How're you doing?

K-car 1: K-3, go.

K-car 3: Roger, I'm clearing down towards the south-east at this time. Just follow me down, I've got something on, over.

K-car 1: K-3, K-1.

K-car 3: Go ahead.

K-car 1: How're you doing?

K-car 3: Yah, we're doing fine. [*Staccato burst of machine-gun fire.*] We're just nearly out of ammo.

141

K-car 1: K-4, K-1.

K-car 4: Roger, we've still got a stoppage. I think they're right down the southern end.

K-car 1: But you'll find they've disappeared down towards the south-eastern corner of the camp, and I'm setting course to take them out. If you will like to join us?

Navigator: They ran straight into the bombs. Couldn't believe it you know.

K-car 4: Confirm you have left the area. Roger, I'm at the southern side of the orbit. There are some of them about to leave. Roger, I'm moving down now. I've got you visual.

K-car Leader: K-1, K-lead.

K-car 1: Go.

K-car Leader: How does it look?

K-car 1: Beautiful, John. [*More bursts of machine-gun fire.*]You're clear straight up now.

Green Leader: A thousand feet. Got to keep it up all day.

K-car Leader: K-2, K-1, K-4 and 3. Got you visual.

K-car 4: K-4 in the middle.

White Leader: K-lead, this is White lead. Have you finished? [*White Section is a flight of ground strike aircraft.*]

K-car Leader: Affirmative. You're clear then. Roger, I think that building you are going for has been taken out completely. You might like to have a leemo back at it just to make absolutely certain.

White Leader: Ah, Roger. White-2, White-lead.

White-2: Go.

White Leader: Roger, what would you like us to take out?

White-2: Roger, sir, if you'd like to look for our strikes, and then re-strike after us.

White Leader: Roger, will do.

White-2: I think if you could...

White Leader: Affirmative.

White-2: If you take out one, and I'll put my guns on the south-east boundary, attacking from the south, over.

White Leader: Roger, copied.

Navigator: Speed's got to go up to three ten. [*Crackle of radios in background.*]

Green Leader: Yah, two of you cheating, hey? [*Laughter.*]

A K-car: K-2 and 3, got you visual.

Kenya Airways Flight 432: Lusaka Tower, this is Kenya four three two.

Lusaka Tower: Four three two, stand by, four three two, stand by.

K-car 1: Hello, Dolphin-3, this is K-car 1.

Dolphin-3: K-car 1, Dolphin-3, go ahead.

K-car 1: Roger. K-car Sections, and White Section, everything's going in okay, over.

Dolphin-3: We've heard nothing from Green Section. Confirm they did go through.

K-car 1: Affirmative. And right on target.

Dolphin-3: Okay, thanks very much.

Green Leader: Dolphin-3 from Green Leader.

Dolphin-3: Green-lead, this is Dolphin-3, go ahead.

Green Leader: Roger, are you listening out on one one eight one?

Dolphin-3: Negative, I've been listening out just on the other one.

Green Leader: Roger, shortly I'm going to ask you to take over on that frequency to pass on certain messages which I'll advise you about. [*Dolphin-3 then prepares to take over the exchanges with Lusaka Tower by changing frequencies. Lusaka Tower asks Green Leader if two civil aircraft may take off.*]

Navigator: Tell them no.

Green Leader: Lusaka Tower, this is Green Lead. Roger, request you hold them for another ten minutes ... I'd better tell him we're going out of range. [*Green Leader now hands over to Dolphin-3, who passes on advice to Lusaka Tower and answers queries. Lusaka Tower seeks permission for a civil aircraft from the north to land.*]

Dolphin-3: Roger, there's no problem on that. You can let him come in and land. The main thing is that if there are any air force, air force, traffic, they are to remain on the ground. [*The Canberras head back for base, leaving control of Zambian airspace to Dolphin-3.*]

Green Leader: The Hunters are fucking sprawling back like scalded cats up here. Fucking leaving trails of white shit in the sky. [*Later the Canberras approach their base at New Sarum near Salisbury.*]

Green Leader: Roger, Green Alpha Section, go radar. Green check.

Green-2: Green-2.

Green-4: Green-4.

Green-3: Green-3 check, Green-3 check.

Green Leader: Radar, Green Section.

Radar: Green Section, Radar.

Green Leader: Flight two five zero, TE five eight. For the field at zero eight and request priority landing for all our aircraft.

Radar: Roger, cleared. One zero six, zero, one eight zero knots, temperature twenty-two. Report at topography.

Green Leader: Roger, Greens reporting at the topography. [*Lusaka Tower asks Dolphin-3 about the civil aircraft from the north.*]

Dolphin-3: I will clear you in one minute's time.

Lusaka Tower: All right, no problem. He can do a wide orbit.

Dolphin-3: You can resume normal traffic, over.

Unidentified voice: Lusaka Tower, are you reading me?

Lusaka Tower: Go ahead.

Unidentified voice: That is our task now complete. We are leaving the area. I repeat we have no quarrel with Zambia or security forces or civilian traffic, and I would like to thank you very much for your co-operation. Thank you.

THE LANGUAGE OF WAR

If the first casualty of war is truth, a second victim is often language. Even before the war the Rhodesian whites had their own *patois* which drew its inspiration from a number of sources. The indigenous languages, Shona and Sindebele, influenced what the Rhodesians called 'English'. To take an example:

A troopie (soldier) who'd had enough *shupa* (trouble) out in the Zambezi valley chasing *gandangas* (guerrillas) and being chased by flat dogs (crocodiles) came home on R and R (leave) to see his *umfazi* (girlfriend). She was really *kengi* (nice) and so were the *shumbas* (beers) they had together. But she gave him a big indaba (caused a lot of trouble) because he wouldn't take any *muti* (medicine) for his hangover.

The slang was not restricted to the other ranks. A new officer straight from England was rather shaken by a briefing from his Rhodesian commanding officer:

Masikati (Good afternoon). Now I'm not going to make a big indaba about this lost *katunda* (equipment) but we've had a bit of a nause (problem) and the main manna (my superior) is flat (upset). Therefore I want to get the whole spiel (issue) straightened out – now now (immediately). Not just now (some time in the future) but now, now. There's a helluva *hanna hanna* (uproar) over the whole scene so some of you okes (people) will have to pull finger (sort it out quickly), OK. Apart from this everything is *mushi sterek* (very good). Any questions?

No doubt, the poor befuddled British officer had too many to dare start asking after this briefing.

Afrikaans was also drafted into use. The Afrikaans word *houtie* (meaning 'wooden head') became the most common derogatory term for blacks. The Rhodesians, however, were not grateful to their white brothers for the loan of such words. Afrikaners were hailed by a wide variety of names: *japies*, hairy-backs, rock spiders and ropes (ie thick, twisted and hairy) were the more polite examples. White Rhodesians were also rude about their darker-skinned compatriots. Whites often referred to themselves as 'European', though liberal whites usually preferred the term 'white African'. A 'European' farmer in Fort Victoria described blacks as 'oxygen-wasters' and coloureds as 'sun-kissed puff adders'. The adders' and wasters' comments about this farmer were mercifully left unrecorded.

With the growing intensity of the war, military slang and abuse flooded the vernacular. American volunteers in the Rhodesian Light Infantry – which produced probably the most distinctive and impenetrable military argot – imported 'gook' from Vietnam, although the most common local slang word for a guerrilla was 'floppy', from the way they allegedly fell when shot. The insurgents had equally colourful terms for their enemy, particularly the Selous Scouts, whom they loathed, and feared. The coloured community, however, indulged in the most prolific spate of phrase-mongering. They had traditionally defended their small community by erecting a linguistic barrier to keep white 'honkies' out of their conversation. As they created a sub-culture, their defence mechanism was transformed into a poor man's poetry. 'What is the time?' became 'bowl me the ages'. 'Let's go' was translated as 'agitate the gravel'. If a coloured wanted a lift into town, he might ask: 'Man, can I have a charity glide into society?' When a group of RDR coloured troops was pinned down on a hill by aggressive guerillas, and were taking heavy casualties, the radio operator calmly said to his white counterpart on the end of the radio-phone: 'You honkies had better start getting it together with houtie chicks otherwise we're gonna get extincted here.'

The military units each had nicknames for themselves and other units. The Police Special Reserves – middle-aged volunteers who patrolled urban streets – were affectionately called 'wombles'. When the 38-50 year-olds were called up, they became known as the 'Salusa Scouts' (after the name of a local tonic for the elderly called Salusa 45 and recalling the image of the elite Selous Scouts who were themselves jokingly referred to, but never to their faces, as 'walking armpits'). When the government scraped the last dregs of the manpower barrel and called up the 51-

60 year-olds, these men were disparagingly termed 'Mashford's Militia' (Mashford's was the name of a Salisbury firm of funeral directors).

The government also played a role in the creation of catchy cant with its various propaganda campaigns. In 1977, for example, the Harmony campaign was launched, to reconcile the racial conflicts. It misfired badly. The catch-phrase became 'harmony terrs have you slotted (killed) today?' Bullets became known as 'harmony pills'. A Rhodesian company, the Beverley Building Society, jumped on the bandwagon with its daily radio 'language clinics' to help whites to speak Shona and Sindebele. Curiously, the initial lessons were about instructions to gardeners and cooks. Perhaps the whites would shout less loudly at their servants in the vernacular.

The war slang encouraged a sense of camaraderie. Slang was elevated almost to the pedigree of patriotism. This happens in nearly every war. But, unlike, for example, the Great War, Rhodesian slang permeated every home and office. It was not entombed in the trenches or in the mess. Because the war was on everyone's doorstep and the troops, particularly the large number of reservists, came home frequently, the wives took their new-fangled colloquialisms to the supermarket and the kids threw around the catch-phrases in the school-yards.

When Mugabe's 'new order' came in 1980 the word 'terrs' dropped out of fashion, though Rhodesians could not stop themselves repeating the joke that the now ubiquitous term 'comrade' was 'simply a Russian word for kaffir'. Young whites started sporting T-shirts with the slogan: 'Rhodesian War 1965-1980: We came second.' They tried to laugh off defeat, while most prepared to emigrate.

According to Brian Annan, the Head of Linguistics at the University of Rhodesia, 'War is innovative for the language. Language is always in a state of change and war brings rapid change. The present war is a healthy situation – for the language.' But it was not a healthy situation for outsiders when it came to translating the confusing semantics of the Rhodesian war.

Chapter Nine

TOWARDS ALL-OUT WAR 1977-1979

The Green Leader raid was part of the Rhodesian strategy of cross-border raids which began in earnest in mid-1977. After the debacle at Geneva, the Rhodesian government concentrated on finding an 'internal solution' to the war. Pretoria would continue to provide the arms to attack guerrilla camps in Mozambique and Zambia, and later Angola. This would 'buy time' to negotiate with moderate black leaders, who would be suitably awed by the still vigorous white military power. Such was the thinking in Salisbury. It meant that the Anglo-American proposals of September 1977, touted by Andrew Young, the American ambassador to the UN, and Dr David Owen, the British foreign secretary, were doomed.

The Patriotic Front was neither awed nor keen to negotiate an end to the war. By April 1977 the Rhodesian government conceded that about 2,350 guerrillas were active in the four operational areas: 500 in Hurricane, 1,000 in Thrasher, 650 in Repulse and 200 in Tangent. New operational areas were opened in central Rhodesia (Grapple), the Salisbury area (Salops) and Lake Kariba (Splinter). As the numbers of guerrillas increased, so did the extent of the penetration and disruption of the government infrastructure. Schools, clinics and mission stations were forcibly closed. In the south-east in May 1977 the government admitted that 22,000 tribesmen in four administrative areas had refused to pay their taxes. All over the country African councils in the rural areas could not function; local council buildings were looted and burnt. Stock theft and attacks on white farms mounted. In August 1977, the rail line to Sinoia was sabotaged on the outskirts of Salisbury. The most devastating guerrilla attack in 1977 was the bomb planted on 7 August at a Woolworth store in Salisbury: 11 people were killed and more than 70 injured. Nearly all the casualties were black. ZIPRA infiltration increased across the Botswana border; the new tempo of Nkomo's effort brought a massive upswing in recruits, many of them schoolchildren, who crossed clandestinely into Botswana. They were then flown to Zambia for training.

Also, ZANLA raids grew more daring. On 18 December at 10.45 pm about 60 ZANLA guerrillas attacked the Grand Reef security force base near Umtali. The troops were watching a film show in the canteen. The show came to an end as rockets crashed on to the area. The guerrillas had seen one RLI unit leave, but they had not noticed the arrival of another RLI Fire Force which returned fire. The guerrillas then disappeared into the night, after killing one African and injuring six whites at the base. A vociferous section of the RF demanded total war on the guerrillas: it wanted a full-scale call-up and urged that, while a large regular army was being created, the security forces should destroy all guerrilla bases in the frontline states. Some hardliners in the RF hatched a plan to appoint a military junta under General Walls, after putting Smith under house arrest. Later 12 RF members, nicknamed the 'dirty dozen', hived off from the ruling party to form the Rhodesia Action Party. (They were all defeated in the August 1977 general election.) But the dissident RF men had a point: the Rhodesian effort was poorly organised. A new War Council was set up to co-ordinate the various ministries directly involved in the war; it also included the service chiefs. A National Manpower Board was established to oversee white conscription. The most important development was the creation of a Combined Operations centre (ComOps) in March 1977 which took over the role of the OCC and the National JOC. ComOps now co-ordinated the activities of the various Joint Operations Commands which remained the HQs of the respective operational areas. ComOps was thus the national JOC for day-to-day administration and also a think-tank for long-range strategic planning. It was headed by Lieutenant General Peter Walls, the Rhodesian-born, Sandhurst-trained, SAS commander and former OC of the Rhodesian Army. There was some canvassing for Air Marshal 'Mick' McLaren, the former air chief, to become the ComOps supremo. McLaren was considered by some to be a more capable commander than Walls; in the end the army, as the larger organization, had more 'pull' and McLaren was made Walls's deputy. Both men were due to retire from the armed forces, but the government was thus able to retain their expertise.

ComOps HQ was appropriately situated in Milton Buildings next to the prime minister's office in central Salisbury. By late 1979 the political-military balance had swung heavily towards Walls. By then, real power in Rhodesia lay in the hands of Walls, not Smith or Muzorewa. Ken Flower, a small, wily Cornishman who headed the CIO, also wielded tremendous power behind the scenes. By this time Smith and Walls were hardly on speaking terms because of disagreements over strategy. Both men were strong-minded and Smith found it easier to get on with Walls's deputy, Mick McLaren. The two ex-airmen spent hours talking about aircraft, often of the World War Two variety. (After the Rhodesian war ended, Walls was asked why he hadn't persuaded Smith of the importance of providing a political strategy for the war. Walls maintained that as a 'simple soldier' he was not in a position to dominate the political leadership, especially a stubborn man like Smith. Bearing in mind the position of the army in the last stages of the war and Walls's personal influence, it is difficult to accept Walls's conventional interpretation of civil-military relations. Perhaps Walls, a former member of the Black Watch, had fully imbibed the Sandhurst principles. The strain between the two men did not develop into a total rift. After Walls's exile to South Africa, Smith continued to recommend that visitors to Johannesburg should look up his former military chief.)

Besides changes at the top, in April 1977 – despite an outcry from the business community – conscription was extended to the 38 to 50 age group and exemptions were severely reduced. The maximum call-up for those under 38 was increased to

190 days a year; those older than 50 were asked to volunteer for police duties. In September the government encouraged national servicemen to stay on for another year by offering Rh$100 a month bonus. The bottom of the barrel was being scraped; the only alternative was to boost the number of black soldiers. Black doctors had already been drafted and apprentices were next on the list, but large-scale black conscription was unnecessary as hundreds of volunteers flocked every month to join the Rhodesian African Rifles. The RAR was augmented with a third and a projected fourth battalion. In addition, the PV programme was stepped up. In June 1977, according to the Ministry of Internal Affairs, more than 145 PVs and 40 consolidated villages had been completed; another 32 PVs were scheduled for construction by the end of the year. The Catholic Justice and Peace Commission asserted, however, that 203 PVs had been erected and that, in August 1977, 580,832 people were living 'behind the wire', often in squalor. Dawn-to-dusk curfews had been imposed on most TTLs and 'no go' areas had been extended along the Botswana and Mozambique borders. The government was trying to pull out all the stops. As Roger Hawkins, the minister of Combined Operations, put it: 'Until now it has been accepted as basically a police operation with military support against criminals. Now it is to be a military operation, mainly by the army, with police support.'

Hawkins also admitted that 'our greatest problem before was lack of decision'. Decisions were now made. The most significant was to escalate the cross-border raids. ComOps personnel had been impressed by the various film versions of the Entebbe raid; in particular, they wanted to experiment with a Dakota fitted out with communications equipment to act as the 'command module' of future raids. And the SAS were arguing for a '1,000-kill' raid. In May 1977, Mapai, about 95 km from the Mozambique-Rhodesia border, was captured by security forces. It was not a successful raid. In spite of the scale of the operation, only 32 guerrillas were killed, although large quantities of equipment were seized. But a Rhodesian Dakota was shot down and the pilot killed at the Mapai airstrip. The raid was prolonged to three days to salvage the plane. ComOps privately blamed the military failure on a tip-off; politically the Mapai raid was a disaster. An irate Vorster phoned Smith to tell him to pull out his troops. Pretoria was still not convinced of the validity of Smith's plan to bomb his way into a constitutional settlement. South Africa did not want an endless war; it was looking to its own military needs (in November 1977 the UN imposed a mandatory arms embargo on the apartheid state).

But then South Africa changed tack. For a number of political reasons, including the need to project a tough image to sidestep the HNP challenge in the November elections, the National Party government began to support the internal settlement plan in Rhodesia. Bishop Muzorewa's UANC looked like going along with Smith; so did Ndabaningi Sithole's wing of ZANU. On 25 September 1977 Smith had flown to see Kaunda in Lusaka to encourage the old warrior Nkomo to return. With his options widening, Smith had in effect rejected the Anglo-American settlement by late September. The Rhodesian government particularly loathed the idea of integrating the guerrilla armies with the Rhodesian security forces during a transition period monitored by a British Resident Commissioner (Field Marshal Lord Carver) and a UN-appointed military supremo (General Prem Chand). Perhaps a show of force before negotiating with Muzorewa and Sithole would work. And this time Pretoria nodded its assent. (On most occasions, until the last few months of the war, the Rhodesians did not consult Pretoria officially in case it disapproved. Salisbury wanted to avoid having to disregard South African advice, though the SADF liaison officers in Salisbury co-ordinated any military support required.)

On 23 November the Rhodesians launched their biggest operation to date. The Rhodesian army, with a crucial SAS core, hit the ZANLA HQ near Chimoio, about 90 km inside Mozambique (roughly opposite Umtali). Three days later a second assault wave overcame Tembue in Tete province (220 km from the Rhodesian border). The double assault, codenamed Operation Dingo, were classic examples of vertical envelopments. At Chimoio 97 SAS and 48 RLI parachutists landed on two sides of the base, while 40 heliborne RLI troops were dropped on the third side. The fourth side of the trap was, in theory, to be sealed by fire from K-cars, after the initial bombing strikes. Chimoio was estimated to hold at least 9,000 ZANLA and Tembue 4,000. Practically the entire air force (42 helicopters, eight Hunters, six Vampires, three Canberras, six Dakotas and 12 Lynx aircraft) was deployed for air strikes and to transport 185 Rhodesian troops. It was almost impossible to air-transport more than 200 troops at one time. Normally, a 3:1 superiority is required for attacking an entrenched enemy; the Rhodesian attackers were massively outnumbered. The element of surprise and air power were supposed to fill the gap. During the first phase of Operation Dingo, ComOps claimed that the Rhodesians had killed more than 1,200 guerrillas. According to ZANU sources, the guerrilla figures were much higher; probably nearer 2,000, many of them women and children. The Chimoio complex contained schools and hospitals, as well as military training sections. On 25 November a ground and air attack hit Tembue. A Hunter dropped flechette anti-personnel darts for the first time in the war. It hit the parade ground, but a hangover had prevented the ZANLA commander summoning his men that day. A personal inspection of the killing ground by the RAF's Peter Petter-Bowyer had left him in no doubt of his invention's potential. ComOps had vetoed their use at Chimoio because an international outcry would have followed the inevitable visit by the UN High Commission for Refugees. In total, ComOps estimated that Operation Dingo had cost ZANLA in excess of 3,000 trained men and approximately 5,000 wounded (and many subsequent desertions). The Rhodesians had suffered two dead, six wounded and one Vampire was downed. On 26/27 November, in Operation Virile, a Selous Scout column with close air support destroyed five key road bridges between Dombe (near Chimoio) and Espungabera to deny ZANLA vehicular access to the Rhodesian border.

The slaughter at Chimoio in particular was to have a big impact on the collective psyche of the ZANU leadership. The mass graves were continually conjured up in political speeches and poetry, particularly after Mugabe's accession to power. After a week's protest, however, the most important leader still in Rhodesia, Muzorewa, decided to return to his negotiations with Ian Smith. Eventually, in March 1978, Smith reached an accord with Muzorewa, Sithole and a pliant Shona chief, Senator Jeremiah Chirau. These four men, nicknamed the 'gang of four', hoped to bring about a kind of majority rule which would end the war and pre-empt a military victory by the forces of the Patriotic Front. It was essentially a formula for white survival: 'Give them the parliament and we keep the banks.'

The Patriotic Front rejected the March Agreement as a sham, another UDI. Nkomo called the three internal black leaders 'small nuts in a big machine'. Nevertheless, Nkomo still kept back the bulk of his army. During 1978 he never deployed in Rhodesia more than 2,000 guerrillas; 8,000 to 10,000 remained in bases in Zambia. ZANU in Mozambique had repaired much of the damage caused by interparty dissension. 1978 was declared the 'Year of the People' in which ZANU intended to achieve a mass political mobilization of the peasantry before 1979, the 'Year of the People's Storm', the final onslaught on the Rhodesian government. ZANLA troops entered Rhodesia in groups 100-strong; by June 1978 at least 13,000 ZANLA troops were deployed in the country. They were assisted by locally trained recruits and thousands of *mujibas*.

In Salisbury, Muzorewa and Sithole, now members of the four-man Executive Council (Exco) which in theory controlled the transitional government established in March 1978, promised that the war would wind down. They argued that, as majority rule was in sight, the guerrillas would have no reason to fight on. Both men claimed to represent large groups of ZANLA guerrillas, but Smith was soon to find out that the two nationalists had deceived both him and themselves. During the rest of 1978 only a few hundred genuine guerrillas responded to the government's amnesty offer.

The internal solution was not working. The war escalated. The main reason why the guerrillas refused to heed Salisbury's call was the fact that behind Sithole's and Muzorewa's rhetoric all real power was still firmly in the hands of the whites. The obvious example was the running of the COIN war. On the same day that the Bishop, Sithole and Chirau were sworn into government, Smith quietly created his own unofficial war council, which had six members: Walls, as head of ComOps, the army and air force chiefs, the Commissioner of Police, the director-general of the CIO and sometimes civilian ministers. The streamlined war council had been set up in September 1976 to co-ordinate the ministerial control of the war; in March 1977 the formation of ComOps had improved some elements of the central command. Smith's personal council primarily aimed at excluding the black co-minister of defence. Black ministers were considered unreliable and prone to security leaks. (The first black minister of defence, John Kadzviti, a Sithole man and a former guerrilla, shortly after his appointment fled the country to escape a murder charge brought by the BSAP.) Smith was officially excluded from the conduct of the war. In fact, however, he worked closely with the service chiefs.

The new administration tried to improve its image. Most of the political detainees were released, executions of political prisoners were suspended and the ban on the political wings of both ZAPU and Mugabe's ZANU was (temporarily) removed. In spite of the military repercussions, many of the PVs were closed, especially in the Mtoko, Mrewa and Mudzi areas. (Some were in regions where the government tacitly admitted it had lost effective control.) This was done to satisfy the UANC's clamour to end the PV programme, which it knew was unpopular with the tribespeople. The main weakness, however, was the tardy removal of racial discrimination. (Four months after the March Agreement, a committee was set up to 'explore' means of removing discrimination.) Smith seemed to regard the tempo of removal of racial inequalities as an exchange for winding down the war. The black leaders had not kept their side of the agreement, Smith argued. In turn the black leaders argued that white intransigence over the race laws had undermined their efforts to persuade the guerrillas to come home. Lacking real power, the three black internal members of the Exco did look like puppets.

Many white soldiers regarded the settlement as an opportunity to Africanize the war under effective white leadership. With blacks in a semblance of power, a tougher policy against the frontline states might be more acceptable to the world. White conscripts continued to agitate for blacks to be conscripted as well. Muzorewa opposed this move (except for blacks already affected – apprentices and doctors). But in September Exco announced that blacks would be conscripted in spite of the massive problems of training this posed for the army. Skilled men were needed in the field; few could be spared as instructors. The light had just dawned upon Muzorewa and Sithole: both leaders belatedly realized that they should flood the army with as many trained political followers as possible. Black Rhodesians, who comprised 80 per cent of the armed forces in 1978, could well hold the balance in future events. It would be just as well to have some soldiers already committed to their respective parties.

Meanwhile, the security forces were determined to show that a black-white coalition in Salisbury did not imply a softly-softly approach to the war. Sometimes excesses resulted. At a village in the Gutu district in May, security forces fired upon a night-time *pungwe* organised by ZANLA troops. At least 50 black civilians were killed and 24 were wounded for the loss of one guerrilla. Despite protests from Muzorewa, such incidents of indiscriminate firing continued. Casualties caused by the guerrillas also mounted. By mid-June fatalities within the country were 100 a week, against three a week in the first five years of the war. Guerrilla attacks became more determined and cruel. On 23 June 12 missionaries, eight adults and four children, were raped, hacked and bludgeoned to death at the Elim Pentecostal Mission in the Vumba mountains near Umtali. (ZANLA denied responsibility, and blamed the Selous Scouts. After the war, regular ZANLA troops were proved to be guilty of the abomination.) In July the first major gun battle took place within the Salisbury city limits. Police units killed three guerrillas in the Mufakosi and Highfields townships, wounded two and captured five others. It was claimed that the guerrillas were part of a suicide squad planning to assassinate members of Exco. The spiralling conflict continued to hit the white core: emigration was edging up to 1,500 a month and taxes were increased. On 20 July the government announced a compulsory national defence levy of 12.5 per cent extra income tax to help to cover a record budget deficit.

Salisbury was also perturbed by international events. In July 1978 the US Senate voted against lifting sanctions. Despite continuing South African backing, Rhodesia under a black-white coalition appeared to be the same pariah it was under unadulterated RF rule. And the Russians were meddling in southern Africa again. The Soviets and the Cubans were accused of encouraging an invasion from Angola of the Shaba province of Zaire. The bestial slaughter of whites in Kolwezi sent shivers down Rhodesian spines, as they prepared to hand over to blacks. Black rule might come in parliament, but the whites were determined to control law and order and the security forces. Rhodesian intelligence sources began to fear that the Cubans would step up their support of ZIPRA, which could be given the means to launch a conventional sortie into Matabeleland. Vassily Solodovnikov, the Russian ambassador in Lusaka, was portrayed by the CIO as the *eminence grise* behind an invasion threat. BOSS had got wind of the plans and so had the CIO. The CIO head, Ken Flower, a genial, unflappable man, rushed off to London. The traditional intelligence links between the rebel state and Britain (as well as the USA) had, like oil, proved too slippery and vital to succumb to the moral dictates of sanctions. London tried to calm the Rhodesians; the British were more afraid of Smith renouncing UDI and handing back to them a Rhodesia which was portrayed by the world's media as completely war-torn. This thought terrified London more than any conceivable Red plot. The British fears were groundless because Smith would never have willingly renounced UDI. He had a pathological distrust of the British. (Although the CIO did have some grounds for alarm, as there was evidence of a conventional build-up, the Russians were playing a waiting game and were planning a long-term strategy. The year 1978 was vetoed. When the Cubans suggested a conventional sortie in mid-1979, ZIPRA rejected the plan even though ZANLA also had made extensive preparations for a conventional incursion. The Russians expected the war to last much longer and were gearing up for a big move in July 1980 or July 1981, depending on military developments.)

In April 1978 the first (and only) foreign war correspondent was killed. It was a sad irony, but it happened to be Lord Richard Cecil, a descendant of Lord Salisbury, the British prime minister who had lent his name to the Rhodesian capital. Cecil, a former Guards officer who had a distinguished record in Northern Ireland, was shot while making a film of the war. Because of his unusually good contacts with the Rhodesian army, he had caused some resentment among other journalists. He also carried a gun, which contradicted the professional ethics of journalists, who claim neutrality. Some journalists did nevertheless carry firearms for self-protection. The insurgents rarely asked for press cards before opening fire.

By mid-1978 Smith knew that his internal experiment was not working. The transitional government was being torn apart by party bickering among the blacks; even some of his own trusted supporters had been involved in a scandal over the theft of defence funds. The war was worsening and no one, not even South Africa, wanted to recognize the beleaguered state. Could Nkomo be brought into the internal settlement? Could ZIPRA and the security forces together wipe out ZANLA? Certainly Zambia and Angola, and perhaps other African states, would recognize a Nkomo-led Zimbabwe.

On 14 August Smith flew to State House, Lusaka, in a Lonrho company jet. Nkomo and Smith talked again, and later Brigadier Joseph Garba, a former Nigerian minister for external affairs, tried to involve Mugabe. The ZANU leader refused. But the secret Nkomo-Smith talks did not blossom into a military alliance, for on 3 September 1978 ZIPRA guerrillas shot down an unarmed Air Rhodesia Viscount with a SAM-7 missile. Of the 53 people on board, 18 survived the crash, but 10 of them, including six women, were massacred by ZIPRA guerrillas. Nkomo said that ZIPRA had shot down the plane, but had not murdered the survivors. During a BBC interview the ZAPU leader incensed Rhodesians by chuckling over the Viscount incident. One RF MP, Rob Gaunt, captured the mood of the whites when he said: 'I believe we have done our utmost in this country to be reasonable and the time, I fear, is now upon us when all Africa is going to see their first race of really angry white men.' Smith called Nkomo a 'monster'; clearly a ZAPU-RF deal was now out of the question. In a subdued speech (Walls had persuaded him to tone it down) Smith declared martial law in certain areas of the country. Although ZAPU and ZANU were later re-banned, Special Branch allowed senior ZAPU personnel, such as Josiah Chinamano, to leave the country before arresting the lower echelon party members. Perhaps when the storm had died down, Nkomo and Smith could try again.

The whites called for a massive retaliation against Zambia. Initially, however, the Rhodesians hit Mozambique. In late September Rhodesian forces launched a four-day airborne attack against ZANLA bases around Chimoio. The area had been extensively attacked in the previous November in Operation Dingo. It had been rebuilt, but dispersed over a much wider area. The Canberras went in low with their Alpha anti-personnel bombs, followed by the Hunters with Golf cluster bombs which were designed to explode above ground. The Rhodesian troops, including South African Recce Commandos in 'D' squadron of the SAS, spent three days clearing ZANLA from the trenches. Nine FRELIMO T-54s were driven off when they came to the rescue, and four Soviet armoured cars were destroyed. The Rhodesians lost no aircraft, but many were hit by ground fire. The Rhodesians suffered one trooper killed in 'friendly fire' during an air strike; a South African Recce serving with the SAS was also killed in a separate incident. Salisbury claimed that large quantities of ammunition had been destroyed and several hundred guerrillas killed. Zambia seemed to have had a reprieve. In early October Kaunda had opened the Zambian border, which had been closed since 1973. The British-owned Benguela railway through Angola was useless because of action by South

African-backed UNITA rebels and the TAZARA line through Tanzania was clogged by mismanagement. Kaunda had no choice but to use Rhodesia to get his copper out and food and fertiliser in.

Then Rhodesian security forces swept into Zambia. Previously Salisbury had launched raids only in the border areas of Zambia. On 18/19 October 1978 Chikumbi, 19 km north of Lusaka, was bombed. Mkushi camp, north-east of the capital, was also bombed and occupied by heliborne troops for two days. Via Green Leader, the leader pilot of the Canberra bombing force, Rhodesians controlled Zambian air space during the Chikumbi raid, and in effect prevented any hostile Zambian air activity for 48 hours. Using a Zambian airstrip (Rufunsa, near the Rhodesian border) as a forward staging base, Rhodesian aircraft created panic in the camps they hit.

During the Green Leader raid the security forces suffered minimal casualties. The Rhodesians claimed more than 1,500 ZIPRA killed as well as a small number of Cuban instructors. In fact, the bulk of Nkomo's 10,000-strong army in Zambia was unscathed, although hundreds of refugees living in and near the camps were killed. From the gunners' sights it was impossible to distinguish innocent refugees from young ZIPRA recruits.

The three-day assault demonstrated the efficacy of Rhodesian firepower and the superior security force training and leadership. Perhaps better weapons could help to fill the gap? Nkomo rushed off to Moscow to ask for further military aid and Kaunda asked Britain to improve on the air defence weapons it had already sent. Besides new equipment such as AA guns, the British Aircraft Corporation sent instructors and a maintenance team to refit the Rapier SAM system which had fallen into disrepair.

The raids into Mozambique and Zambia had boosted white morale, but they had done little to deter the rainy season offensives of both ZANLA and ZIPRA. On 23 October General Walls admitted: 'We have not only had a hard job containing them [the guerrillas] but in some areas we have slipped back a bit.' By December 1978, three-quarters of the country was under martial law. ComOps discussed a 'vital ground' strategy of trying to hold on to key areas of white settlements and farmlands, while effectively giving up on the TTLs. The generals, not a squabbling Exco, held uncertain sway. Courts martial had been set up which could impose the death penalty for acts of terrorism without the right of appeal to higher courts (though sentences were subject to a reviewing authority). The government claimed that more than 22 'frozen zones' (encompassing seven per cent of Rhodesia) were being policed by security force auxiliaries, the guerrillas who had come 'on-sides' and accepted the internal settlement. In fact, only a small proportion were converted guerrillas; the vast majority had either been unemployed or were UANC or ZANU (Sithole) supporters who had been trained in Uganda, Libya and the Sudan. By late 1978 the UANC and ZANU (Sithole) had about 1,000 armed guerrillas each. By late 1979 *Pfumu reVanhu*, as they had become known, had swollen to nearly 20,000. Most were loyal to Muzorewa. In spite of the brief training and supervision provided by Rhodesian whites, the auxiliaries turned on each other as much as they fought the PF. Often looting rather than battle was their main preoccupation. A measure of their military capability was that Selous Scouts often dressed up as auxiliaries to entice the guerrillas into attacking a supposedly 'soft' target. The RF was creating the perfect conditions for its greatest fear – uncontrollable civil war. Five armies were active in Rhodesia by December 1978: ZANLA, ZIPRA, the security forces and the armed followers of Sithole and Muzorewa.

From Salisbury things looked decidedly ugly. The internal elections had been postponed from December 1978 to April 1979 because of the security situation. The internal 'solution' had impressed relatively few guerrillas; even UANC supporters were disgruntled. Moreover, few of the 25,000 Africans affected by the October call-up seemed ready to take up arms against their brothers in the PF. With whites emigrating and blacks reluctant to be conscripted, who would protect the Salisbury government in the future? The war was edging closer to the city suburbs. On 11 November, while Smith was celebrating the anniversary of UDI, guerrillas launched an attack on the exclusive Umwinsidale suburb of Salisbury. On 11 December guerrillas fired rockets and tracers at the central oil storage depot in the heart of Salisbury's industrial sites. Only five guards armed merely with truncheons had been protecting the vital depot. ZANLA forces (although ZIPRA claimed the honours) created a fire which lasted six days and destroyed 25 million gallons of fuel.

The Rhodesian government entered 1979 in dire straits. This was to prove the crucial year. ZIPRA forces were committed in greater numbers; Rhodesia was now safer for them than Zambia. ZANLA, which stopped active recruiting because numbers were too large to train, had infiltrated beyond the Bulawayo-Plumtree rail line. The cities were being surrounded and ZANLA believed they would fall like 'ripe plums' as Mao had foretold. Despite the frictions, in some areas ZANLA and ZIPRA were co-ordinating their strikes. ZANLA was preparing to establish formal liberated zones and to defend them with a locally trained people's militia. The groundwork for the initial, crude structure of administration was being laid.

South Africa also feared the worst. During the white referendum of January 1979 that preceded the April poll, Smith admitted that if things went wrong South Africa had made 'a very generous agreement' to help Rhodesian war widows and the war-wounded. (A year before South Africa had secretly offered Rhodesian special forces, and their families, the option to move south to join the SADF.) Pretoria was also preparing to construct refugee camps in the northern Transvaal. And, like the British, South Africa had considered contingency plans for the military evacuation of Rhodesians if a wholesale carnage among whites was to take place. Against such a scenario of fear, the whites still said 'yes' (85 per cent of the 71 per cent poll) to Smith's plan to elect the first black prime minister of Zimbabwe-Rhodesia. How could Salisbury expect the PF guerrillas to believe that white rule was really over and to hand in their arms, if the unborn republic was to have such an ugly compromise name so redolent of white chicanery?

In the same month as the referendum, blacks had massively boycotted conscription. On 10 January, only 300 out of the scheduled 1,544 blacks turned up at Llewellyn Barracks in Bulawayo. Also, 415 of the expected 1,500 whites failed to show up. Two days later whites aged 50 to 59 were told they would have to serve for 42 days a year. Even 'dad's army' would have to be deployed for the coming general election.

On 12 February 1979, ZIPRA shot down another civilian Viscount aircraft. Air Rhodesia Flight 827 from Kariba to Salisbury was hit by a SAM-7. Fifty-four passengers and five crew members were killed as the plane came down only 50 km from the spot where the first SAM victim had crashed. Nkomo claimed that the intended target had been General Walls, who was aboard a plane which took off just after the ill-fated Viscount. The alleged attempt to kill Walls was probably a post-hoc rationalization: ZIPRA had intended to shoot down a plane just before the referendum. The emotional white backlash might have produced a 'no' to Smith's plans; and this would have disrupted the internal settlement to the benefit of the PF.

A feeling of sullen, resigned anger pervaded the white community, which retreated further into its laager. The roads were unsafe even for convoys; now the sky was dangerous too. Air Rhodesia flights were reduced and old Dakotas with heat-dispersion units around the engine exhausts were introduced on passenger runs. South African Airways cut back its flights and stopped its Jumbo jets from landing at Salisbury airport.

On 26 February the Rhodesian Air Force launched a retaliatory raid deep into Angola, the first major raid on that country. Canberra jets struck at a ZIPRA base at Luso, situated on the Benguela railway and 1,000 km from the Rhodesian border. Thanks to excellent intelligence work, the Rhodesian pilots avoided the British-maintained air defence of Zambia and the Russian-manned radar tracking system in Angola. In this audacious raid 160 guerrillas were killed and 530 injured. The Soviet MiG-17s at the Russo-Cuban air base at Henrique de Carvalho (320 km to the north) did not have time to retaliate. The guiding hand of South Africa was evident, however. The SADF was unhappy about the SWAPO threat to South West Africa and the UN's indifference to guerrilla incursions from adjacent Angola. Rhodesia could act as a cat's paw for the SADF, and SAAF Mirages could provide some emergency protection for the Canberras if things went wrong in Angola, despite their limited combat radius (a factor which also inhibited the Russian MiGs). All seven Rhodesian and South African Canberras returned safely. Ironically, on the same day as the raid ZIPRA did shoot down a Macchi jet fighter north-west of Lusaka, but this plane belonged to the Zambian Air Force. ZIPRA troops were jittery, as the Rhodesian Air Force had made two big raids into Zambia in the week before the Luso sortie. Rhodesians were in a tough mood in February; as one ComOps spokesman discussed the cross border strategy he said: 'If necessary, we'll blast them back into the Stone Age.'

157

Special forces had already attacked Zambian oil depots, with little success. On 23 March 1979, however, the SAS, with South African Recce commando support, hit the Munhava oil depot in Beira. RENAMO was given the credit, a frequently used device for Mozambican coastal raids. But the raiders arrived in Mark-4 Zodiacs, courtesy of ships from the South African Navy. (The navy also regularly supplied and transported RENAMO leaders by submarine.) The oil depot went up in flames and the desperate Mozambicans turned to the specialist unit of fire-fighters in Alberton, near Johannesburg. The South Africans helped in the arson plot and then basked in the applause for their good neighbourliness.

The Rhodesian strategy had always relied upon sound morale and leadership. But by 1979 the prospect of black rule, even by the internal leaders, had sapped white resilience. Grit had been transformed into mechanical resignation. Worse was the infighting within the RF and the UANC. The senior officers of the army were at loggerheads over military developments. An incident in January 1979 exacerbated their strategic (and personal) schisms. On 29 January a bugging device was discovered in Lieutenant Colonel Ron Reid-Daly's office. As Reid-Daly was then head of the elite Selous Scouts, this had serious security implications (though no one was actually monitoring his calls, because the Director of Military Intelligence, Lieutenant Colonel John Redfern, said he had actually 'forgotten' about it, after the Selous Scout monitoring plan was devised in August 1978). All Selous Scouts and SAS operations were immediately suspended. Two days later Reid-Daly launched a personal attack on the army commander, Lieutenant General John Hickman. The occasion was a crowded RLI mess during the drunken celebrations of the regiment's birthday at Cranborne Barracks. An angry Reid-Daly used more than soldier's language to describe his commander. Later described as being 'overwrought and emotional', Reid-Daly turned to Hickman, the guest of honour and began: 'I want to say to you Army Commander for bugging my telephone, thank you very much.' Raucous cheers followed. Everyone assumed Reid-Daly was joking. Reid-Daly repeated his words, and the company went silent. Reid-Daly concluded: 'If I ever see you again, it will be too soon.' The two antagonists immediately squared up for a fight, but senior officers managed to separate them. Reid-Daly was court martialled for insubordination and given a minor punishment. He then resigned. But the Reid-Daly/Hickman row had dredged up many murky facts about the army. There followed a welter of accusations and counter-accusations of gun-running and poaching. (Most prominent was the accusation that the Selous Scouts were using the no-go areas, from which other army units were excluded, to poach big game rather than hunt guerrillas. In some 'frozen' no-go areas on the Mozambique border guerrilla bands would seek refuge in Selous Scouts-patrolled areas and use them as a haven from patrols by other security forces.)

After another embarrassing incident involving too much alcohol, a lady and underwear for military dress code, General Hickman was summoned to the ministry of defence at 7.45 am on the following Monday morning. The co-minister of defence, Hilary Squires, had a file on his desk which contained the full details. The minister, who had a puritanical streak at the best of times, sacked Hickman on the spot. At 7.50 the general was out of a job. (Hickman, who had won the MC in Malaya, later sued, and won, a case for wrongful dismissal. Even though he had won his case on a technicality, he was paid a year's salary minus the pension he had received.) After Hickman's departure, the ministry of defence needed a 'Mr. Clean'. The two choices as Hickman's successor were either Major General Derry McIntyre or Sandy Maclean. McIntyre, although popular with his men, also had a reputation as a playboy, a man who was described as 'a cross between a cavalier and a hooligan'. Maclean had a stable family background and, on the technicality that he was 12 days' senior, was appointed the new army commander.

Hickman's decision to contest his dismissal publicized the problems in the army. Then Reid-Daly sued Hickman (and the minister of defence and combined operations, Muzorewa, the directors of army military intelligence and counter-intelligence, the director of military police, and other senior officers). As the court case dragged on to an inconclusive end, the normally publicity-conscious Hickman dropped out of sight. The death from wounds of his 19-year-old son also severely affected him. A bitter Reid-Daly went to South Africa, where he dabbled in a number of security firms and then, after helping to write his own account of the war, became briefly the head of the Transkei's army.

In spite of the scandals surrounding two of Rhodesia's best-known soldiers, Lieutenant General Maclean tried to give the impression that it was business as usual, for the army had to organize a massive security screen for the April 1979 one-man, one-vote, election. More than 70,000 men were involved in the country's biggest mobilization. The security forces were determined to prevent any PF disruption of the polls, but sometimes the preventive counter-measures were heavy-handed. The security forces also took the offensive across Rhodesia's borders. On 13 April the SAS led an Entebbe-style assault on the ZIPRA military command HQ in Lusaka (the Selous Scouts had done the initial reconnaissance in the city). The raiders tried to smash through the main gates in a Land Rover, but the padlock held the first time and the vehicle had to be used a second time to batter through them. By this time the ZIPRA guards were alerted and the SAS were pinned down by an RPD light machine gun. The delay would have given time for Nkomo, who was thought to be in the building, to escape. ComOps said that it wanted to destroy the ZIPRA nerve centre, but an SAS source later admitted that the aim was to kill Nkomo. Nkomo claimed that he had been at home and that he had escaped through a lavatory window but this was untrue. So complete was the destruction of the building that the ZIPRA leader could not have escaped. He must have been elsewhere, allegedly tipped off by a British mole in CIO. Rhodesian troops also sank the Kazangula ferry which was carrying ZIPRA military supplies from Zambia into Botswana daily. At the same time commandos spirited away ZAPU men from Francistown in Botswana and took them back to Salisbury. Not a single Rhodesian soldier was killed in the dramatic attacks which were executed with total efficiency and accuracy.

But ComOps regarded the April election as its crowning success. Never had a ruling minority done so much to hand over (apparent) power to a dominated majority. As one critical history, *Rhodesians Never Die*, observed about the two elections which marked the end of white rule: 'Rhodesia buried itself with considerable integrity and maximum bureaucratic effort.' Some Rhodesians, and most of the hundreds of pressmen in the country, expected the April internal elections to be wrecked by PF attacks. Instead, the security forces inflicted a high kill rate on the ZANLA forces which had concentrated in the Chinamora, Mhondoro and other TTLs in the Salisbury area. Security forces were deployed near all the static and mobile polling booths; for the first time the auxiliaries were mobilized in a major supporting role in the rural areas. Eighteen of the 932 polling stations were attacked, but none were closed. In a 64 per cent poll (if the population estimates were correct) 1,869,077 voters took part. Even some guerrillas voted. In some areas ZANLA actively encouraged the peasants to vote, although in most cases the PF tried to discourage any involvement in the election. The diminutive bishop, Abel Muzorewa, won 51 of the 72 black seats and so became the first African premier of the country. The election was a success comparable to that in 1966 in war-torn South Vietnam. It proved that the PF was nowhere near 'imminent victory' and that the security forces were still powerful enough to mount a huge logistic exercise. If, as the PF claimed, the turnout was the result of intimidation, it showed who effectively controlled the population at that time.

Rhodesians believed implicitly in Margaret Thatcher's promise, when leader of the opposition, that she would recognize the April poll if the Tory group of observers said the election was fair. The group, headed by Lord Boyd, did indeed submit a favourable report, but the new British prime minister reneged on her commitment. She was swayed by a Foreign Office confidential paper outlining the possible repercussions of recognizing Salisbury, plus personal pressure from Lord Carrington, her foreign secretary. This was a catastrophic setback for Muzorewa. Many Africans rightly interpreted it as lack of faith. If a Conservative British administration would not go along with the internal settlement, who would? And the plain answer was – nobody. The internal settlement's goal had been to bring peace, recognition and the removal of sanctions. The only tangible result was an escalation of the war. When the bishop became prime minister on 1 June 1979 he assumed the additional portfolios of defence and combined operations. By then ZANLA forces numbered more than 20,000 in the country. Could Muzorewa survive ZANLA's 'Year of the People's Storm'?

The PF felt that military victory would come within one or two years at the latest. But what if Western nations recognized Muzorewa and channelled into Salisbury a vast array of military assistance? That would set back the war by years. By mid-1979 ZANLA had amassed a large reserve of conventional weaponry, although the variety of calibres and spares was proving a major problem. (This had been a continuous difficulty; the logistic chain to the forward-based guerrillas in Rhodesia, besides being poorly organized, suffered from the heterogeneous nature of the supplies.) ComOps was aware of the arsenal at Mapai, not far from the ZANLA base which the Rhodesians had hit on a number of occasions. The weapons seemed to be set aside for a special purpose which eluded Rhodesian intelligence. The arsenal had been intended at one time, May 1979, to support Operation Cuba. This was a Cuban scheme to set up a provisional government within a liberated area of Rhodesia. Many Eastern bloc and Third World countries would have recognized it and thus have pre-empted Western recognition of the Muzorewa administration. Mapai could have supplied such a venture in the Chiredzi area, apparently ZANLA's choice. ZIPRA did not want anything to do with the plan and the Cubans withdrew their support. The open terrain in the Chiredzi area and its proximity to South Africa would have made a joint ZIPRA/ZANLA/FPLM/Cuban army an ideal target for a Rhodesian and South African conventional counter-attack. The other area mentioned in Operation Cuba, the north-east, would have been far more viable.

As it happened, the Cuban fear was unwarranted; not even South Africa risked recognizing Muzorewa. But Pretoria did pour equipment, pilots and ground troops into the very area set aside for Operation Cuba. And with the promises of bonuses and security of pensions, many whites in the civil service, security forces and police were persuaded to stay for another two years. Yet after the brief euphoria of the April election, the whites grew disenchanted with Muzorewa's ham-fisted management of the new coalition government. Even his own UANC split with the departure of James Chikerema's Zimbabwe Democratic Party. Then the bishop talked of encouraging skilled whites to return, but demanded a levy of Rh$20,000. In a bizarre attempt to court American opinion, he offered to welcome 1,000 Vietnamese 'boat people' to his country, which had an African unemployment rate of 50 per cent. His biggest failure was his 'campaign for peace'. Muzorewa launched his amnesty programme at the same time as he authorized the RLI to wipe out groups of mutinous auxiliaries. Sithole's men were particularly unruly in the Gokwe area. In this area and others a total of 183 auxiliaries were killed. One group was gunned down by troops hiding in the backs of troop carriers; another was lured into a schoolhouse for a supposed meeting to thrash out discipline problems and was obliterated in a strike by Hunters. Undoubtedly the government needed to control the more lawless bands of *Pfumo reVanhu*, but to kill so many of what the PF considered to be the bishop's own force – just before the amnesty launch – was catastrophic timing. Few PF guerrillas were impressed.

The Amnesty Directorate had been set up on 7 June 1979. It was headed by Malcolm Thompson, the man who had masterminded the administration of the April election. Thompson came from Northern Ireland, a territory not exactly distinguished then for a tradition of fair elections or successful ceasefires. The amnesty call included the exhortation to phone a series of numbers across the country. Most of the numbers were UANC offices. A group of journalists tried to phone these offices in the early evening; most of the numbers were unobtainable because the offices were unmanned. The security force aspects of the amnesty were much more professionally executed. Besides the radio and TV campaigns, trilingual leaflets were scattered across the country. The air force helped with 'skyshouts'. Aircraft would suddenly swoop down on a guerrilla camp. As the guerrillas ran to escape the expected bomb run they were deafened by the blast from enormous tannoys which delivered a dramatic and simple message: 'You are about to be killed by the security forces. Give up and live.' Despite many possible personal doubts about the internal settlement, guerrillas were severely punished by political commissars for listening to amnesty broadcasts. They could be executed for reading an amnesty leaflet.

The internal leaders had promised peace after the March Agreement, in 1978. Then they said the war would end after the one-man, one-vote polls; then after the installation of a black premier...Eventually few whites believed anything Muzorewa or Sithole said. Many emerged from their cocoons of total reliance on 'good old Smithy'. After the April election the disenchantment in the army, particularly among the reservists, was widespread. The bickering among the internal nationalists, which threatened to destroy all the hard work the part-time soldiers and policemen had done, undermined their loyalty. A number of white police reservists refused to guard Muzorewa's house the week after the April poll. They pointed out that the prelate had many bodyguards while their own families went unprotected. No disciplinary action was taken against the policemen. The real bone of contention was still white conscription. Why should the bishop call up 59-year-old whites possibly hostile to the UANC when he refused to conscript his youthful black followers? Only a handful of blacks had been called up. The whites began to feel that their taxes and skills were running the country and yet they were being compelled to fight for a black administration which could soon steal their rights and property. Another issue was the loyalty of the so-called 'new Rhodesians', the roughly 1,400 foreign mercenaries and volunteers in the regular forces. On the night of Muzorewa's election victory, Captain Bill Atkins, an American Vietnam veteran who had been in the Rhodesian army for two years, said:

> A good proportion of the foreign professionals [in the army] will stay – we're not mercenaries. If we find that we're working with a guy we disagree with, we will leave. We're not here for the money. If they [the new Muzorewa administration] back away from the war, as the Americans did in Vietnam, then we'll leave.

But no amount of reluctant military support from South Africa, white Rhodesians or foreign levies could replace some kind of international diplomatic support for Muzorewa. The PF rejected the new leader as a stooge. As one ZANU official put it: 'At least the leader of a so-called Bantustan in South Africa can fire his own police chief.' But Muzorewa could not. Behind the facade, the whites were in control. Even Ian Smith was still there in the Cabinet as a minister without portfolio. But the PF regarded him as the minister with *all* portfolios. And the new Tory prime minister, Margaret Thatcher, was still reluctant to recognize Muzorewa. At the Commonwealth

Conference in Lusaka in August, Mrs Thatcher secured the agreement of her fellow premiers: an all-party conference would try for one last time to cut the Gordian knot of the Rhodesian impasse. Muzorewa was bitter and Salisbury's *Herald* newspaper thundered: 'Is Mrs Thatcher really a Labour Prime Minister in drag?'

The Lancaster House conference opened on 10 September and staggered on until just before Christmas. Both sides struggled to inflict military reverses on their opponents, both to influence the course of the three-month conference and to be in a commanding military position if diplomacy should once again fail. As during the Geneva conference, the guerrillas talked and fought, but this time there were four times as many guerrillas in the country as in 1976. Within 48 hours of Muzorewa's accession to power he had authorized raids into his neighbours' countries. Later, on 26 June, the Rhodesians hit the Chikumbi base, north of Lusaka. Simultaneously five Cheetah choppers dropped assault troops into the Lusaka suburb of Roma where they stormed into the ZAPU intelligence HQ. It contained ZIPRA's Department of National Security and Order, which was commanded by Dumiso Dabengwa, whom Rhodesian intelligence dubbed the 'Black Russian' because he was reputed to be a KGB colonel. With the SAS was a senior ZIPRA captive, Elliott Sibanda. His job was to use a loud hailer to get his former colleagues to surrender and then identify whoever responded. During the fighting 30 ZAPU cadres and one SAS captain were killed. Five hundred pounds of sensitive documents were seized (including documents which, according to Muzorewa's minister of law and order, Francis Zindoga, proved that intelligence information had been passed to ZAPU by white liberals). What had happened to the 150 tons of British air defence equipment which had been sent to Zambia in October 1978 and the Rapier missiles which the BAC team had repaired? Was it plain incompetence, or were the Zambians afraid of protecting PF targets in case Salisbury decided to hit directly at Zambian military installations?

On 5 September, five days before the Lancaster House marathon began, Rhodesian forces hit ZANLA bases in the area around Aldeia de Barragem, 150 km north-west of Maputo. This was part of a new strategy: instead of just targeting PF military bases, Salisbury escalated its strikes to include the economic infrastructures of both Zambia and Mozambique. The attacks on economic targets, especially dropping bridges, were a small part of the ComOps 'final solution' plan. The highly secret proposals estimated that both Mozambique's and Zambia's economic structures could be destroyed within six weeks. The techniques to be used would have gravely escalated the war and almost certainly brought in the major powers. ComOps demanded a clear political green light for total war on Zimbabwe-Rhodesia's neighbours. If Muzorewa had been recognized after a possible breakdown of the Lancaster House talks, then the plan might have been put into action. Instead, only small parts of the scheme were used. It was then poorly organized. Major setbacks resulted and Walls was privately criticized by senior commanders for undue interference, particularly regarding the choice of targets. Some of the final raids were not planned by Walls or the CIO chief, who often had the final say, because both men were in London for most of the Lancaster House talks. Several raids had to be publicly supported by them even though they had been carried out against their better judgment.

In September the Rhodesians tried to destroy much of the transport system in Mozambique's Gaza province, and beyond. More bridges were destroyed by SAS and South African Recce Commandos. Then Salisbury stopped the rail supplies of maize to Zambia through Zimbabwe-Rhodesia. In October and November vital Zambian road and rail arteries were hit. The aim was two-fold: to stop the infiltration of PF guerrillas and supplies, and to induce the frontline states to pressurize the PF into accepting a more conciliatory line towards the Salisbury delegation in London. But such a strategy was not without its costs. ZIPRA had improved with the aid of Cuban, East German and Russian instructors. And FRELIMO had added a stiffening to ZANLA forces. In Zambia the regular army was too small and ineffective to give much conventional support to ZIPRA in its defence against Rhodesian raids, but in Mozambique the position was quite different. The ZANLA bases there were well defended.

The Rhodesian raids were now no walkover. In the three-day Operation Uric (Operation Bootlace for the South Africans) in the first week of September the Rhodesians were determined to stop the flow of both ZANLA and regular FPLM soldiers infiltrating across what the Rhodesians nicknamed the 'Russian Front'. The target was Mapai, the FRELIMO 2nd Brigade HQ and a control centre for ZANLA, a very heavily defended forward base 50 km from the border. Conventional military thinking dictated that in, addition to air support, two infantry battalions supported by artillery and tanks would have been required. As ever, the Rhodesians would make do with far less, relying on the shock of air power, surprise and courage. The aerial order of battle included: 8 Hunters, 12 Dakotas (half SAAF), 6 Canberras (of which 4 were South African), 10 Lynxes and 28 helicopters, including the newly acquired, but worn-out, Cheetahs (Hueys) along with a majority provided by the SAAF: Pumas, Super Frelons and Alouettes. A Mirage and Buccaneer strike force was on cockpit readiness in South Africa, and a battalion of paratroopers, with Puma helicopter transport, was on standby at a base near the Mozambique border. The command Dakota, the Warthog, was equipped with an advanced sensor system capable of locating and monitoring the guidance systems of ground-to-air missile installations and identifying surveillance radar systems. The crew included an intelligence officer and four signallers for communications with friendly forces. The plane was piloted by John Fairy, a scion of the famous British air pioneers. The SAAF had its own AWACS aircraft, a converted DC-4, nicknamed Spook. This was the largest single commitment of the SADF in the war.

The Canberras normally carried the cylindrical Rhodesian-designed Alpha bombs. But these had to be released in level flight, when flying at an air speed of 350 knots and at 300 metres above the ground. When they struck they bounced four metres into the air and exploded, sending out a deadly hail of ball bearings. The flak at Mapai was so heavy they would have been blown out of the sky if they tried a low-level attack. So the SAAF supplied conventional bombs which were dropped at 20,000 feet. A heliborne force of 192 troops went in after the bombers. In all the raiders numbered 360 men in the field, from the SAS, Recce Commandos, RLI and the Engineers. They met very fierce opposition. The fire from the 122mm rockets, mortars, recoilless rifles and machine guns from the entrenched ZANLA/FPLM enemy was intense, the heaviest the Rhodesians had ever encountered. All they had, besides air power, were 82mm and 60mm mortars, RPG-7s, light machine guns and their personal weapons. Soon the battle developed into a grim face-to-face encounter in trenches. The defenders stood and fought, and showed no intention of running from the air power, as they had so many times previously. General Walls, in the Warthog above the battle, wanted a victory not a defeat to accompany the politicking at Lancaster House. Nor did the South Africans want to commit their reserves and so not only risk defeat, but also reveal the extent of their cross-border war with Mozambique.

Two helicopters were shot down. The first was a Cheetah, hit by an RPG-7. The technician was killed, but the badly wounded pilot was extricated by a quick-thinking SAS sergeant. The second, an SAAF Puma, was downed by another RPG-7; the three air crew and 11 Rhodesian soldiers were killed. One of the dead was Corporal LeRoy Duberley, the full back of the Rhodesian national rugby team. The remains of the wrecked Puma were later golf-bombed in a vain effort to destroy the South African markings. Seventeen soldiers were killed in Operation Uric. Walls called a stop to the operation. This was the worst single military disaster of the war. And, for the first time, the Rhodesians were unable to recover the bodies of their fallen comrades. As a book on the Rhodesian SAS later noted: 'For the first time in the history of the war, the Rhodesians had been stopped dead in their tracks.' The RLI and the SAS were forced to make an uncharacteristic and hasty retreat.

The Rhodesians had underestimated their enemy. They were outgunned. Their air support had proved unable to winkle out well-entrenched troops and they were even more vulnerable when the aircraft – even when the whole air force was on call – returned to base to refuel and rearm. Combined Operations had decided to use more firepower. Surveillance from the air was stepped up by deploying the Warthog. The South African air force became heavily involved in these last months, both in the fighting and as standby reserves, as in the case of Operation Uric in September 1979. Super Frelons and Puma helicopters were difficult to pass off as Rhodesian equipment, but the Canberras and Alouettes also on loan were practically indistinguishable from their Rhodesian counterparts, except when they were shot down. The combined Rhodesian-South African efforts were approaching all-out war in the region. In late September, the Rhodesians hit the reconstituted ZANLA base known as New Chimoio. They also hoped to kill Rex Nhongo, the ZANLA commander, who narrowly escaped the first air strikes. ComOps claimed that this operation (Miracle) was a success, but the air force lost an Alouette, a Hunter and a Canberra. At the end of the climactic raid on New Chimoio, one Selous Scout admitted: 'We knew then that we could never beat them. They had so much equipment and there were so many of them. They would just keep coming with more and more.' The Rhodesians also attempted to stall the conventional ZIPRA threat to Kariba. RLI and SAS troops found themselves outgunned during this operation (Tepid). ZIPRA forces stood their ground, although they did eventually make an orderly withdrawal. On 22 November Walls ordered ComOps to stop all external raids.

The political warfare at the conference table was almost as bitter as on the real battlefields in southern Africa. The PF haggled over every step of the negotiations. Muzorewa had conceded easily. But Ian Smith had to be brought into line by the toughness of Lord Carrington, the conference chairman, as well as by a series of lectures from Ken Flower, General Walls and D C Smith, the RF deputy leader. David C Smith had played a pivotal role. Bishop Muzorewa had not wanted to include Ian Smith in his delegation to London, but David Smith had talked the bishop into it and said that he himself would not go if the RF leader were excluded. But Ian Smith's presence was counterproductive for the Salisbury team. The RF chief did his best to undermine the bishop's leadership. Gradually the PF was pushed into a diplomatic corner. The British had bugged all the hotel suites, especially the PF's, and knew exactly how far to push the guerrilla leaders. The Rhodesians realized that their hotel was bugged and sometimes used an irritating device which made squawking noises to hide conversations. More often they talked about confidential matters out-of-doors. Lord Carrington told the PF he would go ahead and recognize Muzorewa if the conference broke down. None of the frontline states wanted the war to continue and they exerted a continuous leverage on the hardline PF coalition. Josiah Tongogara, who had more influence over ZANLA than did Mugabe, believed that a political compromise was possible. Nyerere also urged moderation and he persuaded Britain that more than 'metaphysical' force was needed to set up a ceasefire monitoring group. Samora Machel was also a vital ally of Carrington's. In spite of Mugabe's threats to go back to the bush, Machel privately told him that he wanted peace, and without Mozambique as a sanctuary ZANLA would collapse. Machel told Mugabe: 'We FRELIMO secured independence by military victory against colonists. But your settlers have not been defeated, so you must negotiate.' Angola, Nigeria and Zambia, for different reasons, wanted a speedy end to the conflict. There had been too much suffering for far too long.

If the guerrillas had not been put in an arm-lock by their backers, especially in Mozambique, and had walked out of the conference, Lord Carrington had warned that he would go for the 'second-class solution': recognition of Muzorewa. Paradoxically, the very success of the military raids, especially on the economic infrastructure (including the SAS-Recce Commando raid on Beira harbour on 18 September), was probably politically counter-productive. The raids raised the morale of the white hardliners in Salisbury, but it ensured that the frontline states kept the PF sitting around the table. A tactful lull in the externals might well have prompted Mugabe to go for the unconditional surrender option, and walk out, and thus force Carrington to hand the baton to Muzorewa.

On 12 December Carrington took a gamble and sent Lord Soames as the new British governor of Rhodesia. Britain was officially in full control, for the first time in the colony's 90-year history. It was a highly risky venture – 'a leap in the dark' in Soames's own words. Final agreement on the complete process of drafting a new constitution, a return to British rule, a ceasefire and a new election had not been reached. But the rebellion was over. As soon as Lord Soames stepped down on Rhodesian soil, the revolt against the British Crown was quashed and sanctions were removed. But the civil war went on.

Walls had long predicted privately that the war would end in a military stalemate, and so it was. On 21 December 1979, after an epic of stubborn last-stands, all parties to the conference signed the final agreement. Ironically, it was exactly seven years to the day since the real war had begun with the attack on Altena farm in the Centenary district. Robert Mugabe was resentful. He said later: 'As I signed the document, I was not a happy man at all. I felt we had been cheated to some extent, that we had agreed to a deal which would... rob us of the victory we had hoped we would achieve in the field.'

On 28 December the ceasefire creaked uncertainly into life. By 4 January 1980 more than 18,000 guerrillas had heeded the ceasefire and had entered the agreed rendezvous and assembly points inside Zimbabwe-Rhodesia. Just as the ceasefire began, one of the main architects of compromise, Josiah Tongogara, was reported killed in a motor accident in Mozambique. As the most prominent soldier on the ZANLA side, his voice of moderation – especially regarding relations with ZIPRA – would be sorely missed. Because 'motor accidents' had been staged throughout the Rhodesian saga as a means of removing opponents, ZANU went out of its way to try to prove the incident an accident; even to the extent of sending a white employee of a Salisbury funeral service to Maputo to embalm the body. But a strong suspicion of murder lingered at the time. Nevertheless, no firm evidence of this has surfaced, though ZIPRA was convinced that an East German specialist in 'road accidents' had arranged Tongogara's demise. Later, even in ZANLA, it was accepted that he had been murdered. Senior ZANU men had agreed to his removal because of several general factors, including his desire to work closely with ZIPRA and his emphasis on encouraging whites to remain in the country. But the specific reason may have been his alternative plan, discussed privately during the Lancaster House talks, if the conference had failed. He argued that the three main armies (ZIPRA, ZANLA, the Rhodesian security forces) could guarantee a peaceful, five-year transition to civilian rule. A council of four parties (the RF, UANC, ZANU and ZAPU) would provide the administration, with a council of the military leaders acting as a watchdog. During this period the armies would be integrated. Then, after five years, or sooner if the integration was completed, elections would be held. Sir Humphrey Gibbs was suggested as a compromise candidate for the transitional presidency. ZIPRA apparently went along with the plan, but the constitutional conference reached agreement before Walls could be consulted by Tongogara. With hindsight such a plan appears bizarre, but it certainly paralleled Tongogara's public demands for conciliation.

Certainly some reconciliation would be needed to rebuild the devastated country. The long war had exacted a sad toll. More than 30,000 people had been killed (though some historians have offered a lower figure). Operation Turkey had destroyed a vast acreage of peasant crops to prevent food reaching the guerrillas. The International Red Cross estimated that 20 per cent of the seven million black population was suffering from malnutrition. More than 850,000 people were homeless. The maimed, blinded and crippled totalled at least 10,000. The Salvation Army reckoned that of the 100 mission hospitals and clinics which served the rural population, 51 were closed, three had been burnt to the ground, and most of the others were badly damaged and looted. More than 100,000 men in the towns were unemployed. At least 250,000 refugees waited to be repatriated from camps in the frontline states. About 483,000 children had been displaced from their schools; some had gone without schooling for five years. Half the country's schools had been closed or destroyed. Finding a real peace was only half the problem; a massive reconstruction programme would have to follow.

Many outside observers and most whites in Rhodesia expected the fragile truce to erupt once more into full-scale war which a British governor with only 1,300 Commonwealth troops would have to contain. Ninety-five per cent of the country was under martial law when Soames arrived. Extra regular troops had entered the conflict. FPLM soldiers from Mozambique were fighting alongside ZANLA. On the other side, the South African army's commitment had grown. By November 1979, South Africans were operating in strength in the south-east, particularly in the Sengwe TTL and along the border. They were supplied by air from Messina and their HQ was at Malapati. They were using artillery bombardment to create guerrilla movement, a technique the Rhodesians could not afford with 25-pounder shells costing $150 each. By December the SADF was operating north of Chiredzi. The aim was to put one battalion, each with a company-sized Fire Force, into each major operational area, making the total commitment five battalions. The news of South African involvement was deliberately leaked to boost sagging white morale.

If the ceasefire collapsed, more foreign regulars would be sent to fight in the civil war, a war that could have engulfed southern Africa. A grave responsibility rested on the man at the epicentre of the storm: Lord Soames, who had no previous experience of African affairs. As the London *Observer* warned: 'A bomb disposal expert would be the best British Governor to send to Zimbabwe-Rhodesia. The country lies ticking, a black and white booby trap with many detonators.' Would the ceasefire hold?

URBAN BATTLE

A section of 10 ZIPRA guerrillas, heavily laden with weapons and munitions, filtered across the Zambezi from forward bases in Zambia in March 1978, and made its way to Salisbury. The guerrillas' mission was to blow up power pylons and bridges within the Salisbury area. The section was commanded by a demolitions expert whose code name was Democrat. His right-hand man was another Soviet-trained sabotage expert whose nom de guerre was Bond.

The guerrillas infiltrated to the area between Glen Norah African township, on the south-west outskirts of the capital, and the Hunyani River. They did not trust the crowded, teeming townships to give them cover for their operations, and they set up their small base camps and arms caches in the bush outside the city. The area was European farmland and relatively open, and the guerrillas had to be extremely circumspect in setting up their operations base. They remained undetected until mid-July, when one of their arms caches and several resting camps were discovered by Rhodesian police units.

But the cadres themselves remained operational until one guerrilla broke discipline and robbed a beerhall in Mufakose township. A Police Anti-Terrorist Unit stick reacted to a report from one of the beerhall's employees and arrived in time to engage in a gun battle with the guerrilla outside the building. The guerrilla was forced back inside the beerhall but was trapped in a back room. By this time a police SWAT section arrived on the scene. Despite attacks with small arms and grenades, and wounds, the guerrilla was able to hold off the Rhodesian policemen single-handed with his folding-butt AK-47.

The police considered calling in an army demolition squad to blast out the beerhall's back wall to get at the guerrilla, but first they tried to talk him into surrendering. Through a loud-hailer he was told that he was surrounded and that resistance was futile. He surrendered. Under interrogation by Special Branch operatives he quickly pinpointed the house in Highfields township where four other guerrillas were hiding. A PATU task force was assembled and sped to the township. The captured guerrilla pointed out the house where his comrades were hiding.

At first light the Rhodesian force surrounded the house, deploying into two sections to cover the front and rear. A police officer called on the occupants to surrender, but only an African woman and two children came out. Two policemen went up to the front door and shouted to the other occupants to surrender. There was no answer from the guerrillas, who prepared the grenades they carried to hurl at the surrounding forces. The guerrillas were heavily outgunned as they carried only one grenade each to avoid being conspicuous as they moved about the townships. The policemen kicked open the door. One guerrilla crouched ready near the doorway and pulled the pin of his grenade, but a Rhodesian policeman emptied his pistol magazine into him at point-blank range. The guerrilla dropped his armed grenade, which detonated and killed him. The two other guerrillas in that room were killed when they dropped their grenades, which exploded. When the grenades went off the Rhodesian police riddled the building with small arms fire.

When the occupants of the house were again called on to surrender a man and a woman came out. They reported that there were four guerrillas inside, three of them dead. The woman was forced back inside the house with orders to drag out the guerrilla corpses, and to tell the survivor to capitulate. The woman pulled the bodies into the open one by one, then the surviving guerrilla emerged with his hands in the air. By then a SWAT squad had arrived and it cleared the house by throwing grenades into each room.

The captured guerrilla told Special Branch interrogators where another guerrilla was hiding in Highfields. A raid was carried out on the house, but the guerrilla had moved on. One of the men arrested in the raid pointed out another Highfields house as the new hiding place. A follow-up raid resulted in his arrest and identification as a guerrilla. In the continuing breaking of the chain this guerrilla led Special Branch agents and a SWAT team to a further hiding place and the wounding and capture of a seventh guerrilla.

The captured guerrillas pointed out their caches and bases to the Rhodesian forces, including one near Arbor Acres chicken farm on the city boundary. The Rhodesians' haul was five AK-47 rifles, 136 slabs of TNT, 39 hand grenades, nine Soviet anti-personnel mines, one NATO anti-personnel mine, 50 detonators, 1,700 rounds of AK ammunition and webbing and medical packs.

The three surviving members of the ZIPRA section, including the commander, were soon mopped up by the Rhodesian security forces. The incident showed the vulnerability of urban guerrillas inside Rhodesia. As long as they remained totally inactive they were able to survive, but as soon as they moved into action their operations quickly disintegrated under the swift and ruthless counter-measures devised by the Rhodesians. It is usually supposed that the police informer network was responsible for the guerrillas' vulnerability, but the group was compromised by the reporting of an armed robbery, a normal crime procedure. It was the guerrillas themselves who destroyed the network, swiftly targeting their comrades for the Rhodesian forces. The guerrillas' urban warfare was essentially a series of sporadic, hit-and-run raids or commando operations. They were never able to use the urban jungle to build up the same sort of operational infrastructure as they could among the rugged kopjes and in the villages of the dense Rhodesian bush.

Chapter Ten
AFTERMATH

CEASEFIRE

Nobody in Rhodesia really believed the ceasefire would hold. Despite the mountain of pessimism, the British governor and his staff were determined to try to make it work. No British government for 15 years had dared to contemplate sending British troops to Rhodesia. Now a predominantly British Commonwealth force was being sent into the middle of a war with only light arms and the responsibility of having to defend itself against attacks from the guerrillas or the security forces or both. It was a high-risk venture. The fact that it succeeded can be attributed mainly to the personality of the new governor and the courage of the Commonwealth Monitoring Force.

Soames was an excellent choice as the Empire's last pro-consul. As one Foreign Office insider said of the well-fleshed, ex-Etonian and Sandhurst man: 'He's large, noisy and impossible to ignore.' His Churchillian connections (he had married Churchill's daughter, Mary) appealed to the old-fashioned patriotism latent in many white Rhodesians and his blunt patrician manner earned him the respect of the African leaders. As one of Nkomo's aides said: 'We Africans get on with old fashioned Tories better than modern Labour politicians.' Soames lifted sanctions, opened the closed borders, put an end to secret trials and released dozens of political prisoners. But could he stop the rival armies rupturing the ceasefire, and, even more difficult, could he ensure that elections be held amid the barrage of intimidation and violence?

The Commonwealth force was the key to peace. The force, 1,300 strong and led by Major General John Acland, was made up of 159 Australians, 75 New Zealanders, 51 Kenyans and 24 Fijians, with the rest British troops from 35 different units. Their task (code-named Operation Agila) was to supervise the movement of PF guerrillas from the various rendezvous points to the 17 Assembly Points (APs) and then to make sure they stayed there. By 6 January 1980, 15,730 guerrillas had assembled. Their numbers ranged from 30 in one AP to 6,000 in others. By 9 January more than 20,634 had gathered and the numbers gradually increased to about 22,000. Small groups of Commonwealth troops camped near the APs to give a reassurance that the Rhodesian air force would not bomb the area. Even though most APs were turned into fortresses by the guerrillas, Commonwealth troops were told not to make their own defensive measures obvious. Although they were supposed to be merely a 'psychological barrier', in areas near some APs British troops began to dig deeper foxholes.

Another danger was the presence of land mines. Tens of thousands of mines were laid by the Rhodesians along 750 km of the border. Some maps of the minefields were incomplete; even in well-mapped areas the rains had shifted many of the devices. Twenty-five security force engineers were killed and 91 lost their limbs while putting the mines down. During the ceasefire the guerrillas sometimes helped to point out their mines in the vicinity of APs and their access routes, but the random nature of guerrilla plantings would cause tragedies long after the end of the war.

Although the Rhodesian commanders had warned that most of the Commonwealth groups would be 'taken out' on the first night, remarkably few incidents ensued. By and large, the Commonwealth force, particularly the British members, worked with tremendous tact, courage and good humour to persuade the guerrillas that the ceasefire was not a trick. Besides reassuring the guerrillas, the Commonwealth force became responsible for feeding and housing 22,000 people. Everything from film shows to panties (for the hundreds of female guerrillas) had to be provided. Rations were issued on a scale equivalent to an African soldier in the Rhodesian army. It was a logistic nightmare. Meat, 450 tons, was bought from South Africa and 90 tons was airlifted for immediate distribution. Eighty per cent of the goods were provided locally, but the initial demand for 23,000 of everything (from toothpicks to sets of knives and forks) meant purchases from Britain, Hong Kong, America and South Africa.

Food, clothes and entertainment were crucial. Many of the guerrillas were angry and bored. They did not want to stay cooped up for two months until the election results were announced. Many of them wanted to get out and join the guerrillas who remained outside the APs. Of the 22,000 in APs, about 16,500 were ZANLA and 5,500 ZIPRA. But many of these men were not guerrillas: a large percentage were *mujibas* or in some cases just camp followers. At least 7,000 fully trained ZANLA troops remained outside. They had been ordered to stay out and organize for the election even if (as happened) their commander, Rex Nhongo, should order them via TV and radio broadcasts to go to the APs. More than 500 fully trained ZIPRA troops also remained operational outside the APs. In addition, according to ComOps figures, 17,000 guerrillas were still in Mozambique and 10,000 in Zambia; many of these were infiltrating across the border after the 4 January deadline for assembly of guerrillas in the APs. ZANLA infiltration and political harassment were escalating, and the removal of Rhodesian security forces to their bases had also led to a massive upsurge in banditry and crime. The increasing violence threatened to swamp the fragile ceasefire. The small groups of Commonwealth troops around the 15 APs (two were disbanded) were extremely vulnerable, even though British troops were in reserve in Kenya and RLI Fire Force troops were ready to spearhead rescue attempts for endangered Commonwealth troops.

On 6 January Lord Soames authorized the redeployment of the security forces, with the order to use minimum force. As well as the regular units, more than 15,000 auxiliaries were included. Soames was forced to rely upon the security forces and the police, as well as the civil service, if he was to administer effectively the transition. From the viewpoint of many African states, as well as guerrillas, this was bound to encourage a pro-establishment bias during the run-up to the election. Soames was further criticized for allowing South African troops to remain in the Beit Bridge area. (Officially they were removed on 30 January; unofficially some regular SADF troops donned Rhodesian uniforms. Mugabe insisted that 6,000 South African troops were still operating in the country. Three thousand, he said, had just been disguised as Rhodesian troops and 3,000 had been serving for some years as volunteers.) The other major criticism was of Lord Soames's deployment of the auxiliaries, who often acted like thugs in the TTLs.

After a few weeks it looked as though from a military perspective the ceasefire was a success. The guerrillas were being fed and clothed, although they were still jittery about possible attack, especially from the air. Occasionally they would overreact. In one incident the guerrillas surrounded the entire 'Echo' AP with machine guns, RPG-7s and mortars trained on the Commonwealth troops. And, on the other side, in spite of contacts with 'unlawful' guerrillas (those who had not moved into APs or had strayed from them) Soames appeared to have the Rhodesian security forces under control. But this was an illusion; towards the end of the war, the Rhodesian military had begun to act as a state within a state. It was only the personal contacts between Smith and his service chiefs which kept the fiction of political supervision intact. With 95 per cent of the country under martial law, military dominance was inevitable. Soames was in fact at the mercy of the Rhodesian high command.

The key figure was still Walls. A confidential memo in the files of the Foreign Office's Rhodesia section described him as the right man in the right job at the right time – 'One of the more comforting aspects of the Rhodesia complex.' Walls had earned the respect of the 'Brits' at the Lancaster House conference by backing Ken Flower's reading of the riot act to Ian Smith when the RF leader was the odd man out in the Salisbury delegation's acceptance of Carrington's initial proposals. In the end, Walls, not Soames, was to prove the final arbiter of war and peace in Rhodesia.

Another key figure for British intelligence was Derry McIntyre, one of the most popular senior officers in the army. MI6 had fingered him as the man who might be sufficiently daring, able and charismatic to lead a coup. Many of the Commonwealth soldiers showed true grit during the exigencies of the ceasefire, but some of the officers were playing fast and loose with the Rhodesian women. The most egregious example was the British commander himself: Major General (later Sir) John Acland. The unconventional Scots Guards officer was foolish enough to seduce, over a game of bridge, Major General McIntyre's attractive wife. The understandably irate Rhodesian general intended personally to shoot the offending British commander. This could have collapsed the very delicate peacekeeping exercise, and possibly led to general war in the region. McIntyre was eventually dissuaded from an almost justifiable homicide. Nevertheless, he was completely distracted at a time when a coup was highly possible. Whether Acland was acting under orders in the service of his Queen or whether he was dangerously indiscreet is not known. Experience of the British officer corps might suggest the latter, especially considering Acland's record for impulsive behaviour during his long (and distinguished) career. Acland, happily married for over 50 years to his charming wife 'Turtle', died in 2006.

Behind the scenes, the security forces worked to ensure a Muzorewa victory. The auxiliaries were busy in the villages 'teaching people how to vote'. And the army illegally distributed anti-Mugabe leaflets. Security force members, mainly Selous Scouts, were also responsible for a number of 'dirty tricks', including attacks on churches (while leaving false evidence of ZANLA complicity) and the destruction of the pro-Mugabe Mambo Press in Gwelo. The security forces denied any involvement, particularly the planting of a massive bomb which nearly succeeded in killing Mugabe when he was on a visit to Fort Victoria on 10 February. Mugabe had led a charmed life. The CIO at the very last minute had aborted an attempt to assassinate him in London during the Lancaster House talks. At least nine other Rhodesian attempts on his life were foiled or aborted. The last one was scheduled for 2 March 1980, when the SAS planned to use a SAM-7 Strela to shoot down a plane carrying Mugabe and 22 members of his central committee as it came to land at Salisbury airport. Some SAS operators objected to killing the crew as well. ComOps cancelled the plan at the last minute. The dirty tricks and assassinations, which came under the code name Operation Hectic, were poorly planned, partly because of constant in-fighting and vacillation in ComOps. Operation Hectic was distinct from the later Operation Quartz, which had involved a great deal of careful staff planning.

Meanwhile, ComOps lambasted Mugabe's dirty politics and mass intimidation, while denying any underhand measures of their own. Although evidence indicated Special Branch/Selous Scout involvement, the denial by some security force commanders could have been entirely genuine. After independence, many senior Rhodesian military leaders were surprised, and disgusted (or pretended to be), when they found out about some of their own side's undercover adventures. Just as the Wehrmacht's Abwehr (the German army's counter-intelligence until 1945) distanced itself from the excesses of the Gestapo, some Rhodesian commanders tried to dissociate themselves from the dirty tricks perpetrated by the CIO and SB. In fact, most of the dirty tricks were committed by SB and the Selous Scouts. The SB'S head, Mike Edden, was on the ComOps staff, and the Selous Scouts, like the SAS, were directly, though sometimes separately, controlled by ComOps. Chief Superintendent 'Mac' McGuinness ran the SB element of the Selous Scouts and kept a lot of information close to his chest. Information was also compartmentalized because of the unadulterated mutual loathing of BSAP Commissioner Peter Allum and CIO boss Ken Flower. It is difficult, however, to absolve the service commanders, who were also part of ComOps, of complicity in at least some of the atrocities of the secret war, especially in the final days.

One of the unexpected aspects of the pre-election turmoil was that nobody tried to assassinate that fine, fat target of a man, Nkomo. Like Mugabe, he was protected by men from Scotland Yard, as well as his own bodyguards. A South African organization had put a price of R100,000 on his head, but because of the Viscount massacre many whites would have happily *paid* to dispatch the ZAPU president. Like Mugabe, Nkomo had also led a charmed life: he had escaped a number of assassination attempts arranged by the Rhodesians. Besides the attack on his HQ in April 1979, a contract to kill Nkomo had been given to a single assassin by Rhodesian agents. Ironically, Nkomo was also in continuous contact with Rhodesian intelligence through most of the war, in a fascinating London-Salisbury-Lusaka triad of conspiracy. Tiny Rowland, the head of Lonrho, was the key figure in this triangle. Nkomo had also established close ties with British establishment figures in the early Sixties. During his long years of detention in Rhodesia, senior members of the British Liberal Party were negotiating with Kenneth Kaunda to help to spring Nkomo by using a small group of Israeli mercenaries.

As election fever spread in February, intimidation on all sides mounted. It was clear that the bulk of violence originated from ZANLA, and Soames warned that ZANU(PF), the Mugabe party, would be banned from campaigning in areas where intimidation was rife. One ZANU(PF) candidate, the fiery Enos Nkala, was prevented from campaigning after uttering particularly bloodthirsty threats to voters. Walls urged Soames to ban ZANU(PF) completely because a large army of guerrillas, led by commissars, were active outside the APs and were making clear to the Shona peasantry that they could vote for only one man. The governor was unresponsive. After all, Lord Soames said – with a refreshing lack of political correctness – when he arrived in Salisbury:

> You must remember this is Africa. This isn't Little Puddleton-on-the Marsh, and they [black Africans] behave differently here. They think nothing of sticking tent poles up each other's whatnot, and doing filthy, beastly things to each other. It does happen, I'm afraid. It's a very wild thing an [African] election.

ELECTIONS

The election was to be held on the last three days of February 1980. What worried the Commonwealth troops were the possible reactions of the guerrillas in the APs if their respective leaders did not become prime minister. Would the 16,000 pro-ZANLA men march out of the APs with guns blazing if either Muzorewa or Nkomo won the election? Every one of the Commonwealth contingents wanted to withdraw before the election results were announced on 4 March. Eventually General Acland persuaded the Ceasefire Commission – made up of representatives of the security forces, ZIPRA and ZANLA – that small security force detachments should replace Commonwealth troops in the APs (small police units had already been positioned). This would act as an insurance against air attacks and be the first step on the road to the integration of the three armies once a new government was installed. British officers at Government House drew arms and readied to defend themselves at dawn against the Rhodesians. 'It was shades of the Indian Mutiny,' according to one historian.

As a final piece of old-style security, Lord Soames requested that 570 British policemen should stand near the polling booths in their regular uniforms. And so it was that 2,702,275 men and women, in the middle of African rainstorms, voted under the watchful eye of British Bobbies, traditional helmets, boots and all. If the estimate of the population was correct, it was a 93 per cent turnout. Senior Rhodesian intelligence officers had predicted that Muzorewa would win at least 30 seats. Indeed, both Walls and Peter Allum, the Commissioner of the BSAP, had spent the last days of February on a morale-boosting tour to tell their men that Muzorewa would win, and there was no chance of a Marxist takeover. The defeat of Muzorewa, although a major intelligence failure, should be seen in perspective. The much larger CIA, for example, failed abysmally in its forecasts on Iran under the Shah. During the Russian invasion of Czechoslovakia, which the Americans did not anticipate, the CIA lost track of the Soviet army for two weeks. Another example is the Tet offensive in Vietnam which caught the Americans unawares. Nevertheless, most of the security elite failed to predict Mugabe's win because they did not want it, and because they did not want to believe, or could not interpret, the evidence which was all around them. In the last year or so of the war, but especially in early 1980, Rhodesian intelligence was swamped by data. 'Never had so much intelligence been collected to so little point,' was the post-war verdict of Professor Ray Roberts, the University of Zimbabwe historian. Right from the start, the interpretation of the war – that it was a non-political criminal issue to be dealt with primarily by the police – was misguided. As late as 1977 the police had an equal voice with the army in all decisions. Ian Smith tended not to listen to military advice but for too long heeded his Secretary for Internal Affairs, Hostes Nicolle, who represented the old Native Department tradition, and who, it was said, 'could misunderstand Africans in three [indigenous] languages'. By the war's end, the much-vaunted Rhodesian flair for innovation and invention had produced a command structure of Kafkaesque proportions. The creation of ComOps tended to increase rather than diminish inter-service and inter-departmental rivalry. Military Intelligence, Special Branch, CIO and the Selous Scouts often conducted their own wars inside and outside the country. They all had different notions of what kind of war they were fighting and accordingly disparate methods of countering it.

No one except ZANU(PF) expected any one of the nine contending parties to win an overall majority of the 80 black seats in parliament. Despite a multi-million dollar campaign, backed by Rhodesian businessmen and South African funds, as well as the loan of a fleet of helicopters, Muzorewa's UANC won only three seats – fewer seats than he had choppers. Nkomo's Patriotic Front (ZAPU) won 20 seats, mainly in his Matabeleland base. The remaining 57 seats went to Robert Mugabe's ZANU(PF). It was the first time in Africa that a Marxist had been voted into power. The internal settlement had merely hastened genuine black rule by allowing Muzorewa to play Kerensky to Mugabe's Lenin. Although ZANU(PF) had actually predicted 57 seats some weeks before the election, Mugabe was obviously stunned by the extent of his triumph. ZANU(PF) had been so long geared for war that the ZANU boss worried that his party might not be ready for the reins of government. Hence his request that Soames stay on for at least six months.

Nkomo was shattered. He said sullenly: 'You give them one man, one vote and look what they do with it.' The whites were panic-stricken. Some had their petrol tanks full ready for the 'Beitbridge 500', the 500 km drive to the South African border. Other whites prayed for a white security force coup. Contingency plans did certainly exist under the name of Operation Quartz. The most persistent version of the conspiracy was based on Mugabe being defeated. This could have happened because of an elaborate plan to stuff the ballot boxes with Muzorewa votes. A few (highly deniable) nods and winks came from Britain's MI6 and Pretoria. Ken Flower, however, firmly vetoed the subversion of the democratic process. But if Mugabe had been defeated fairly, and resumed the war, the Rhodesian army would have wiped out ZANLA in the APs and (perhaps) joined forces with ZIPRA to finish off the rest. Then a Nkomo-Muzorewa-white alliance would have run a pro-capitalist Zimbabwe.

Quartz, then, was a plan for a *counter-coup*, not a coup. ZANU(PF) would have lost the election or been proscribed by Lord Soames because of the massive intimidation. Mugabe would have led ZANLA back to the bush to continue the armed struggle. The first military stage of the operation involved SAS and the Rhodesian Armoured Car regiments, with their new T-55 tanks, surrounding buildings occupied by returned PF leaders. The SADF provided a range of sophisticated monitoring systems. The ZANLA leadership element was specifically targeted for destruction, ZIPRA would have been allowed the chance to surrender if trapped in the same locations. At the same time, the air force and the RLI and Selous Scouts would wipe out ZANLA assembly points. South African forces would assist where necessary. ZANLA's ambitions would be set back 20 years. Quartz was a military plan, but it contained elements of political sensitivity, especially the need for ZIPRA to at least acquiesce initially, and later co-operate, in backing a Nkomo-Muzorewa-Smith coalition. But, it must be repeated, Quartz was dependent on Mugabe's return to the battlefield. Many of the NCOs and junior officers, who had got wind of, or were involved in, the contingency, may have misinterpreted the deployment as a pre-emptive coup. Many wanted one.

So, despite a massive display of troops and armoured vehicles around the main government buildings, road junctions and communication points just before and after the announcement of the election results on 4 March, no coup materialized. Some British newspapers reported (erroneously) that Walls had vetoed a planned coup three hours before it was due to be triggered off. The misinformation may have leaked from Whitehall, not Salisbury. British intelligence was certainly suspicious about a Rhodesian *coup de main*. And Muzorewa was approached by ZAPU officials on 1 March to discuss a possible coalition. Then, on 2 March, as the extent of the Mugabe landslide was becoming apparent from leaks, Muzorewa was asked by some whites to consider backing a coup. He refused. The most powerful military leader, Walls, also refused to countenance a rebellion. He made it clear to ComOps staff that Rhodesia would not'copy the rest of Africa'. However much he might have questioned the validity of the electoral process, he clearly recognized that the political consequences of a pre-emptive coup would have been disastrous.

Many whites expected one but it did not happen. In fact the country had been much closer to a coup on other occasions. During the 1974-5 detente period there had been rumblings within the RF party of a coup to depose Smith because he was *delaying* a settlement by his hardline stance. Then, during the Kissinger period, some rumours had circulated of a coup from the right to *slow down* the pace of change. In the period 1977-8, some young army officers talked of a military government which would wage an effective all-out war. In the end, the British convention of military subservience to the civilian authority was formally observed. Despite being at the peak of its deployable size and alertness, and augmented by South African forces, the Rhodesian military reluctantly accepted Mugabe's electoral triumph. A rapid exodus of South African troops and equipment followed. Special Branch shredded its files and the Central Statistical Office destroyed its more sensitive information, particularly the records of Rhodesia's illegal trade with Eastern bloc nations. Many of the Cabinet papers were spirited away to South Africa.

Walls had kept his promise to Machel. Just before the election he and Ken Flower had flown to Maputo (and brought back two large boxes of prawns, a delight Rhodesians had been denied since 1976). Machel promised to abide by the results of the elections if the Rhodesians promised not to launch a coup if Mugabe won. Despite Mugabe's threats to go back to war during the election campaign, it was clear that Machel did not favour a resumption of hostilities. At most he would have offered Mugabe a quiet exile if he lost the election. A Rhodesian coup could not have worked against the massive vote for Mugabe. Even without intimidation, he was clearly the favourite son of the masses. Above all, the people wanted peace. A coup, with South African support, could have precipitated an even worse civil war, even if such countries as Zambia had recognized a coalition which included Nkomo.

And yet recent evidence, particularly in works written and published by Peter Stiff, a former officer in the BSAP and prolific writer of southern African militaria, points to an elaborate but separate South African plan to thwart Mugabe's win at the polls. A week after the elections, the Rhodesian security machine had been wound down, and the elite troops had been confined to barracks, but the South African forces had mobilized the powerful Battle Group Charlie near the border. South African and ex-Rhodesian special forces were preparing a series of roadside bombs (disguised in electricity sub-stations and traffic light control boxes) placed in Jameson Avenue in Salisbury. The intention was to detonate them by remote control on 17 April when a VIP motorcade was due to pass on the day before the independence celebrations. The prime targets included Lord Soames, Mugabe and Prince Charles. The killings were expected to trigger off a mass ZANU reaction to the death of their leader, especially from Rufaro stadium where the *povo* were to celebrate their freedom. Mass revenge on white Rhodesians would replicate the worst days of the Congo. The hog-tied Rhodesian forces and the tiny British monitoring force could have done little. So the South African battlegroup would cross the border to 'restore order'. The British could hardly object to a humanitarian intervention, especially after the shock of the death of the heir to the throne, nor did they have the military reach to protect the numerous white British passport-holders. Pretoria would have installed a temporary administration of Muzorewa and Nkomo, whose regular ZIPRA formations would also move rapidly into the country to spell an end to ZANLA. With ZANLA men and supporters running riot in the country, they would be considered unfit to govern. Zambia would welcome the re-birth of Nkomo's power, while the other frontline states, utterly exhausted from the war, would do little more than protest. Mugabe would have been cheated of his victory, and thousands of whites would have been murdered, but Pretoria would have kept the Marxists from power, and installed, finally, a pliant black administration which was beholden to South Africa. CIO's Danny Stannard got wind of the plot and the foreign special forces in the country were forced to flee. The South African invasion force stood down. Such was Stiff's interpretation of a very febrile few days in Salisbury. Certainly, Pretoria's frenetic military activity fitted this interpretation.

INDEPENDENCE

Once again Mugabe survived the machinations of his numerous enemies. On 18 April 1980 Zimbabwe became independent with Mugabe as premier. The Rhodesian albatross slipped off Britain's neck. Soames, the amiable Tory, had accomplished his 'mission impossible' and handed over a British colony to a Marxist guerrilla leader. The new black leader took over a white-constructed dictatorship with the panoply of secret courts, secret hangings and emergency powers. Would Mugabe now turn those weapons the other way? If he did, and the whites fled, what good would peace be to an economically prostrate country?

After the first tidal waves of shock, some whites responded to Mugabe's calm calls for reconciliation with comments about a 'miracle'. As one right-wing white said: 'The war's over and we've got a strong leader. There's no mucking about with a coalition that could have triggered off a civil war.' Mugabe appeared on television to ask for understanding between the races. 'Let us deepen our sense of belonging,' he said, 'and engender a common interest that knows no race, colour or creed. Let us truly become Zimbabweans with a single loyalty.' Some whites accepted Mugabe's call, while many prepared to quit Zimbabwe. Others could not because the financial restrictions on emigration grew even tighter.

Under the averted gaze of the British, the SADF flew out or drove out much of their loaned equipment, although some Rhodesian officers, keen to appease the new government, back-tracked on an agreement to return 800 brand new MAGs and the Eland armoured cars. The majority of white regulars in the armed forces and the BSAP (renamed the Zimbabwe Republic Police) left. Some joined the South African Police, but afterwards found the strong Afrikaans orientation uncongenial.

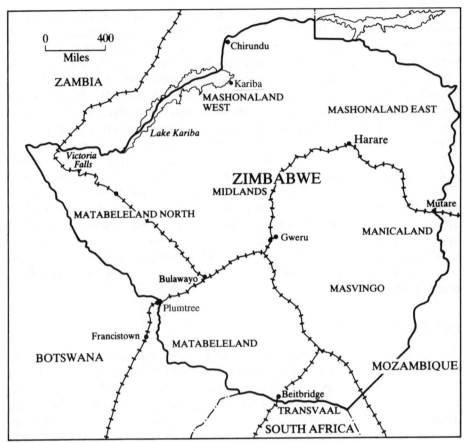

Zimbabwe

The RLI was officially disbanded with some dignity on 17 October 1980; its last deployment was an anti-poaching operation. ZANLA commanders detested the Selous Scouts (who quickly disbanded with very little ceremony), but Mugabe asked the SAS commander, Lieutenant Colonel Garth Barrett, to stay on as a form of Praetorian Guard. Barrett politely refused. Many SAS men joined the Reconnaissance Commandos based at Durban, South Africa, while others went to assist the training of the Territory Force in South West Africa. The regiment's silver was presented to the 22-SAS Regiment in Hereford. Some specialized vehicles and weapons, as well as records, were transported back to South Africa, reportedly along with a very large consignment of ivory. A few SAS men joined the British equivalent, while some RLI men returned to conventional British regiments. Former black security force auxiliaries were trained in the Northern Transvaal; South African intelligence officers wanted the option of staging a successful southern African variant on the Bay of Pigs invasion. None of the turned black guerrillas in the Selous

Scouts went south, despite being invited by the SADF, even though many were murdered soon after independence. Morrison Nyati, the turned Scout who had been a guide at the raid on Nyadzonya, was flayed alive. Twenty-eight volunteer black Scouts joined their white colleagues in Phalaborwa, in South Africa. White members of the Rhodesian forces were in action against SWAPO guerrillas in Namibia within months of the ceasefire north of the Limpopo. Overall, Rhodesian tactical skills and some soldiers were quickly absorbed into the SADF, though the strategic implications may have been conveniently ignored, at least for the time being.

Black Scouts who remained (or survived), along with remnants of the RAR and RLI, became the nucleus of the newly formed special forces unit of the Zimbabwe National Army, 1 Parachute Battalion. It was commanded by Colonel Dudley Coventry, a former SAS commander. The ZNA took time to find its feet, but one immediate change took place at ComOps HQ. The magnetic markers and arrows on the maps showing ZANLA bases in Mozambique and ZIPRA deployments in Zambia were cleared away. The new locations were of South African bases. The change of enemies was dramatic.

Transitions from war to peace make fascinating history, and the emergence of Zimbabwe from the ruins of Rhodesia was full of bizarre incidents as the old and new orders warily merged. Special Branch officers, used to harassing or planting 'disinformation' on foreign journalists made startling confessions about the murkier side of the war to the same newsmen. Edgar Tekere, a Cabinet minister, donned combat fatigues to lead an attack on a white farm, and then holed up in a Salisbury apartment block with a small arsenal. Former members of the disbanded RLI hijacked truckloads of the weapons they had used throughout the war from their abandoned barracks and spirited them away by air from the country. (Apparently the daring raid was performed by ex-RLI soldiers who had joined the SADF. The venture had been sanctioned by superior officers, but not the army commander. The SADF did not need the weapons, but it has been suggested that it was a piece of private enterprise to embarrass the new Zimbabwe army. At the time there was speculation that the weapons had gone to the Mozambique resistance movement, the IRA or ZIPRA, but the destination of the hijacked weaponry was South Africa.) Crime rates in Salisbury's African townships soared 400 per cent in weeks. South African agents armed to the teeth with small arms and sophisticated SAM-7s scrambled back across the Limpopo when they were stopped at a roadblock. Weapons marked 'Special Branch Rusape' were seized by South African commandos in a raid on a South African African National Congress base in Maputo.

Despite the strange happenings, rumours of coups and the bitter taste of defeat, many whites were prepared to give Mugabe a chance to prove that he could bring real peace. And peace rested upon three main pillars: the retention of white expertise, economic aid for reconstruction and the re-establishment of law and order. Long after independence, banditry was endemic, particularly in the Goromonzi and Mtoko areas. P K van der Byl, still a vociferous RF member of parliament, described parts of Zimbabwe as a 'sort of Wild West'. The police could do much to round up bandits, but the chief problem in Zimbabwe was the delay in the integration of the three rival armies. In a magnanimous gesture, Mugabe asked Walls to supervise the creation of a Zimbabwe National Army (ZNA) from elements of the former rival armies. A Joint High Command was established. By mid-1980 it consisted of the ZANLA chief, Rex Nhongo, the ZIPRA commander, Lookout Masuku, the army commander, Lieutenant General Sandy Maclean, the head of the air force, Air Marshal Frank Mussell and the Secretary of Defence, Alan Page. (The JHC was initially chaired by Walls, then, after his dismissal, by Alan Page, or his deputy Harry Oxley. The chairmanship then passed permanently to Emmerson Mnangagwa.)

CIVIL WAR

Although Britain had withdrawn its monitoring forces before independence, Mugabe asked the British army to assist in the integration process. One hundred and forty officers and NCOs were soon to play a vital role in preventing the ZANLA and ZIPRA factions from destroying the ZNA. Although ZAPU, along with two whites, was represented in the new Zimbabwe Cabinet, ZANU(PF) ministers such as Enos Nkala (an Ndebele himself) were publicly contemptuous of ZAPU and its president, Nkomo. The self-styled 'Father of Zimbabwean nationalism' was nevertheless in the Cabinet as minister of home affairs (this ministry controlled the police, but many of the security and paramilitary functions had been removed). ZIPRA leaders objected to the increasing dominance of ZANU(PF) in the civil service, army, police and the constant stream of ZANU(PF) propaganda in the newly controlled press, radio and TV. Eventually, in November 1980, ZIPRA and ZANLA skirmishes erupted into full-scale fighting in the Entumbane suburb of Bulawayo. More than 55 people (mainly innocent civilians) were killed and more than 400 injured in the fighting which went on for two days. Air force Hawker Hunters thundered over the battling guerrillas and new units of the national army, stiffened by the still white-officered RAR, stood by to intervene. Zimbabwe hovered on the brink of civil war. Finally, senior ZIPRA and ZANLA commanders gained control over their troops in Bulawayo and in other centres where guerrillas were gearing up for a general conflagration.

In February 1981 more than 10,000 ZNA troops were again involved in ZIPRA-ZANLA faction fighting in the Bulawayo area and at camps in the Midlands. Once more the core of the forces which quelled the mutinies was made up of RAR and the air force. Mugabe had wanted to disband the RAR but had been dissuaded by Walls and the secretary of defence. Without the RAR and its white officers the fighting in February 1981 – which included the use of BTR-152 armoured cars and the threat of ZIPRA tanks at the Gwaai river AP – might not have been contained. The whites in Zimbabwe silently cheered on 'their' RAR as it once again went into combat against guerrillas, but this time on the orders of Robert Mugabe. Obviously the referee role of the white-officered RAR could not last long in the new Zimbabwe. A North Korean-trained 5th brigade, based in Inyanga, took over the role of Praetorian guard. Nearly all the 3,000 troops in the brigade were Shonas loyal to ZANU(PF). The unit operated totally independently of the rest of the army; not even the army commander, Lieutenant General Maclean, exercised any jurisdiction over the obsessively secretive brigade, which was soon to indulge in a genocidal frenzy in Matabeleland.

The remaining whites in the armed forces (despite some determined foot-dragging) and the 140 British instructors managed, just, to keep the ZNA together in the first demanding year of independence. (A small group of British BMATT instructors were to repeat the miracle with South Africa's nine different armies after 1994.) Walls's initial appointment as supremo of the three armies did a great deal to prevent a white exodus. It also obviated the need to select a ZIPRA or ZANLA chief of the ZNA. But Walls could not prevent the clashes between the rival guerrilla forces and, to many whites, he appeared as a sell-out. Unfounded rumours abounded that Walls had received a large sum of money outside the country in order to stay on. In some messes, white officers gave a 'balls to Walls' toast. They talked about 'Rhodesia's Wall Street Crash'. Stung by this harsh criticism, and privately admitting to a heart condition, the general asked Mugabe for permission to retire. Walls was also angry that Mugabe had refused his promotion to full general. Walls had argued that he needed the extra rank to deal with the truculent ZANLA commanders such as Rex Nhongo (who were technically the equivalents of a lieutenant general). In two indiscreet TV interviews, Walls publicly criticized the government. He admitted that he had telegraphed Thatcher just after the elections to request that she should declare the results null and void because of the massive intimidation. Walls sent his message to Mrs Thatcher via Pretoria; if he had sent it from Salisbury there was the possibility that Soames might have intercepted the crucial cable. Walls had good reason for contacting the British prime minister. First, there was indeed massive intimidation and ZANU(PF) was largely responsible. Second, besides taking tea with the Queen Mother, Walls had held a secret meeting with very senior British Cabinet members during the Lancaster House talks. (He was the only Rhodesian present; Ken Flower, who was supposed to attend the meeting, was delayed by bad weather en route from Paris.) Walls had been told that he had the right to contact Thatcher directly if he felt that something was seriously amiss with the election process. Therefore, in his view, Walls did not breach protocol in going over Soames's head. The Zimbabwe government, however, enacted a special law to exile Walls even though he had been born in the country. It was a sad end to an illustrious military career.

Emmerson Mnangagwa took over as the country's overall security co-ordinator. The highly intelligent Mnangagwa understood that the transition from war to peace would be full of pitfalls. Many of the highly politicized ZANLA commanders found it difficult to adapt to low-key professional soldiering as ZANU(PF) switched from guerrilla warfare to government administration. The ex-ZANLA commander Mnangagwa had an intellectual equivalent in ZIPRA: Dumiso Dabengwa. Dabengwa, the urbane, Russian-trained intelligence chief of ZIPRA, had been the prime link between Nkomo and his army, as well as a useful counterweight and collocutor with the powerful Mnangagwa.

The rival guerrilla armies settled into a fitful and uneasy peace. Even though a ZIPRA coup was rumoured to have been planned for Christmas 1980, it gradually appeared that tribal animosities would not explode into all-out war. As most of the remaining whites in the ZNA and police began to leave, ZANU(PF) dominance looked like slowly penetrating all areas of administration outside Matabeleland. ZIPRA had shot its bolt and Nkomo's 'second coming' seemed remote. It had been mooted that Nkomo might have tried to repeat the experience in Katanga and declare his own UDI in Matabeleland. But this could only have survived with Pretoria's (continuing) connivance, perhaps in exchange for a promise to prevent ANC troops infiltrating through ZAPU-held territory. ZAPU officials were alleged to have approached South Africa, but it was made clear that another UNITA-type campaign was just not on. The feeling in Pretoria by the end of 1980 seemed to have become: better the pragmatic devil [Mugabe] we know than the one [Nkomo] we don't. And, in contrast to ZAPU, the South African government shared Mugabe's distrust of the Russians. Nevertheless, Pretoria had long favoured Nkomo over Mugabe; South African intelligence had been in touch with Nkomo for years. But the ANC/Moscow links prevented a closer relationship. After independence, Pretoria was impressed by Mugabe. The government-controlled South African Broadcasting Corporation was allowed to air a long and flattering interview with Mugabe on the prime-time *Midweek* TV programme. The honeymoon did not last long, however.

And so the *Chimurenga* war stuttered on into a new decade. Zimbabwe in 1981 was still not free from the rattle of AKs or the crump of Chinese stick grenades. Yet a year after the election which had formally ended the struggle for black rule, the conditions for further internal military upheaval had considerably diminished. The threat from ZIPRA had subsided. And for the whites the anxious days immediately after the election gave way to a less hysterical tension. The disbandment of the Selous Scouts, the RLI and the SAS raised not even a murmur of protest: the white heroes of the war became an embarrassment. The white elite, whose heads still lay uneasily on their pillows in the suburban bungalows they had feared the triumphant guerrillas would confiscate, were relieved that the ZANU(PF) government did not fit the image painted by Rhodesian Front propaganda. The all-white units of the Rhodesian forces could disappear, as long as the life-style they had fought so long and hard to preserve remained intact for the privileged.

But Robert Mugabe's government continued to fight a protracted war against the whites. There was no immediate confrontation, no direct assault on the citadels of white supremacy. Initially, government propaganda was careful to castigate only 'racists' and 'colonialists', naming no names or racial groups. But the position of the whites was inexorably undermined, first in one area then in another. It was a peaceful and skilfully handled phase of the long guerrilla struggle for the political, social and economic dominance of the majority.

The military structure in Zimbabwe continued to be a big headache for the young republic. The departure of the whites caused severe administrative deficiencies in the armed forces, despite the British army's attempts to train replacements. (For example, inadequate control caused the army to lose millions of dollars in fraud, mainly due to the payment of bogus guerrillas.) The problems of housing and feeding such a large number were immense. A year after independence the army numbered about 65,000, including the ZNA and guerrillas awaiting integration. Although the Zimbabwean ministry of defence had calculated that the optimum size of the army was between 25,000 and 30,000, for political reasons the figure 35,000 was finally decided upon. Finding civilian jobs for these disgruntled men (and women) had been a thankless task. Operation Seed (Soldiers Employed in Economic Development) had failed. Few soldiers had the agricultural skills or the inclination to till the land. As 'heroes of the revolution' they had been taught to expect good jobs, houses and cars in the city, not to be dumped in the *bundu* [bush] with just a *badza* [hoe]. Attempts to integrate the ex-guerrillas into the police also produced ragged results.

Zimbabwe needed to spend its money on large reconstruction programmes, not on a big army. Salisbury, renamed Harare, had also ordered Hawk trainer/strike jets from Britain. The trouble with possessing a large regular army in Africa is the temptation to use it externally in order to channel attention from internal woes. But Zimbabwe's prime minister was then a man of unquestionable intellectual powers and apparent political moderation. It was clear to him that his country's stability precluded a direct conflict with South Africa. Mugabe vowed that he would not allow either the ANC or the PAC to establish military bases in Zimbabwe, but that he would provide shelter to refugees and political exiles. This was exactly what Zambia had declared, with the result that Rhodesian forces had been blasting away at guerrilla bases that were said to be refugee camps. As the darling of the OAU, Mugabe had been nudged by the organization to adopt a more radical stance over South Africa and Namibia. After independence he cut off diplomatic ties with Pretoria and soon South Africa began to apply a tourniquet to Zimbabwe's economic lifeblood. Mugabe maintained that South Africa was preparing to destabilize Zimbabwe by military as well as economic means. Pretoria did arm and train Ndebele dissidents who were dubbed 'Super-ZAPU'.

THE LAST WHITE REDOUBT

The war had locked Zimbabwe into the South African economy. Ninety per cent of its exports passed through the transport system of the apartheid state in 1980. Despite the official policy of reconciliation, the top echelon of the ruling ZANU(PF), educated in hate during exile and war, became a 'hothouse of restless paranoia, hostility and conspiracy'. Much of this bitterness was played out in the arcane clan politics of the central committee which continued to rule as if it were still running a liberation movement, not a government. The one thing they could all agree on, however, was their hostility to apartheid, but the harsh facts of economic life dictated a *modus vivendi*. The financial nexus worked both ways: Zimbabwe was a main route for South African trade with Zaire, Zambia and Malawi.

Nevertheless, Pretoria served up its spiciest and most varied destabilisation menu: economic pressures, particularly in 1981 and 1982, support for Zimbabwean dissidents, selective assassinations, sabotage and propaganda, but it generally stopped short of direct military intervention. Zimbabwe was not like Angola or Mozambique. It was a Commonwealth state where British army instructors trained the (still large) security forces. Washington would not have countenanced direct SADF entanglement, as it had in Angola. But Pretoria still had the best cards: economic dominance, a large potential fifth column of white agents and sympathetic white businessmen in Zimbabwe, a big reservoir of revanchist Rhodesians attached to, or incorporated in, the SADF, and, most important, the glowing embers of tribal passions in Matabeleland. South African destabilization fanned the inherent paranoia in the ruling ZANU(PF), which tended to characterize even indigenous political opponents as 'enemies of the state'. Thus, the state of emergency was retained, with all the same abuses of human rights inherited from the days of Ian Smith. Drought, corruption, excessive bureaucracy and doctrinaire socialism played a part in Zimbabwe's economic woes, but in the first decade of independence South Africa's destabilisation was also to blame.

Pretoria demanded that South African insurgents in Zimbabwe be ejected. Mugabe quietly rounded them up and dumped them back in Zambia. Then the economic squeeze began. In July 1980 South African Railways began to withdraw its technicians and engineers loaned to the *ancien régime*. 'Inexplicable' bottlenecks in the ports and especially on the railways followed. The 'notoriously drunken stationmaster at Messina' (the small railway town near Zimbabwe's main border post at Beit Bridge) became a legendary figure in this blackmail scenario.

Pretoria also took an active interest in the series of mutinies in the half-integrated Zimbabwe National Army (ZNA). In November 1980 full-scale fighting had erupted in Bulawayo. In February 1981 more than 10,000 ZNA troops were involved in internal faction fighting. Without the white-officered elements of the old Rhodesian forces, especially in the air force, the ZIPRA troops, armed with BTR-152 armoured cars and tanks, might not have been contained. South Africa viewed these events and considered Mugabe ripe for toppling. It was alleged that South African agents had twice tried to kill him. South Africa withdrew more locomotives. On 16 August 1981 a mysterious explosion destroyed the armoury at Inkomo Barracks near Harare. At the time, some blamed it on vengeful ex-Rhodesian and South African infiltrators but it now appears that the destruction was caused by the new Zimbabwe Army's incompetence in storing explosives and old, Rhodesian-made gas containers in the same area. Disregarding basic regulations, troops were making fires inside the explosives storage area. Leaking gas caught fire, which rapidly developed into a series of massive munitions explosions. Nonetheless, the incident reinforced and spread fears that South Africa-based saboteurs were everywhere and poised to strike the new regime. On 18 December 1981 a blast ripped though the Harare ZANU(PF) HQ. One senior SADF officer warned: 'If it came to a showdown, we could wring Mugabe's neck like a chicken.'

Pretoria was planning something more sinister than rail stoppages or seizure and destruction of arms: 'Super-ZAPU'. Ndebele dissidents, some genuine ex-ZIPRA guerrillas, were trained in the Transvaal. The ZIPRA insurgents argued that in order to cross a river one sometimes has to ride on the crocodile's back. In February 1982 large arms caches were 'discovered' on properties, especially farms, owned by ZAPU. Nkomo and three of his Cabinet colleagues were kicked out of government by an angry Mugabe. Much ZAPU property was confiscated. Many of the demobilized ZIPRA troops had put all their army severance pay into these confiscated farm co-operatives. Hundreds of serving ZNA troops joined their demobilized tribal compatriots who took to the bush in revolt. The former ZIPRA commanders, Dumiso Dabengwa, and General Lookout Masuku, were charged with treason and were detained at Chikurubi maximum security prison, even after they were acquitted by the courts. This crisis fuelled the rebellion in Matabeleland. Three sometimes rival groups ranged across vast swathes of rugged bush: bandits feeding on the anarchy; genuine ZIPRA dissidents held together by a disciplined command structure, with support from sanctuaries in Botswana, and loyal to Dabengwa and Masuku, with perhaps only titular allegiance to Nkomo; and Super-ZAPU, supplied by South Africa. Harare lumped them all together as disorganized bandits contaminated by Pretoria's agents.

In March 1983 a propaganda station, disseminating very simplistic material, broadcast that it was operating from Matabeleland. It emanated, however, from SABC studios near Johannesburg. Pretoria also supplied ZIPRA and Super-ZAPU (never more than a few hundred men) with weapons, once the pre-independence arms caches were exhausted. Pretoria's Ndebele strategy was based upon a number of factors. Firstly, the troubles in Matabeleland undermined the policy of conciliation, and thus hastened the white exodus, especially of white farmers. More than 60 members of the white farming families in Matabeleland were killed by dissidents, far more than during the liberation war. Whether the whites were killed by ZIPRA, bandits or Super-ZAPU was impossible to discover in the prevailing chaos. This further undermined the economy and discouraged foreign investment. Secondly, it drew off ZNA troops from the Mozambique front, where South Africa was backing the RENAMO rebels. Thirdly, it encouraged Mugabe to overreact. The ZNA, especially the ruthless, red-bereted North Korean-trained 5th Brigade, exacted ferocious reprisals, killing 15,000 men, women and children, at a conservative estimate. (Ian Smith put the figure at 30,000.) The campaign was deceptively dubbed *Gukurahundi*, a Shona word meaning 'the early rain which washes away the chaff before the spring rains'. Though it was poorly covered by the international media, the massacres and mutilations provoked an international outcry, as well as strong domestic condemnation from the churches. Mugabe took Smith's place in the moral pillory, and thus relieved some of the pressure on Pretoria. As a bonus, the saturation of ZNA forces in southern Matabeleland discouraged ANC penetration of the northern Transvaal.

On 25 July 1982 six foreign tourists were abducted on the road south from the famous Victoria Falls. Their bodies were not found for two years, though ZIPRA dissidents were blamed immediately. Tourism had been dealt a major blow. Two days later, a quarter of Zimbabwe's air force was sabotaged at Thornhill base near Gweru (Gwelo). Thirteen fighters and trainers, including Hawk Mk60s recently purchased from Britain, were blown up. Six white air force officers, including an Air Vice Marshal, were detained, tortured, acquitted, redetained and, eventually, released and expelled from the country. The six men were innocent. It was a South African special force operation, assisted by ex-Rhodesian SAS. The audacious raid virtually eliminated the jet strike capability of the air force and propelled a mass exodus of the remaining white pilots and technicians.

In the next month, three white soldiers from a larger SADF raiding party were killed on the wrong side of the Limpopo river. The three, ex-Rhodesians who had served in the RLI and SAS, were said by Pretoria to have been on an unauthorised raid, a freelance operation, to rescue political prisoners held in south-eastern Zimbabwe. Undeterred, former SAS soldiers continued to attack Zimbabwe's oil lifeline through Mozambique. By December 1982 Zimbabwe was down to two weeks' supply of petrol. Eventually Washington told Pretoria to desist, but South Africa had made its point. It could turn off the tap whenever it wanted. South African intelligence chiefs then had a series of high-level meetings with Harare to set up a liaison committee to prevent what one Zimbabwean minister termed 'nuclear war by accident'. An informal and uneasy truce lasted about 15 months.

From 1980 to 1984, under Project Barnacle and Operation Mute, various branches of South African intelligence had run a sophisticated penetration of Zimbabwe, deploying ex-Rhodesians in South Africa and Zimbabwe. Duplicate keys of every cell-block in prisons and police stations, duplicate keys of police Special Branch and CIO cars, and detailed architectural plans of security installations such as army bases had been sent to South Africa (where the hoard was lost). But the operation was wound down by Pretoria. Part of the reason was the murder of white farmers by ZIPRA dissidents, although many were killed by turned dissidents acting in a pseudo role under the control of the ZNA. Harare was applying the lessons learned from the Selous Scouts. Pretoria also accepted that Nkomo was unlikely to displace Mugabe. It is likely that Major General H Roux, of South Africa's Directorate of Special Tasks, pulled the main plug in 1984, although a number of operations continued from within the Byzantine system of agencies. For example, the SADF's radio intercept service continued to monitor the radio traffic from Zimbabwe's security forces.

Pretoria appeared to put on the brakes, and at the same time the ZNA swamped the dissidents, particularly during the run-up to the general election of June 1985. Nkomo, who had fled and then returned from exile in Britain, called the elections a 'fraud before they started'. He had said the same about Smith's election in 1979. Any election he did not win was bound to be a fraud. Nkomo said that the Mugabe government was 'led by fascists, not even comparable to Herr Hitler...We stand a cursed people. Independence has meant nothing to us.' Bishop Muzorewa, however, was released after ten months' detention, to compete in the 'fraud'. The whites were still blinkered enough to argue that Mugabe was unpopular and Muzorewa and Nkomo would make a comeback, if the polling were fair. Not a single white liberal had been elected for the 20 seats reserved for whites (out of 100) in the lower house of parliament. Some of Smith's 20 MPs had defected to form an independent group, leaving the former premier with a rump of seven members. The repackaged RF managed to secure 15 seats in the 1985 poll; the independents, all conservatives, got the rest.

Mugabe interpreted Smith's surprising comeback as a rejection of his conciliation policy. Many whites, however, saw the 1985 election as their very last chance to show their disapproval of Mugabe's march to a one-party state. After the results were announced – ZANU(PF) had increased from 57 to 64 of the black seats – Mugabe made it clear that he intended to revise the British-engineered constitution: the white seats would go and ZAPU would be merged with ZANU(PF) to form one ruling party with himself as executive president. White politics now reversed the UDI pattern. White liberals – at least those who had chosen actually to live under the black rule they had so long advocated – embraced the idea of one-party rule as the 'last best hope of stability'; the faithful followers of Smith juggled with unaccustomed theories of pluralism and tolerance as devices to stall a one-party Zimbabwe. The Zimbabwean whites, however, were now finished as a political force. Mugabe's enemy was Pretoria. A month after the election, dissidence flared up again in Matabeleland and, in the east, ZNA troops poured into Mozambique for a major offensive against RENAMO.

In May 1986 the SADF openly raided Harare, as part of its military assault on three Commonwealth states in the region – in order to sink the Commonwealth Eminent Persons' Group's peace drive. An ANC house and office were hit. Mugabe seemed to have lost his temper publicly when he talked of 'killing Boers'. He went to the brink of declaring all-out sanctions against South Africa, only to be restrained by his more pragmatic Cabinet colleagues. Kenneth Kaunda also shouted for sanctions, but the economic chaos in Zambia crowded out dreams of kamikaze heroism in Lusaka.

By 1987 Ndebele dissidence had diminished because of harsh repression. Pretoria lost interest in Super-ZAPU partly because the Mozambican war was fully occupying the ZNA. In the vital Beira corridor through Mozambique, the ZNA manned the bunkers on the railways and concentrated on trying to keep the convoys protected. Supplies got through, but nowhere near enough to replace the South African routes. RENAMO was left to roam around outside the defended areas. FRELIMO and the ZNA could operate in daylight, but RENAMO owned the night. The Mozambican rebels started to hit targets throughout eastern Zimbabwe in 1986. The ZNA had to resort to recreating the war-time protected villages to defend some of the more isolated peasant settlements. Mugabe edged once more towards imposing sanctions on South Africa. He also flirted with a new defence pact with Moscow. London reacted by supplying new aircraft. Britain was not only Zimbabwe's largest aid donor, but also its major Western military backer. British army military advisers had played a key role in the integration of the three main armies after independence. Thereafter, the British Military Advisory Training Team (BMATT) had helped, *inter alia*, to retrain the bloodthirsty 5th Brigade.

Mugabe offered Nkomo his final chance to merge his party with ZANU(PF). This time the exhausted veteran nationalist took the bait. The successful shotgun marriage led to an amnesty campaign for ZIPRA dissidents still active. But raids and sabotage from South Africa continued. The excuse was the still same – 'crazy gangs' of ex-Rhodesians were trying to 'rescue friends and relatives off their own bat'. Yet, it was strange that, after nearly a decade after their defeat, ex-Rhodesians were still so bitter and so well-organized and well-financed that they could attempt sophisticated missions, without the knowledge of the highly efficient South African intelligence services. The 'unauthorised raid' excuse was wearing more than thin.

Just as the Rhodesian war engulfed the whites who stayed on in Zambia, so the remaining whites in Zimbabwe risked being dragged into the anti-apartheid struggle. One farmer's wife, a veteran of the UDI bush war, said simply: 'We had a paradise here once, now we must adapt to joining the real world.' Despite all its homemade problems and Pretoria's troublemaking, Zimbabwe had survived as a multi-racial society of sorts. During the 'unrest' in South Africa during 1984-86, hundreds of ex-Rhodesian exiles, disillusioned with life in the apartheid republic, and afflicted by a sense of *déjà vu*, made a reverse trek back to their former homeland.

But Zimbabwe had become an integral part of the apartheid regime's war of destabilization in the whole region. The undeclared war between Zimbabwe and South Africa was to continue until the end of apartheid in the early 1990s. South Africa boosted the RENAMO guerrillas in Mozambique, and UNITA in Angola, as well as arming dissidents in Zimbabwe. But Pretoria was forced to retreat from South West Africa, which became independent as Namibia. For a decade after 1980 the question still remained: how much had Pretoria learned from the strategic errors made by the Rhodesian politicians? The Rhodesian security forces had fought well, but it was all to no avail. The South African Defence Force was much stronger, and it was nuclear-armed, but would it also fight to the bitter end to defend the indefensible? The Afrikaner government may well have heeded the obvious lessons of the Rhodesian war. From 1990-1994 the two lawyers, President F W de Klerk and Nelson Mandela, the ANC leader, managed to negotiate a relatively peaceful transition to majority rule.

In this sense the Rhodesian war may have saved numerous lives in South Africa. But many of the tens of thousands of white Rhodesians who had fled to South Africa now felt they had to pack their bags again, and join other 'ex-Rhodies' in the UK, Australia, New Zealand and America. Another exodus was in progress too: millions of black Zimbabweans had to flee Mugabe's dictatorship and its collapsing economy, especially after 2002. Perhaps, in the end, Ian Smith was right. Black rule, he warned, would bring a Shona tyranny which would first destroy its old tribal enemies, the Ndebele, and then throw the whites off the land. But the white Rhodesian rebellion may have transformed Smith's warning into a self-fulfilling prophecy. For all except a small group of cronies around Mugabe, the end of the Rhodesian war had not brought wealth or stability, but the self-annihilation of a once-prosperous land. Rhodesia was killed off in a lost war, but Zimbabwe committed suicide. Mugabe could no longer scapegoat his troubles on settler revanchism, ex-Rhodesians still fighting their lost war, backed by the South African military. The weather apart, after 1994, most of Mugabe's wounds were self-inflicted.

Chapter Eleven

THE LONGER PERSPECTIVE

The Rhodesian war ended officially at the end of 1979, nearly three decades ago. Some memories of the participants may have faded, though bitterness remains. An overwhelming sadness also pervades interpretations of Zimbabwe because of the almost unique self-destruction of the country since independence. Perhaps as many as 80-90 per cent of its white population have left, as had millions of black Zimbabweans. This was on a scale equivalent to Pol Pot's ravages in Cambodia. Inflation reached nearly 5,000 per cent in mid-2007. Life expectancy had halved. The former breadbasket to the whole region was now wracked with famine. The country imploded, socially and economically. But, at the time of writing, Mugabe was still the absolute ruler who had crushed nearly all political opposition. In 1980, despite sanctions, war and no international aid, Rhodesia boasted a highly effective economy. Two decades later, despite massive international aid, peace and fraternal trade with all its neighbours, the economy started to collapse. Rhodesia to Zimbabwe was the substitution of an efficient racist white elite by an inefficient racist black elite.

The country's status as a failed rogue state is bound to prompt the question: would Rhodesians have fought even harder had they known that their worst nightmares would – eventually – come true? Perhaps not, because short-termism dominated white politics. Ian Smith implied at the end of the war that UDI had been worth all the pain. It had bought 15 more years of 'the Rhodesian way of life,' he argued. Equally, some aspects of white privileges and life-style survived for another 20 years after 1980. It was Mugabe's determination to seize back the ownership of white commercial farms from 2000 onwards which accelerated the economic meltdown.

Mugabe has often been accused of madness, but he has displayed a logical consistency in transforming his country. The second *Chimurenga* of 1965-79 was based partly on the historical grievances of the original uprising of the 1890s. After 1980 he waged a so-called 'third *Chimurenga*' against all his perceived enemies: first the Ndebele, then trade unionists, who supported the opposition parties, and finally white farmers and businessmen. Along the way, he silenced the churches, the media, the judiciary, social activists and especially the gay and lesbian community. He stayed in power by bribing his cronies, particulary in the security services. Mugabe's intervention in the war in the Congo helped to bankrupt Zimbabwe, but the mining concessions also helped to make his favoured generals very wealthy. After nearly three decades of independence, millions of Zimbabweans were literally starving, while Mugabe's party bosses lived in new palaces in Harare. The liberation war had often deployed an image of the stone walls of Great Zimbabwe to remind the guerrillas of their country's historical heritage. The whites preferred the term 'Zimbabwe Ruins', an apt description of the modern state.

NEW HISTORY

Most of the international media had damned Rhodesia as a racist state, though conservative newspapers often praised its anti-communist credentials and the efficiency of the security forces. Sympathetic obituaries of the country also mentioned the many old-fashioned Home Counties virtues of neighbourliness, civic pride, politeness, efficiency, discipline, practicality, pluck and a little light charity. To quote the *Guardian*, in a 2000 interview with Ian Smith, 'It was as though the world was defied for a decade by some gigantic local bowls club.' Generally Rhodesian stubbornness was derided as 'Surrey with the lunatic fringe on top'.

This was all about the colonial connection – the past. What mattered more was the future. After 1980, Zimbabwe published revisionist school books expunging settler history, and black artists extolled the struggle in music, poetry and books, pathfinders on the way to an exciting democratic future. Whites also produced excellent literary works, most notably Alexandra Fuller's *Don't Let's Go to the Dogs Tonight*. But the majority of the new military information on the war was written by former members of the security forces, often brooding in far-away exile. Much documentation on the intelligence war, especially on the British and American side, still languished in vaults in London and Washington. The fall of apartheid, however, permitted many South African secrets to be divulged.

The truth about the Battle of Sinoia was revealed soon after the war. The heroes of the revolution in this encounter were actually working for Rhodesian intelligence. Accounts of the SAS and Selous Scouts provided intriguing details of the bravery and ingenuity of the special forces, especially the use of pseudo forces, but they also vividly illustrated how the escalation of the war had almost swamped white resources by 1979. Also, fresh research on RENAMO showed exactly how it had been created by Ken Flower's CIO and nourished later by Pretoria. It was a text-book example of how to destabilize a neighbouring state, at minimum cost, by deploying a surrogate army.

New data on sanctions-busting has amply demonstrated the crass hypocrisy of the UN measures: Rhodesia traded more with the Eastern bloc than the West. And the Smith regime dealt with most of Africa's leaders. Ken Flower observed in his memoirs, 'In Africa we went where the spirit moved, easily attracting mercenary rulers such as Mobutu of Zaire, or the leaders of Biafra, Togo and Chad who used our services in fighting their own wars. One of the few countries in Africa to spurn us was Somalia, when we offered assistance in their war with Ethiopia.' And, according to the CIO chief, one of the most valuable connections in Europe was in the Vatican.

There is also new information on Pretoria's direct involvement, not least the backing of the South African Air Force. South African Alouette helicopters and Pumas (after 1977) were vital ingredients of the COIN strategy. The Cessna 185 (Kiewets) were also useful additions. Three SAAF Canberras provided back-up for the Luso raid on Angola. SAAF transport aircraft also visited Rhodesia for military liaison and political visits, but no Mirage or any other strike aircraft crossed the Limpopo, though Mirages were posed to attack if they were given the signal to take out Assembly Points in the Operation Quartz plan, for example. Peter Petter-Bowyer, a senior Rhodesian air force officer, has provided much useful background in his book, *Winds of Destruction*. Peter Stiff, in a number of books, but especially *The Silent War*, has detailed the extensive South African special forces' activity in Rhodesia and Zimbabwe. Interestingly, though understandably, the full story of white Rhodesian collaboration with the guerrillas has not been extensively told. Some whites, including bank managers and urban housewives, let alone dangerously isolated white farmers, actively or passively, supported the insurgents.

One of the most fascinating aspects of the war was the intelligence game, especially the 'dirty tricks' operations. The murder of Herbert Chitepo, ordered by the CIO and carried out by a Welshman who had served in the British SAS, Alan 'Taffy' Brice, disrupted the insurgency for years. The CIO also eliminated another top guerrilla leader, J Z Moyo, who was allegedly a senior agent for Special Branch. If he was a spy, then Rhodesians scored an own goal of World Cup standards. Edson Sithole's fate was long clouded, though there is little doubt now that he was helped down a mineshaft by Special Branch. One of the nastiest incidents in the war was chronicled by Flower in his memoirs. He said that Reverend Arthur Kanodareka was shot in 1978 because, although a CIO agent, he had become a loose cannon. He had been responsible for distributing poisoned uniforms to guerrilla recruits. Hundreds suffered a slow, agonising death in the bush. The reverend was terminated by the CIO before what Flower calls the 'diabolically successful' operation was exposed. Evidence of unconventional warfare emerged in South Africa's Truth and Reconciliation process. Pretoria used Rhodesia as a laboratory for its bio-weapons programme. Even during the war it was known that the security forces used to deliberately poison wells on guerrilla infiltration routes, and there were recorded examples of occasional inadvertent use of these same wells by Rhodesian troops. Cholera was also deliberately encouraged on a number of occasions in the neighbouring states. But it took 20 years for more detailed evidence of the use of anthrax to emerge, which was also supported by interviews in a July 1998 BBC Panorama programme, *Plague Wars: The Secret Killings*.

THE GREAT BETRAYAL?

Long after Mugabe's victory, many Rhodesians could not accept that they had lost. Many of the books published abound in conspiracy theories, most notably by the great recalcitrant himself, Ian Smith, who entitled his book, *The Great Betrayal*. Lord Carrington was the favourite scapegoat, but also included in the litany of culprits were the short-sighted Afrikaners (also myopic British and Americans), and alleged deceptions by Flower (often unjustly accused of being a double agent for the British), as well as Walls. In the end, Rhodesians should blame no-one but themselves. Smith in 1985 laid much of the blame on Pretoria: 'To put it bluntly, we were the sacrificial lamb.' Commenting on Pretoria's meat-axe diplomacy, the ex-premier added: 'In the end it was Vorster who we had to accept. If it had been Kissinger, I could have said "Hop off!" If it had been the British I could have said the same. There was only one person in the world to whom I could not say that and that was Vorster.' John Vorster sold the Rhodesians down the river, or saved them from themselves, depending on the perspective, because it was in South Africa's interests to do so. (Vorster had the balls to ditch Smith, despite the kith and kin arguments; President Thabo Mbeki of South Africa never displayed the same courage or realpolitik to do the same to Mugabe, to save Zimbabwe, even though once more Pretoria held all the levers.)

In-fighting in the Rhodesian elite also hastened their demise. Little has been written on the civil-military relations, but it is clear that Walls and Flower essentially directed the war, in the last days, not Smith. Many RF politicians, often intoxicated with their own propaganda, grew out of touch with the realities of the war. Smith and P K van der Byl, predictably, opted usually for the mailed fist, whereas Walls and Flower knew that to prevent defeat, a political compromise was imperative. Much of the debate about political versus military solutions centred on the question of martial law. By 1979, warlordism was rampant. Besides ZANLA, ZIPRA, the security forces and two rival auxiliary armies loyal to Muzorewa and Sithole, dissident guerrillas as well as plain armed bandits all stirred the pot of anarchy. At one stage the Selous Scouts were going their own way to such an extent (including poaching and selling ivory) that the SAS was being considered as the only force capable of physically constraining them. Flower described the Scouts, long after the war, as 'vainglorious extroverts and psychotic killers'. Their commander, Ron Reid-Daly, denied this publicly and vehemently retorted that this was the 'venom of a bumf wallah'.

It was sad that, in defeat and exile, former leaders of some of the most professional soldiers in the world should have turned on each other. Denis Beckett, a South African writer, aptly captured the mood in the early 1980s:

> Shades of Vietnam. Side A has overwhelming firepower, radio communications, a monopoly of air support, and all the access to public propaganda. Side B has nothing but rifles and boots, and even operational commands are conveyed by hand-written scraps foot-slogged through the bush. Side A's propaganda machine makes much of 'winning the hearts and minds of the people'. But its soldiers in the field think this is a lot of pious nonsense and place their faith instead in the Nixonian amendment: 'When you've got them by their balls, their hearts and minds will follow.' Side B is perceived by the majority of the population as its liberators…And it all comes to its inevitable end. Side B in the seat of government desperately trying to restore a shattered economy. Side A is writing books in the past tense about

distant places, its former officers all blaming each other for their failure.

It bears repeating that despite the welter of recriminations and details of the derring-do of the Rhodesians, the political, social, economic and military structures of white power were collapsing. Lancaster House, despite all the alleged slipperiness of the British, was a necessary alternative to surrender or defeat. British treachery is the leitmotif of much post-war Rhodesian opinion and writing. At Lancaster House, the British said they wanted Muzorewa to win. Soames was said to represent the ABM school – Anybody But Mugabe. British diplomacy, however, has traditionally consisted of being, and promising, all things to all men to gain maximum tactical flexibility. As one very senior Rhodesian defence official said ten years after the war: 'In Lord Carrington's view the only way to stop the fighting was to hand over to Mugabe. He was probably right. It was a convenient way of getting rid of the problem. It was dishonest, immoral…but effective.'

Some authors have developed idiosyncratic analyses of the war. Anthony Verrier, for example, argued that Britain had to accept the vagaries of South African policy on Rhodesia because London needed to secure continuous supplies of Pretoria's gold and uranium. André Astrow took an entirely different tack by extending the conspiracy theory: Mugabe, he argued, betrayed the revolution by co-operating with white capitalists – socialism had been compromised in Zimbabwe. Few white Zimbabweans would agree.

A FINAL VERDICT

At the end of Chris Cocks's remarkable personal account of the war from the viewpoint of an RLI troopie, *Fireforce*, he asks what was the point of all that bravery and death. Why did 30,000 people have to die? In 1945, bereaved Britons could console themselves with the thought that it was worth it: humanity, democracy and freedom had been saved. Hitler was defeated. In Rhodesia the man castigated as the 'black Hitler' had triumphed. And in the end he too committed genocide and left the country in ruins.

On the technical level, the operational achievements of the security forces will be studied in military colleges throughout the world. Failures there surely were. The PV programme, for example. And projects such as the auxiliaries could have been successful, or disastrous, if the war had continued. The covert operations, especially the pseudo gangs of the Selous Scouts, continued to fascinate military specialists. So did the sheer bravado of the external raids. The most notable innovation was the amazingly successful Fire Force concept. The SADF soon copied the Fire Force, externals and RENAMO models. Indeed, the South Africans turned the RENAMO technique into a would-be counter-revolution. In Angola and Mozambique, as in Afghanistan, Soviet generals had seen their supposedly infallible Marxist tactics emasculated by new 'liberators' in the form of pro-Western guerrillas. But Pretoria could not sustain the manpower or political and financial costs of these counter-revolutions, without US support.

No matter how brilliant its military techniques, a conservative counter-revolutionary war must be based upon a clear political strategy. This is as true of Iraq today, as of the white regimes in Rhodesia and South Africa of yesteryear. No distinct political strategy emerged in Salisbury. Political transformation to black rule was the only viable, if initially unacceptable, option for the white rulers. Instead the RF created a mountain of propaganda which the whites, but not the blacks, swallowed. The whites made the cardinal error in being gulled by their own propaganda. They became blinkered by a siege mentality largely of their own construction. This instilled a fatal blindness. Most, though not all, whites became unwilling or unable to comprehend the real nature of African nationalism. Black demands for social justice, equality and, much later, majority rule were distorted by the RF into a curious amalgam of communist threat and Western duplicity. The Rhodesian government failed to appreciate not only the fundamental character of the black challenge, but also the possible effects of the international and local lobbies which the nationalist campaign could expropriate. The RF failed to perceive both the political and military elements of an expanding guerrilla war. Rhodesian leaders never constructed a political design which could satisfy, counter or contain black demands. Maintenance of white supremacy and later the installation of a pliant black government were not convincing political strategies. Despite their operational achievements and determination, the Rhodesians not only fought an unwinnable war, but they fought it in a particularly unwinnable way.

Foreign interests which tried to end the war also sought peace in an unwinnable way. If black rule was inevitable then it was almost inevitable that the Rhodesian whites were unlikely to accept their fate without a considerable struggle. That conflict was bound to be prolonged if, firstly, the black nationalist movements were to become divided and, secondly, if international pressures, especially sanctions, were not comprehensively and effectively applied. A full recognition of these factors by all the major players involved in the crisis would have been necessary to prevent the years of bloodshed.

The crisis in Rhodesia, although frequently expressed in legal terms, had always been about power, not law. Force and primitive fears, not fancy franchises, became the essential determinants of delayed settlement. Rhodesia's Catch-22 was that the most effective method of preventing, then of curtailing, the civil war – forging a precise understanding of the comparative strengths and aims of the contestants – was attained only by actually fighting, almost to the finish. All the major powers, the frontline states and South Africa, as much as the combatants themselves, blundered when assessing the intensity and likely duration of the conflict. The RF's failures of perception, or stubbornness on the part of its more prescient minority, led relentlessly – almost in the manner of a Greek tragedy – to rapidly diminishing political options for the whites. Compared with terms offered at the *Tiger* and *Fearless* talks, Lancaster House was an abject white surrender. From 1966, as the political horizons narrowed, the war escalated. From 1976-9 the security forces were fighting a lost war. Tightening sanctions compounded the problem. By 1979, senior members of the military and intelligence elite were in a dominant position in the white power structure, not only to force stubborn RF leaders to settle, but also to make independent overtures to Western powers and sometimes guerrilla leaders themselves. Flower, the longest-serving Western spymaster, shuttled back and forth, intellectually at home in London, Paris and Washington. The less cerebral Walls thumped the planning table in Salisbury and threatened RF diehards that both he and the RF might be replaced by a military junta, first white and soon thereafter by a black variant, if they did not accept the realities of the situation. When it came to the crunch, the white military elite remained committed to political compromise. Walls put the lid on the possibility of a coup in the frenetic days of March 1980.

The RF suffered continuously from acute strategic myopia. After the war intelligent men such as Flower and Walls made it clear in interviews and in a book that they had realised the war was unwinnable long before 1979. So why were such competent leaders not able to stop the drift towards the disaster they said they had long foreseen? Most military men, of course, like to sound wise after the event. Flower blamed Smith's stubbornness. Walls insisted that he was just a simple soldier (and it is true he was no intellectual). In fact, both men had tremendous power, much more than Smith in the last period of the war. They could have acted more forcefully, so why didn't they, if they knew that defeat was staring Rhodesia in the face? The very competence of the Rhodesian military machine provides one convincing answer. During the period of unqualified Rhodesian military achievements in 1974-5, for example, the more successful the security forces were in containing the war, the less pressure on the RF to settle. It was their own military accomplishments which encouraged the politicians to believe that the war could actually be won. Senior security officials took on more and more political power, especially after martial law spread throughout the country. By 1979 Walls and Flower were more engaged in political issues such as the Lancaster House talks and combatting Smith's last-ditch opposition than in fighting the war. Ironically, some RF politicians tended still to search for military 'solutions', while some of the military and intelligence elite spent much of their time politicking.

It is said that guerrillas do not win wars but their adversaries often lose them. Despite the Rhodesians' tactical ingenuity and their courage, they lost sight of the one obvious strategic truth: what exactly they were fighting for. Smith had no definitive goal for his excellent army to strive for. According to one senior member of Combined Operations: 'We relied 90 per cent on force and 10 per cent on psychology and half of that went off half-cocked. The guerrillas relied 90 per cent on psychology and only 10 per cent on force.' Rhodesia's generals consistently demanded a clear political strategy; Walls constantly stressed that the solution was 80 per cent political. When a strategy of sorts emerged – an internal settlement to satisfy British stipulations – it was too late. By then the representatives of 'the wretched of the earth' were not fighting for Harold Wilson's six principles. They wanted a total revolution to follow the military climax of their *Chimurenga*.

Could Rhodesians ever have 'won' in strictly military terms? Years after their defeat some ex-Rhodesians still argued that their war was winnable. They asserted that detente in the mid-1970s was mere appeasement, that the nationalists in detention should have been shot or imprisoned indefinitely, that the guerrilla camps should have been obliterated in the early 1970s and that they should not have waited for a massive infiltration to prompt belated cross-border raids. 'War is war,' argued white conservatives, 'so why didn't we bomb Lusaka, or "do a dam-buster" on the Cabora Bassa dam and knock out Mozambique in one single blow?' Such an escalation depended upon the whole-hearted support of Pretoria, which was never forthcoming. Any successful long-term containment of the guerrillas would have depended upon diplomatic recognition and military aid from the West. Yet that would never have been given to a white-dominated government. If a plausible political solution, perhaps an assertive Muzorewa administration in 1976, had been conceded by the RF, then Anglo-American military support might have led to a defeat of the PF if the guerrillas had fought on. But the RF always gave far too little, far too late.

In the end, Rhodesia collapsed because the highly efficient security forces fulfilled their 20 per cent of the axiomatic demands of counter-insurgency, while the political leadership fell dismally short of delivering their expected 80 per cent of the political context. The security elite's growing influence helped to reverse the political balance within the disintegrating white power structure, and this created the conditions for a reluctant political settlement in December 1979. The Rhodesian war, by reversing the normal meaning of the 80/20 axiom, suggested a lesson, perhaps applicable elsewhere, that greater force may be needed against politicians to settle than against insurgents fighting in the field. Later, the apartheid regime groped by fits and starts to heed the lesson of Rhodesia and of French philosopher Raymond Aron: 'When a party gives itself the right to use force against all its enemies in a country in which to start with it is in a minority, it condemns itself to perpetual violence.'

GLOSSARY OF PRINCIPAL ABBREVIATIONS

The English versions are used here for consistency, not the Afrikaans or Portuguese original.

ANC	African National Congress (South Africa) and African National Council (Rhodesia)
BMATT	British Military Advisory and Training Team
BOSS	Bureau for State Security
BSAP	British South Africa Police
CIO	Central Intelligence Organisation
COIN	Counter-insurgency
ComOps	Combined Operations HQ, Salisbury
FPLM	FRELIMO's military wing
FRELIMO	Mozambique Liberation Front
FROLIZI	Front for the Liberation of Zimbabwe
JOC	Joint Operations Command
MNR	*See* RENAMO
OAU	Organization of African Unity
PAC	Pan Africanist Congress
PATU	Police Anti-Terrorist Unit
PF	Patriotic Front
RENAMO	Mozambique National Resistance
RAF	Rhodesian Air Force
RAR	Rhodesian African Rifles
RBC	Rhodesian Broadcasting Corporation

RF	Rhodesian Front
RLI	Rhodesian Light Infantry
RR	Rhodesia Regiment
SAAF	South African Air Force
SABC	South African Broadcasting Corporation
SADF	South African Defence Force
SAP	South African Police
SAS	Special Air Service
SB	Special Branch
TTL	Tribal Trust Land
UANC	United African National Council
UDI	Unilateral Declaration of Independence
UNITA	National Union for the Total Liberation of Angola
ZANLA	Zimbabwe African National Liberation Army
ZANU	Zimbabwe African National Union
ZANU (PF)	Zimbabwe African National Union (Patriotic Front)
ZAPU	Zimbabwe African People's Union
ZIPA	Zimbabwe People's Army
ZIPRA	Zimbabwe People's Revolutionary Army
ZLC	Zimbabwe Liberation Council
ZNA	Zimbabwe National Army

SELECT BIBLIOGRAPHY

When the original version of this book was published in 1982, very little written material was available. The authors relied largely on their own experiences of the conflict and extensive interviews with the major participants. The following books are suggested as further reading on the subject.

Arbuckle, T, 'Rhodesian Bush War Strategies and Tactics: An Assessment',
    Journal of the Royal United Services Institute, 124: 4, 1979.

Astrow, André, *Zimbabwe: A Revolution that Lost its Way?* (Zed, London, 1983).

Bailey, Martin, *Oilgate* (Coronet, London, 1979).

Beckett, Ian F W, 'The Rhodesian Army: Counter-insurgency, 1972-1979' in
    Ian F W Beckett and John Pimlott, eds. *Armed Forces and Modern
    Counter-Insurgency* (Croom Helm, Beckenham, Kent, 1985).

Bhebe, Ngwabi and Terence Ranger, eds., *Soldiers in Zimbabwe's Liberation War*
    (Currey, London, 1995).

Binda, Alexandre, *The Saints: The Rhodesian Light Infantry*
    (30° South Publishers, Newlands, Johannesburg, 2007).

Blake, Robert, *A History of Rhodesia* (Methuen, London, 1977).

Brickhill, Jeremy, 'Zimbabwe's Poisoned Legacy: Secret War in Southern Africa,'
    Covert Action Quarterly 43 (Winter 1992–93).

Caute, David, *Under the Skin: The Death of White Rhodesia* (Allen Lane, London, 1983).

Cilliers, J K, *Counter-Insurgency in Rhodesia* (Croom Helm, Beckenham, Kent, 1985).

Cocks, Chris, *Fireforce: One Man's War in the Rhodesian Light Infantry*
    (Galago, Alberton, 1988).

Cole, Barbara, *The Elite: The Story of the Rhodesian Special Air Service*
    (Three Knights, Amanzimtoti, 1984).
    Sabotage and Torture (Three Knights, Amanzimtoti, 1988).

Cowderoy, Dudley and Roy C Nesbit, *War in the Air* (Galago, Alberton, 1987).

Doro, Marion E, *Rhodesia/Zimbabwe: a Bibliographic Guide to the Nationalist Period*
    (Hall, Boston, 1984).

Ellert, Henrik, *The Rhodesian Front War* (Mambo Press, Gweru, 1993).

Flower, Ken, *Serving Secretly: An Intelligence Chief on Record* (John Murray, London, 1987).

Frederikse, Julie, *None But Ourselves: Masses vs Media in the Making of Zimbabwe* (Raven Press, Johannesburg, 1982).

Fuller, Alexandra, *Don't Let's Go to the Dogs Tonight: An African Childhood* (New York: Random House, 2001).

Gann, L and T Henriksen, *The Struggle for Zimbabwe* (Praeger, New York, 1981).

Godwin, Peter and Ian Hancock, *Rhodesians Never Die: The Impact of War and Political Change on White Rhodesia* (Oxford University Press, Oxford, 1993).

Hanlon, Joseph, *Apartheid's Second Front* (Harmondsworth: Penguin, 1986).

Hills, Denis, *The Last Days of White Rhodesia* (Chatto and Windus, London, 1981).

Hudleston, Sarah, *Face of Courage: Morgan Tsvangirai* (Double Storey Books, Cape Town, 2005).

Kriger, Norma, *Zimbabwe's Guerrilla War: Peasant Voices* (Cambridge University Press, Cambridge, 1992).

Lake, A, *The 'Tar Baby' Option: American Foreign Policy Towards Southern Rhodesia* (Columbia University Press, New York, 1976).

Lan, David, *Guns and Rain: Guerrillas and Spirit Mediums in Zimbabwe* (Currey, London, 1985).

Linden, Ian, *The Catholic Church and the Struggle for Zimbabwe* (Longman, London, 1980).

Martin, David and Phyllis Johnson, *The Struggle for Zimbabwe* (Faber and Faber, London, 1981).
The Chitepo Assassination, (Zimbabwe Publishing House, Harare, 1985).

McLaughlin, Peter, 'The Thin White Line: Rhodesia's armed forces since the Second World War', *Zambezia* (1978).
Ragtime Soldiers: The Rhodesian Experience in The Great War (Books of Zimbabwe, Bulawayo, 1980).

Meldrum, Andrew, *Where We Have Hope: A Memoir of Zimbabwe* (John Murray, London, 2005).

Meredith, Martin, *The Past is Another Country: Rhodesia, 1890-1979* (André Deutsch, London, 1979).
Robert Mugabe: Power, Plunder and Tyranny in Zimbabwe (Jonathan Ball, Johannesburg, 2002).

Moorcraft, Paul, *A Short Thousand Years* (Galaxie, Salisbury, 1980).
Contact II: The Struggle for Peace (Sygma Books, Johannesburg, 1981).
'Rhodesia's War of Independence,' *History Today*, Vol. 40, September 1990.
'The Fall of the Republic: The Collapse of White Power in Rhodesia, 1976–1980' (doctoral thesis, Pretoria, University of South Africa, 1988).
African Nemesis: War and Revolution in Southern Africa, 1945-2010 (Brassey's, London, 1994).
Guns and Poses: Travels with an Occasional War Correspondent (Millstream Press, Guildford, 2001).
and Phil Taylor, *Shooting the Messenger: The Political Impact of War Reporting* (Potomac, Washington, 2008).

Munnion, Chris, *Banana Sunday: Datelines from Africa* (William Waterman, Rivonia, South Africa, 1993).

Nkomo, Joshua, *Nkomo: The Story of My Life* (Methuen, London, 1984).

Nyangoni, C and G Nyandoro, *Zimbabwe Independence Movements: Select Documents* (Rex Collins, London, 1979).

Parker, Jim, *Assignment Selous Scouts: Inside Story of a Rhodesian Special Branch Officer* (Galago, Alberton, 2006).

Petter-Bowyer, Peter, *Winds of Destruction: The Autobiography of a Rhodesian Combat Pilot* (30° South, Newlands, Johannesburg, 2004).

Ranger, Terence, *Peasant Consciousness and Guerilla Warfare in Zimbabwe* (Zimbabwe Publishing House, Harare, 1985).

Reid-Daly, Ron, as told to Peter Stiff, *Selous Scouts: Top Secret War* (Galago, Alberton, 1982).
    'War in Rhodesia – Cross-border Operations' in Al J. Venter, ed., *Challenge: Southern Africa within the African Revolutionary Context* (Ashanti, Gibraltar, 1989).

Sisulu, Elinor, (Introduction to) *Gukurahundi in Zimbabwe: A Report on the Disturbances in Matabeleland and the Midlands 1980-1988* (Jacana, South Africa, 2007).

Sithole, Masipula, *Zimbabwe: Struggles within the Struggle* (Rujeko, Salisbury, 1979).

Smith, Ian, *The Great Betrayal* (Blake, London, 1997).

Stiff, Peter, *Taming the Landmine* (Galago, Alberton, 1986).
    The Silent War: South African Recce Operations (Galago, Alberton, 1999).
    Cry Zimbabwe; Independence – Twenty Years On (Galago, Alberton, 2000).
    See You In November: The Story of an SAS Assassin (Galago, Alberton, 2002).

Thompson, C, *Challenge to Imperialism: The Frontline States in the Liberation of Zimbabwe* (Westview, Boulder, CO, 1987).

Verrier, Anthony, *The Road to Zimbabwe* (Cape, London, 1986).

Wigglesworth, Tom, *Perhaps Tomorrow* (Galaxie, Salisbury, 1980).

Wilkinson, Anthony, *Insurgency in Rhodesia 1957-73* (IISS, Adelphi Paper 100, 1973).

Windrich, Elaine, *The Mass Media in the Struggle for Zimbabwe: Censorship and Propaganda under Rhodesian Front Rule* (Mambo, Gwelo, 1981).

Wood, J R T, *The War Diaries of André Dennison* (Ashanti, Gibraltar, 1989).

INDEX